Macmillan Building and Surveying Series

Series Editor: Ivor H. Seeley
Emeritus Professor, Nottingham Trent University

Series Standing Order (Macmillan Building and Surveying Series)

If you would like to receive future titles in this series as they are published, you can make use of our standing order facility. To place a standing order please contact your bookseller or, in case of difficulty, write to us at the address below with your name and address and the name of the series. Please state with which title you wish to begin your standing order. (If you live outside the United Kingdom we may not have the rights for your area, in which case we will forward your order to the publisher concerned.)

Customer Services Department, Macmillan Distribution Ltd
Houndmills, Basingstoke, Hampshire, RG21 6XS, England.

Economics and Construction

Andrew J. Cooke

Department of Economics and Public Administration
The Nottingham Trent University

MACMILLAN

First published 1996 by
MACMILLAN PRESS LTD
Houndmills, Basingstoke, Hampshire RG21 6XS
and London
Companies and representatives
throughout the world

ISBN 0-333-62111-5

A catalogue record for this book is available
from the British Library.

10   9   8   7   6   5   4   3   2   1
05 04 03 02 01 00 99 98 97 96

Printed in Great Britain by
Antony Rowe Ltd
Chippenham, Wiltshire

To Mum and Dad

Contents

Preface

Economics is concerned with resource allocation. It confronts explicitly the problems we all have to face: as householders choosing between commodities on the basis of the income and time we have at our disposal; and as owners or employees of firms or public sector organisations deciding which goods and services should be produced. Nowadays many students encounter economics as a subsidiary subject within their programme of study, not only within social sciences courses but also within humanities and applied science degree courses. This book is intended for students whose field of study lies within the activities associated with the construction industry, such as surveying, estate management and civil engineering.

For many, this will be their first experience of having to learn economics. The aim of this book therefore is to provide a self-contained framework that describes the basic principles of economic analysis in a relative context. The discussion is arranged into eight chapters, which build upon each other in a manner consistent with most economics textbooks. It will be shown that economics provides a clear framework within which construction activity can be analysed. As a result it is important for the student not only to understand the terminology used in economics, but also how to apply it in a relevant way. Consequently the economics is introduced in an order that facilititates an understanding of the subject rather than being contrived to fit in with construction-related issues.

The assumption underpinning Chapter 1 is that most readers will be picking up an economics book for the first time. It therefore provides a brief outline of some of the more general assumptions and definitions that underpin economic analysis. Essential to the successful application of economics to the construction industry, or indeed to any other industry, is an ability to be able to locate and utilise relevant data in essays, presentations, reports and other pieces of written work. To facilitate this process, Chapter 1 not only includes a section that identifies some of the publications that provide useful data, but also a discussion of some the problems that can arise when interpreting such data. This section should not be taken to imply that the rest of the book contains a seemingly endless supply of statistical tables. Rather, the commentary simply uses relevant data where appropriate to emphasise or illustrate particular points. Figures are more easily remembered and utilised if they are presented in a memorable way. Tables are usually forgotten when it comes to writing essays or exam answers.

The remaining seven chapters encompass four broad topic areas, each related specifically to the construction industry: the economics of markets; the economic appraisal of projects; the economics of production; and the analysis of government policy. Chapters 2 and 3 focus on the factors that determine the way buyers and sellers behave towards each other and the characteristics of the markets that emerge as a result. It will be seen that, in some cases, governments choose to intervene in markets if it is felt that without such intervention 'undesirable' outcomes may result. Governments are likely to adopt a paternalistic approach if they perceive buyers and sellers to be ill-informed and/or opportunistic in their behaviour. Either can result in an undesirable mix of commodities being produced in tandem with an undesirable set of prices, for example cheap heroin and expensive health care. Furthermore, unregulated markets may impose costs on others without them receiving compensation in return. For example a factory that does not have to account for its actions may take no account of the pollution it produces if legislation does not require it to. To illustrate the principles that underpin the analysis of markets and the ways in which they may be perceived to 'fail', specific reference will be made to the housing market.

Chapter 4 addresses some of the problems that confront economists when they are asked to carry out appraisals of construction projects. It will be seen that the economist's approach goes beyond a simple cost-accounting process to identify both the costs and the benefits that are expected to arise from the development in question. With specific reference to the construction of roads, the discussion highlights a number of problems that economists frequently have to address: how to take account of the differential timing of the costs and benefits associated with projects; the problem of valuing commodities that are not traded explicitly on markets (and hence do not have a market price, for example the environment); how to take account of the possibility of uncertain outcomes; and whether it is possible to present results in a clear and unambiguous way.

The analysis contained in Chapters 5 and 6 focuses explicitly on firms and the industries to which they belong. Chapter 5 is concerned with the relationship between the inputs firms use and the outputs that can be derived from them, while Chapter 6 analyses the way in which the behaviour of firms is often determined by the degree of competition that exists between them. Given the emphasis the economics literature frequently places on the advantages of large-scale production, it is noted that the construction industry is characterised by a number of unique features that allow it to persist as an activity carried out by a large number of relatively small-scale firms.

The final two chapters are concerned with government policy, both in terms of the variables governments seek to control (for example inflation and unemployment) and how the policies that result impinge on the construction sector. Chapter 7 is overtly theoretical, but this is necessary if the reader is to understand the rationale underpinning the policies that successive governments have adopted since the Second World War. It will be seen that until the mid-1970s, government policy (whether Conservative or Labour) reflected a belief that the government could 'fine-tune' the level of activity taking place within the economy. Subsequent governments, particularly since 1979, have adopted an alternative view: that such policies are not sustainable in the long term if the underlying state of the economy is not itself satisfactory. Hence the emphasis has been on policies intended to provide a stable economic environment, within which economic agents can operate effectively. As the output of the construction industry is used by many commentators as a crude barometer to measure the 'health' of the economy at any given time, the discussion identifies the ways in which changes in government policy have affected the performance of the industry.

In common with all other disciplines, economics has its own terminology. The same principles apply to learning economics as to learning a foreign language in anticipation of a holiday abroad: it is not only important to be able to memorise the vocabulary but also to understand the grammar and rules associated with it. Thus, although a glossary of the basic terms introduced in each chapter is provided at the end of the text, it is important to realise at the outset that time needs to be set aside to become familiar with the principles covered at each stage of the text. Although some people may initially deny that economics is a logical subject, it will soon be found that it can provide a consistent framework within which the construction industry can be studied and evaluated.

ANDREW J. COOKE

Acknowledgements

It would be very wrong of me to accept sole responsibility for the completion of this text. Although I have been the one to sit in front of the word processor with face contorted, numerous people have, unwittingly, provided me with help and inspiration. Grateful thanks are offered to my wife Vivien, my children Rebecca and Joe, my mother and father, as well as my friends and colleagues. May I also thank Notts County Football Club and Nottinghamshire County Cricket Club for having seasons that did not distract me unduly from my literary aspirations.

Although it was a deliberate intention not to overburden this book with numerous tables, the author and publishers would like to thank the Controller of Her Majesty's Stationery Office for permission to reproduce Table 1.2. and Chapman & Hall Ltd for permission to reproduce the figures contained in Table 6.2 and Table 8.1.

ANDREW J. COOKE

1 What is Economics? Some Initial Concepts

INTRODUCTION

The aim of this chapter is to provide an overview of the principles and techniques that underpin this book. Initially the discussion focuses on economics as a distinct discipline. It stresses the fact that economics, contrary to popular opinion, is not just a subject intended to explain how businesses or individuals can make a profit or accumulate money. Rather it is concerned with the broader issue of finding the best use for the scarce resources at society's disposal. Like all disciplines, economics is guided by a set of principles. Thus the initial aim is to provide an insight into what makes economists 'tick' and the issues that economists consider important. This overview will provide a backdrop for the remainder of the chapter, which focuses specifically on the role economics can play in providing an effective framework within which the construction industry can be analysed. Thus we shall consider what makes 'construction economics' different from 'environmental economics', or indeed 'economics' in general. With a view to encouraging readers to find their own evidence to illustrate the economics they use, this chapter also identifies some of the more important sources of statistical information.

WHAT IS ECONOMICS?

As a general discipline, economics is concerned with the analysis of two interrelated problems that confront everyone on a daily basis: *scarcity* and *choice*. Put simply, because human desires are infinite yet the resources we have at our disposal are limited, choices have to be made. As a result economists consider resource allocation in terms of its *opportunity cost*. This is a measure of what is forgone when scarce resources are committed to a particular choice. For example the opportunity cost of a road widening scheme may be seen in terms of the bridge that cannot now be built across a nearby river. Confronted with the opportunity cost problem, economists are often asked to carry out appraisals of particular spending programmes. As we shall see in Chapter 4, the aim of such analyses is to identify and compare the costs and benefits that would arise from alternative spending programmes.

1

Resource allocation decisions are made at every level of society, from supranational organisations all the way down to individual householders. The most obvious example of the scarcity and choice problem involves the allocation of incomes, revenues and budgets. Such examples are given in Table 1.1.

We often forget that another important resource *everyone* has finite amounts of is *time*. Biological requirements dictate that all individuals, whether rich or poor, have to set aside a certain amount of time for sleeping and eating. Thus organisations have to organise their production so as to enable their workforce to take rests and meet basic biological requirements. Similarly individuals have to organise their day in order to work, travel to work, carry out household tasks (for example cleaning and washing), relax, eat and sleep. Of course some of these activities are complementary: some commuters are able to work while they travel, while a visit to a restaurant is a leisure pursuit as well as the fulfilment of the basic need to eat and drink. Even children face time constraints, despite having few responsibilities. For example they are required to go to school five days per week, and in addition they often have to fit into the schedules of their carers. Thus, unwittingly, we are all economists facing the twin problems of scarcity and choice.

UNBRIDLED MARKETS OR PLANNING?

An ongoing area of debate within the economics literature is the role governments should play in the resource allocation process. At one extreme, the government has an extremely limited role, its responsibilities confined to coordinating armed defence against external attack and establishing a legal framework to protect individuals and property. Land and capital is owned by individuals and general resource allocation is guided by prices that emerge naturally in markets inside and outside the economy. The process by which this occurs will be explored in detail in Chapters 2 and 3 of this book. When all resource allocation takes place through the *market mechanism*, we have a system of *pure capitalism*.

At the other end of the spectrum, economies can operate using a *command system*, which at its most extreme operates without the intervention of any market forces. This is known as *pure socialism*. Under this scenario, land and capital is owned by the state. Resource allocation decisions affecting the production of goods and services (concerning what type of outputs should be produced and the types of input used to create them) are determined administratively, initially at the national level and then coordinated at regional and local levels. Al-

Table 1.1   Confronting scarcity and choice

Level of decision making	Nature of decision
European Union	Allocation of the EU budget between different spending headings, for example the Common Agricultural Policy or its social policy programmes.
National government	Allocation of revenues between different public spending priorities, for example the National Health Service, the armed services and road construction.
Individual firm	Distribution of revenues between shareholders and the firm. Allocation of resources between different product lines, choices of technology and between different functional departments (for example research and development, marketing).
Individual household	Spending of income to meet basic needs (food, shelter and clothing), transport requirements, leisure pursuits and precautionary savings.

though this system is often associated with Karl Marx, its establishment as a realistic mechanism of resource allocation is better attributed to Walter Rathenau, who organised Germany's production during the First World War (1914–18). Let us consider each of these resource allocation systems in more detail and the degree to which it has been possible to implement them in practice.

A *market* is formed when buyers and sellers are able to communicate with each other. Markets can emerge for the buying and selling of just about anything, ranging from the most basic building materials to the most sophisticated scientific instruments. Indeed advances in telecommunications and computer technology have made it possible for buyers and sellers to be in contact with each other without ever meeting formally. Under a pure market system, no differentiation is made between the desirability or morality of the goods and services traded and the distribution of income between individuals within the economy that emerges subsequently. Prices are determined by relative scarcity and individuals choose between products according to their tastes/preferences and the amount of income they have at their disposal. Markets do not operate independently from each other. For example a decision by a person to produce a commodity is likely to require him or her to use the labour market to hire workers, the capital market to raise finance for any equipment needed, a market for each piece of machinery used in production, a market for each raw material input and so on. It is the interaction between individual markets that determines how resources are ultimately allocated in a market-based economy.

Important to the long-term survival of the market system is the existence of *entrepreneurship*. Entrepreneurs find new ways of making and marketing established products or create entirely new goods and services, and back their belief in the commodity by taking risks with their own money and that of others. As a result the entrepreneur is the agent of change. According to economic theory, the reward for successful entrepreneurship (which may be attributable to good fortune as well as entrepreneurial skill) is *profit*, the revenue that remains after all the inputs used in the productive process have been paid for. Conversely a financial loss or even bankruptcy results if the entrepreneur is unsuccessful. It is the risky nature of entrepreneurial activity that distinguishes the entrepreneur from other types of worker.

Under a pure command system, resources are allocated by administrative decision. Plans made centrally dictate not only *what* goods and services should be produced but also *how* they should be produced. The prices of any inputs used in the production process and the outputs that result are also determined centrally. Thus, unlike the market system, the distribution of income between different groups within the economy is ultimately at the discretion of the planning committees. In theory, decisions made centrally reflect planners' views about which sectors of the economy should grow and which should contract. As a result the average individual has little if any opportunity to express a preference about what is to be made available in the shops.

The success of a planned economy is measured in terms of *targets*, which, if exceeded, attract bonuses to those responsible for achieving them. However this system can promote inertia, which can lead to a deterioration of product quality and a desire not to exceed an output target by too much. If ambitious politicians set too high a target, then the chase for quantity may well result in a reduction in quality. Conversely, should a target be achieved easily, then a higher target may be set in the future, making bonuses more difficult to obtain. In the pure market system, inefficiency that results in too high a price or too low a level of product quality may ultimately force a producer to leave an industry. In contrast the enterprise in the planned system is afforded state protection, which provides no direct incentive to innovate and rectify any problem that emerges. Another feature of the market economy is that all firms must trade with each other in order to obtain supplies of the inputs they need. Should any such inputs be unsatisfactory with respect to price, quality, delivery time or specification, the purchaser has the option of finding an alternative supplier. In contrast enterprises in a planned system receive their inputs through a distribution network. Should the distribution network break down for any reason, then the problem will have a knock-on effect throughout the system.

As a result the degree to which one manager can meet a particular target will in part determine the ability of other managers to meet theirs. This can result in a high degree of uncertainty. Furthermore managers cannot resort to an alternative supplier if the inputs they receive are substandard or not delivered on time. By definition, this system can be extremely bureaucratic and as a result it can be extremely inflexible when it comes to correcting any mistakes that arise.

No country can be said to have adopted either of these extreme systems of resource allocation, though it is possible to identify Japan and Singapore as countries that have exhibited many of the characteristics of a pure capitalist economy, while in China and the former Soviet Union, revolution enabled a relatively comprehensive system of planning to be established. Resource allocation in the majority of countries has embraced a mixture of market and central control mechanisms. For example, although Sweden has what is essentially a market-based system, the state plays an active role by providing a highly developed welfare system, thereby avoiding many of the potential failures of an unbridled market system (such as environmental pollution, inequality of access to welfare services and a potentially inequitable distribution of income). Similarly, since the Second World War countries such as France, South Korea and Kenya have at times employed a more diluted form of planning known as *indicative planning*. Under this system the government not only plans its future levels of expenditure but also how it expects the economy to perform in the future in the light of this expenditure. If the private sector can be convinced of the validity of these predictions, then it will invest accordingly. In other words, private sector investment and general behaviour is *influenced* by the official plan rather than commanded by it. The general term that economists use to refer to a country in which resource allocation occurs through the combined action of the state and the market mechanism is a *mixed economy*.

Britain is another example of a mixed economy. For three decades after the Second World War the amount of government intervention in the British economy was allowed to grow beyond that which had existed prior to 1939. This reflected two factors. First, the fundamental weakness that characterised the British economy after six years of global warfare suggested to many politicians that the market mechanism needed a high degree of assistance if recovery was to be sustained. Second, the writings of John Maynard Keynes during the 1920s and 1930s provided many governments with an explicit rationale for intervening in their respective economies in order to correct any shortfalls in economic activity. Over the last two decades, however, there has been considerable debate concerning the degree to which governments should participate in the resource allocation process, both as regulators of markets and as direct providers of goods and services. In particular it was seen that the state now had too large a role and was in part responsible for the economic difficulties that Britain found itself in. In 1979 a Conservative government was elected with a mandate to 'roll back the frontiers of the state'. However it is easy to overstate the degree of economic change that has taken place since then. More fundamental has been the transformation that has taken place in the economies of Eastern Europe. Whereas Britain has retained its credentials as a mixed economy, albeit more market oriented than before, political change has seen highly developed systems of central planning replaced by more market-oriented structures. This not only includes the states that used to be part of the former Soviet Union but also its former satellite countries, such as Poland.

A country's progression from a command economy to one in which the market plays a much more dominant role involves a significant amount of change. Most significant is the creation of what economists term *property rights*. These are legally enforceable rights conferred on individuals or groups of individuals to own and use resources and commodities. By definition, the establishment of property rights also requires the creation of a legal system capable of protecting each individual's interests, whether it be the right to own a house, to engage in some sort of manufacturing activity or not to be subjected to the adverse effects arising from the activities of others. Even when a person has the right to construct a building on a piece of land, she or he must still adhere to health, safety and environmental regulations. In addition to the establishment of property rights, the introduction of a market-based system requires the creation of a financial system that is not only capable of facilitating transactions but also of maintaining the confidence of economic agents inside and outside the country. Indeed much of this development has been modelled in such a way that it is consistent with practices elsewhere in Europe.

ECONOMICS AS A DISCIPLINE

In many respects the discipline of economics is no different from that of any other science. However, although economists endeavour to utilise scientific methods in their work, the main problem they face stems from the fact they are unable to take advantage of controlled laboratory conditions. A simple example may serve as an illustration. If a person was asked to prove that water boils at 100° centigrade, he or she would need to carry out a series of experiments. The necessary apparatus would include a thermometer, some sort of heating device, a flask of water and of course somewhere to carry out the experiment.

After a series of repeated observations it would be possible to determine that water boils at around 100° centigrade. However we may wish to obtain a figure that is more exact than just 'around 100° centigrade'. In such circumstances we would need to ensure that our thermometer is calibrated correctly, the water used in the experiment is pure and attention is paid to the height above sea level at which the experiment is being conducted. In other words, the conditions of the experiment may need to be controlled very precisely.

Just like scientists, economists seek to observe and identify the principles that determine the relationship between the variables operating within an economic system. With such knowledge it is possible to predict how an economy might react to a change in the environment within which it operates. Unlike many scientists however, economists cannot test their hypotheses under controlled laboratory conditions. Although the governments of developed countries generate data sets that provide insights into almost every facet of the economy, each is influenced by factors that are outside the control of the observer. In the case of the simple experiment outlined above, it was seen that a researcher can take direct account of variables that affect the boiling point of water. However the conditions that affect the 'laboratory' where the economist conducts experiments are changing all the time in response to events that cannot always be predicted, such as a hasty reversal of government policy or, more seriously, a war. Problems may also arise from the quality of the data used as an input into the research, even from official sources. For example estimates of a country's trading performance with other nations (known as a country's balance of payments) are calculated using information supplied by all the country's importers and exporters. However firms may have an incentive to conceal or distort the information they give (for example, for tax reasons). If the researcher has to obtain a specialised or highly localised data set, it may not be possible to use official statistics. Care must then be taken to ensure that the sample used, whether it be of households or firms, is a representative one and that the format of the survey does not generate biased results.

Thus economists must be extremely aware of the difficulties they are likely to confront. Despite the potential inconsistencies that may be imported into a study, economists use a scientific approach to their work. This often involves the building of a *model*, which usually takes the form of one or more mathematical equations that describe the relationship between the variables believed to be influencing a particular event. Because there are so many of these variables in the real world, economists only include the ones deemed to be the most important. However this does not prevent some models from being extremely complex equations, particularly if they are expected to describe the workings of part or all of a national economy. Once the economist has established the basic format for his or her model, the next stage of the analysis involves comparing its predicted outcome against observations taken from the real world.

CROSS-SECTION AND TIME SERIES DATA

Data used by and produced by economists falls into two distinct categories. *Cross-section* data provide a 'snapshot' of one or more variables at a specific point in time. An example of a statement using cross-section data set is: 'of the 155,000 private sector house completions in England and Wales during 1993, 15 per cent had one bedroom, 34 per cent had 2 bedrooms, 33 per cent had three bedrooms and 18 per cent had four bedrooms or more' (*Social Trends*, 1995, p. 175).

In contrast, other data sets contain a time dimension, so that the past values of a particular variable can also be considered by the reader. Using *time series* data it is possible to identify *trends* affecting a particular variable, for example whether it has been rising, falling or has remained constant. Returning to our example of private sector house completions, an example of a statement based upon time series data would be: 'in 1971, the percentage of completions with one bedroom was 15 per cent, whereas in 1981, 1986 and 1993 the figures were (respectively), 22 per cent, 14 per cent and 15 per cent' (*Social Trends*, 1995, p. 175). On a broader level, the British national accounts, produced by the Central Statistical Office, are also in a time series format to allow commentators to make judgements about how well the economy is performing relative to previous years.

Although the remainder of this chapter is devoted to locating and understanding appropriate data sets, future chapters neither reproduce nor refer to tables containing endless statistical trends. Very few readers will ever remember them. Instead, when data is used to provide an insight into a particular trend, comparative figures will be referred to in the main commentary. The aim is to familiarise the reader with 'bite-sized' facts that can easily be reproduced in essays, reports and exam answers. If anyone wishes to see an entire trend from which a particular statistic has been drawn, he or she should locate it in the original publication.

Interpreting time series data

Index numbers

Sometimes, sets of time series data are presented as *index numbers* rather than absolute figures. This involves selecting an appropriate *base year* within the time period under consideration (usually a mid-point) and assigning each variable a score of 100. Values arising in other years are then redefined proportionately. Thus, if the actual figure for the base year (*t*) is 800 and the corresponding figures for the previous two years (*t* − 1 and *t* − 2) are 600 and 400 respectively, then year *t* would assume a figure of 100 whereas the respective figures for *t* − 1 and *t* − 2 would be 75 and 50. Currently (1995), official statistical sources use 1990 as the base year for calculating index numbers. Examples of (time series) data sets presented in this way include national output figures, industrial output figures, earnings data and expenditure data. To illustrate this approach, consider the following figures, which refer specifically to the construction industry (Table 1.2).

In Table 1.2, 1990 is used as the base year. Since all three variables, namely output, employment and output per person are expressed as index numbers, it is possible to analyse these time series data quickly since all three columns use the same units. For example the figures show that although in 1988 output and employment were both below their 1990 levels, output per person was marginally higher. Indeed this is a more significant feature of the two other years identified after 1990, namely 1992 and 1994. Had column three of Table 1.2 been omitted, it could also be seen quickly that employment in the construction industry has fallen more quickly than output since 1990, a comparison that would have required the reader to use a calculator had raw employment and output figures been used instead. A more detailed analysis of this trend will be undertaken in Chapter 5.

Real and money values

Data used by economists falls into one of two categories: that which identifies *physical* changes over time, for example our previous example of the number of one-bedroom house completions over time in selected years or the number of people employed in the construction industry; and that which involves a *monetary* or *price* dimension, for example changes in the value of output over time or changes in the level of earnings over time (earnings are simply the 'price' employers pay for labour). In the latter case the economist or statistician has to address the question of how *inflation* has affected the 'meaning' of the data.

Table 1.2   Employment and output in the construction industry, 1986–94

Year	Output	Employment	Output/person
1986	76.0	82.6	92.1
1988	92.3	92.1	100.2
1990	100.0	100.0	100.0
1992	88.3	84.1	105.0
1994	90.8	82.8	109.0

Source: *Employment Gazette*, February and May 1995, Table 1.8.

Put simply, inflation is the term economists use when price levels are rising. As a result, a particular sum of money will buy progressively fewer goods and services over time. The rate of inflation quoted on the television or in newspapers is calculated according to the impact of price increases on a weighted 'basket of goods' bought by an average family. For reasons that will become clear later on in this book, different commodities are associated with different levels of inflation. For example, in December 1994 the general rate of inflation was 2.9 per cent whereas for housing, food, clothing and footwear and leisure goods the respective figures were 4.8 per cent, 2.6 per cent, 0.2 per cent and −1.4 per cent (*Employment Gazette*, February 1995, Table 6.5). As politicians remind us frequently, awareness of the presence of inflation always prompts the same basic response from the economic agents affected by it: workers demand wage increases from their employers, firms increase the price of their goods or services and governments are forced to pay higher welfare benefits. As we shall see in later chapters, inflation can be a destabilising influence on an economy and it frequently prompts governments to adopt policies that are intended to slow down the rate of inflation. For the time being, our concern with inflation relates to its potential implications for our interpretation of time series data.

The specific problem to confront us is that if, for example, we are attempting to place a value on a particular type of output using prices that prevail in each year, then the value of that output will also reflect the rate at which prices are increasing. Thus we may be confronted with a misleading situation in which identical quantities of output (in physical terms) appear to grow in value over time. Similarly, if our data set measures household incomes between two dates, then it may appear that incomes are rising when in reality householders are becoming worse off in terms of what goods and services they can actually buy.

In order to identify the real changes that are taking place over time, economists identify a base year from which all prices are taken, regardless of the year actually being analysed. For example, let us assume that we wish to compare the value of Britain's national output in 1990 and 1993. If we use *current prices*, in other words the prices that prevailed during those years, the respective figures are £478 886 million and £546 733 million (*Monthly Digest of Statistics*, July 1995). However, if we use the prices that prevailed in a base year for our calculation, currently 1990, the respective figures are £478 886 million and £476 162 million. In other words, by using *constant prices* it is possible to show that in the context of 1990, the value of Britain's national output *fell* in 1993 rather than rose. When economists use a base year in order to remove the potential ambiguities arising from the existence of inflation they refer to *real* figures, whereas when constant prices are used they refer to *nominal* figures. Thus, in the case of the previous example, the nominal value of Britain's output rose between 1990 and 1993 whereas in real terms it fell. In the same context, economists also refer to *real incomes* and *nominal incomes*, the former reflecting the degree to which householders' overall spending power has increased (or decreased) over time when the effects of inflation are taken into account.

POSITIVE AND NORMATIVE ECONOMICS

Although economists attempt to test their ideas using scientific procedures and sets of data (time series or cross sectional), it should be clear from what is discussed in the media that economics also involves opinion. Political parties are frequently debating which economic policies should be used in order to bring about a change in some part of the economy. This requires us to make a distinction between *positive economics* and *normative economics*. Positive economics is concerned with developing hypotheses that can be tested empirically. Thus the statement 'an increase in the average level of household income will bring about an increase in the level of expenditure on do-it-yourself products' is a positive one that can be tested using income and expenditure data. In contrast, normative statements are concerned with what 'ought to be done' or 'ought to happen' and are therefore open to debate (which may be prompted by alcohol!). Examples of normative statements include 'the government ought to spend more money on road building and road improvement', and 'people should encouraged to become home owners'. Both these issues are frequently included on the manifestos of political parties but cannot be tested empirically as statements.

MICROECONOMICS AND MACROECONOMICS

It is usual to classify economics under two broad headings: *microeconomics* and *macroeconomics*. The difference between the two relates to the level of aggregation that characterises the analysis in hand.

Microeconomics is concerned with economic issues affecting individual decision-making units. Thus the scarcity and choice problems that confront individual householders in Table 1.1 are microeconomic issues. Similarly, microeconomics also embraces the economic analysis of individual firms and industries. Just as with individual householders, firms do not have infinite budgets and therefore, in the light of market conditions, decisions have to be made with respect to how best to use the resources at their disposal.

Macroeconomics involves the analysis of much broader aggregates. Thus, whereas an attempt to explain changes in the consumption pattern of a group of households is essentially a microeconomics issue, an investigation into the changes in the value of total consumption within an economy falls into the sphere of macroeconomics. Similarly macroeconomics embraces a whole variety of aggregated variables reported on the television or in newspapers: unemployment, inflation, interest rates, international trading performances, changes in the money supply, international currency exchange rates and so on.

This book addresses both microeconomic and macroeconomic issues as they apply to the construction industry. Initially the analysis will be microeconomic in nature, for example it will look at the factors that influence consumers when they are deciding whether or not to buy a house or have an extension built. Throughout the analysis it will be emphasised that all economic units, whether households or firms, are forced to respond to some degree to macroeconomic changes taking place around them. If interest rates are historically high, both consumers and firms will be reluctant to engage in activities that involve large amounts of borrowing. Later chapters will analyse the rationale underpinning past and present government policies and identify explicitly how the government's macroeconomic strategy can impinge on different sectors of the economy, particularly the construction industry.

WHAT IS CONSTRUCTION ECONOMICS?

So far the discussion has referred to economics within a general disciplinary context. However for a number of years now the titles of textbooks and degree courses offered at universities and other institutions of higher education throughout the world have tended to identify specialised courses of study that imply the emergence of a range of sub-disciplines. Examples include business economics, environmental economics, financial economics, international economics and urban economics. Given this trend it is perhaps no surprise that reference to the specific disciplines of 'building economics' and 'construction economics' has become an increasing feature of the literature, particularly since the mid-1970s. In this respect some readers may ask why the construction or building industry merits such special attention whereas other industries, for example the car industry, do not.

To answer this question one must look at the distinctiveness of the industry relative to other industries: it is a major source of jobs (officially the construction industry employs over 1.5 million people); its output accounts for around 7 per cent of Britain's national output (excluding the work undertaken in the 'hidden economy'); the final output of much of the industry is 'lumpy', not only in terms of its seasonal nature but also in terms of the physical size of much of the output (houses, bridges and roads cannot be transported easily); unlike the manufacturing industry in general, the construction industry continues to be dominated by a large number of relatively small firms operating in a series of geographically determined submarkets rather than one national market; the 'health' of the construction sector is often used as a crude indicator of the well-being of the economy as a whole – when prospects appear good, householders are more willing to move house or improve their existing property while local authorities and the government are more willing to initiate major building projects, whereas if prospects appear poor, housing markets stagnate and major public works programmes are postponed.

An extremely useful overview of the evolution of building economics and construction economics as distinct disciplines is provided by Ofori (1994) in an article that all students of economics in a construction-related field should read at least twice – once before they embark on their studies and once when they are about to complete them. It is not surprising that one of the key features of Ofori's paper is that there is no real consensus about the exact definition of building economics or construction economics. The perspective that will underpin the approach taken in this text will reflect that adopted by Hillebrandt (1985, p. 1), who sees construction economics within a broad context, with its foundations rooted firmly in the general economics literature. For example she argues that construction economics is 'the application of the techniques and expertise of economics to the study of the construction firm, the construction process and the construction industry'.

This approach can be distinguished from that adopted by other commentators who employ economics within a quasi-accounting framework, which emphasises the measurement of relative costs of different design processes or building projects and the comparison of investment decision criteria. A recent example of this approach can be seen in the work of Mann (1992). In more advanced courses, readers are likely to refer to Seeley (1983, 1995), whose approach to building economics is centred around the securing of building projects that satisfy the client's requirements with regard to cost, time, function and quality and where cost encompasses occupancy cost throughout the life of a building. At this introductory level, however, the basic organisation of this text resembles that of many other economics textbooks, though its focus will be determined by issues that characterise and affect the construction industry and its activities.

THE STANDARD INDUSTRIAL CLASSIFICATION

It should already be clear that 'construction industry' is an umbrella term that embraces a wide variety of economic activities. A helpful guide to the components of this or any other industry is provided by the standard industrial classification (SIC). A number of statistical publications, for example the *Employment Gazette* (see below), use the SIC as a basis for organising information.

The SIC was introduced in 1948 to provide a template for the documentation of official industrial statistics. Productive economic units are classified under a specific heading according to the type of activity in which they are involved. Periodic revisions have been made to these headings in response to changes in the nature and emphasis of production. Since 1948 there have been four revisions of the SIC headings: in 1958, 1968, 1980 and 1992. Readers are informed of the SIC system being used in a given table, such that figures based on the 1980 classification include SIC(80) or SIC(1980) in the heading. The main advantage of the new system is that it has almost 600 activity headings, as opposed to the 344 of its predecessor. However, because of the lead time that exists between the collection and publication of statistics, the new system is not be included in publications prior to 1995. Readers gathering time series data covering the 1980s and 1990s are thus likely to encounter two different classification systems and therefore should be careful when making comparisons between years.

At this point it is possible to outline briefly the main SIC headings that relate to the construction industry, both for the 1980 and the new 1992 system. Under SIC(1980), the main construction activities have the prefix 50 and these are furhter subdivided into the following headings:

- 5000 – general construction and demolition work
- 5010 – construction and repair of buildings
- 5020 – civil engineering
- 5030 – installation of fixtures and fittings
- 5040 – building and completion work

There are two other major prefixes: 24 and 46, which cover many of the inputs used in construction activity. The former includes the production of structural clay products under heading 2410 (for example brick and tile manufacture), the production of cement lime and plaster (2420) and the production of 'other building materials of concrete' (2430), for example kerb edging and precast concrete products. Wooden inputs for construction activity have the prefix 46. For example, the manufacture of wood for floors falls under the heading 4610/2 while prefabricated roof timber resides under the heading 4630. Outside these general headings, but clearly within the remit of the construction industry, are activity headings 8420 (the hiring out of construction machinery and equipment) and 8500 (owning and dealing in real estate).

The definition of activities under SIC(1992) is similar to that identified for SIC(1980), though the numbering is slightly different. In this case 'construction' falls under Section F and each category begins with the prefix 45:

- 45.1 – site preparation
- 45.2 – the construction of complete building or parts thereof and civil engineering
- 45.3 – building installation
- 45.4 – building completion
- 45.5 – renting of construction or demolition equipment with operator

As before, each of these headings is subdivided further. This time, however, each subcategory is ascribed a specific number, so that, for example, 45.21 refers to the 'general construction of buildings and civil engineering works'; 45.22 the 'erection of roof covering and frames'; 45.23 the 'construction of highways, roads, airfields and sport facilities'; 45.24 the 'construction of water projects'; and 45.25 'other construction work involving special trades'.

Bricks, ceramics and cement-based products fall under the general heading of 'manufacture of other non-metallic mineral products' and have the prefix 26, specifically 26.40, 26.20 and 26.60 respectively. The manufacture of builders' carpentery and joinery products has the SIC classification 20.30 and falls under the general heading (20) 'manufacture of wood and wood products'. Other relevant categories include

14.11 (quarrying of stone for construction), 70.11 (development and selling of real estate) and 70.12 (buying and selling of own real estate).

SOURCES OF DATA FOR ESSAYS AND REPORTS

One of the reasons why economics is included as a non-specialist subject in a wide variety of courses is that it provides an analytical framework within which issues can be addressed. Although lecturers or tutors stress the need to get to grips with some introductory economic theory, particular emphasis is usually placed on how the economics can be *applied*, for example how an increase in Britain's money supply affects the economy in general, and in particular the construction industry. The information needed for successful essay and report writing falls into two distinct categories: (1) that which is general in context but nevertheless can be used to provide direct or indirect insights into the factors affecting construction activity; and (2) sources that are derived specifically for the analysis of the construction industry and the environment within which it operates. At the outset it should be recognised that incorporating statistical evidence into an essay or report is not an end in itself. A good economics essay or report in the context of this book is one that synthesises relevant statistical evidence with relevant economic theory to provide a particular insight into the activities of the construction sector. This said, let us consider some potential sources of information, first the more general publications and then the more specialised ones.

General sources of information

Under this heading, five basic information sources will be highlighted: *Social Trends* and its sister publication *Regional Trends*, the *Employment Gazette*, the *National Accounts*, *Economic Trends* and the government's own *Expenditure Plans*.

Perhaps the most user-friendly source of data is *Social Trends*. This is produced annually and on a chapter-by-chapter basis provides information on a wide range of economic and social indicators. This publication is particularly useful since it draws together information from a variety of official sources and is held together by a commentary that analyses the key changes taking place. Although a specific chapter is directed towards the analysis of housing issues (Chapter 10 in the 1995 edition), it should be emphasised that this is not the only source of information for readers interested in the construction industry. For example, chapters headed 'Income and Wealth' and 'Expenditure and Resources' also include tables and commentaries on issues that have direct links to the construction industry and construction activity in general.

Although *Social Trends* contains a limited amount of regional data, readers interested in the difference between different regions of the country with respect to construction or any other aspect of economic activity should consult *Regional Trends*. Like *Social Trends*, *Regional Trends* is divided into chapters. Initially the information is extremely generalised: Chapter 1 provides a series of general profiles of regions in Britain,[1] while Chapter 2 focuses on general European Union statistics. Beyond Chapter 2, the format is more like that of *Social Trends*, with chapters focusing specifically on such issues as housing (Chapter 6), education and expenditure. The housing chapter provides a wide variety of statistics, which include stocks of dwellings, new completions, mortgage advances and sales of local authority dwellings.

While the format of *Social Trends* has increasingly reflected the government's attempts to make statistics more accessible to the general public (*Regional Trends* to a lesser extent), other general publications that provide useful information from a construction industry point of view have a more explicit research bias. Highly accessible however is the *Employment Gazette*. Each monthly issue contains two basic sections: (1) a series of articles written by industrial and labour market specialists (though there has yet to be a survey based on the construction industry), and (2) a seventy-page set of official labour market and general economic statistics. Unfortunately some of the statistics are highly aggregated. For example construction industry statistics are organised according to the general SIC (1980) classification 50, rather than the more specific subgroups (such as 50.10 – 'general construction and demolition work'). Nevertheless within this single publication it is possible to gain a great deal of insight into the construction industry in general. For example, from the February 1995 edition it is possible to obtain information on the following trends, usually between 1981 and September 1994 (provisional) (the relevant tables in the *Employment Gazette* are shown in parentheses):

- Overall employment figures within the construction industry (Table 1.2).
- A breakdown of employment figures into the numbers of male and female workers in the construction industry (Table 1.4).
- General construction employment figures by region (Table 1.5).
- Changes in the level of construction output and the level of output per person employed in construction activities using index numbers (Table 1.8).
- Numbers of working days lost in the construction industry due to industrial disputes (Table 4.2).
- Average earnings in the industry broken down according to manual

and non-manual workers, male and female workers and overall (Tables 5.3, 5.4, 5.5 and 5.6).
- Annual changes in the price of construction products (Table 6.5).

When presenting information of the type listed above, it is often useful to set construction industry figures within a more general context by also considering the corresponding figures for other industries (for example manufacturing).

Additional, but less 'user-friendly' sources of information are the *National Accounts* (also referred to as the 'Blue Book' and produced annually) and *Economic Trends* (produced monthly). In some respects these publications provide similar insights and both are broadly macroeconomic in perspective. Of the two, *Economic Trends* is perhaps the most useful, though this is not to say that readers should not browse through both in order to gain an idea about the information provided in each. Being a monthly publication, *Economic Trends* provides up-to-date statistics on a wide variety of macroeconomic indicators. Although some explicit information on construction activity is provided – for example fixed investment in new buildings, the level of output and orders in home and export markets, and the proportion of national income arising from the construction industry – most information has a general orientation. Nevertheless it is important information given the complex interrelationships that exist between economic activity and macroeconomic performance. Examples include rates of inflation, levels of personal disposable income and levels of unemployment (though some of this material is duplicated in other publications, for example the *Employment Gazette*).

The *government's expenditure plans* are produced every November. They are released on a departmental basis and provide a breakdown of intended expenditure for the coming financial year, set in context with prevailing government policy and past spending. From the point of view of the construction industry, the volume that documents the plans of the Department of the Environment is perhaps the most useful. Commentaries and tables focus explicitly on such spending programmes as house building, land reclamation and infrastructure investment.

Construction-related statistical sources

The publications that fall under this heading may be divided into two: (1) statistical publications produced by the government and (2) non-government reports. Falling into the former category are a number of publications produced by the Department of the Environment. Three will be noted here: *Housing and Construction Statistics 1983–1993*, a quarterly edition of *Housing and Construction Statistics* and the *Digest of Data for the Construction Industry.*

Housing and Construction Statistics 1983–1993 is one of a series of annual reports providing a ten-year overview of key construction statistics. Examples include the value of orders and output in housing and infrastructure, the number of people employed in different construction-related crafts and their earnings (such as carpenters, plasterers and electricians), the rate of house building per one thousand population and per region, levels of repair and maintenance work, slum clearance, the socioeconomic composition of people receiving building society mortgages and the value of investment in public construction in Britain and abroad. *Housing and Construction Statistics* is the most current version of this statistical series, providing quarterly updates of many of the indicators identified in the ten-year digests together with the price and usage of a variety of construction inputs, for example sand and gravel, bricks and concrete.

The *Digest of Data for the Construction Industry* is only in its second edition (January 1995). Chapters provide a variety of insights into the construction industry. Although this publication presents information in a much clearer format than the two other publications, there is little explanation of its numerous tables and graphs. In addition to data provided in other Department of the Environment reports, this digest provides additional insights, such as an international comparison of building costs for residential, office, retail and industrial construction activity.

Many academic libraries house reports by private sector market research companies, often in the statistical section. Particularly invaluable insights into the construction industry can be derived from *Key Note*'s market review of the construction industry, currently in its fourth edition. Headings used in this document reflect insights into industrial structure, demand profiles for construction work, the contractors engaged in building and civil engineering work, construction materials, fixtures and fittings, and plant hire. For readers interested in even more specific aspects of the industry, *Key Note* also provides specialised reports, for example on windows and doors, heating and ventilation, and DIY and home improvement.

A number of publications are produced by firms and organisations within the construction industry. Three in particular come to mind. The first is the *Quarterly State of Trade Survey*, produced by the Federation of Master Builders. This provides information under a number of headings, including workload and capacity of firms, available labour and employment levels. This is complemented by the House Building Federation's *Housing Market Report*, the National House Building Council's *Quarterly Statistics*, the Joint Forecasting Committee of the

Construction Industry's *Construction Forecasts 1994–1995–1996* and Barclays Bank's *UK Construction Survey*. The first two of these publications are, by definition, limited to house building rather than construction activity in its wider sense. The *Housing Market Report* includes a commentary on changes in the macroeconomic performance of the country, such as changes in inflation, unemployment and the money supply. Although the Barclays Bank survey does not provide macroeconomic information, it does embrace non-residential construction, such as shops, offices, industrial premises and factories. However the best overall source is *Construction Forecasts 1994–1995–1996*. This not only provides detail about housing and infrastructure building but a highly integrated and detailed macroeconomic survey of the performance of the world, European and British economics. Readers interested in gaining an insight into how the construction industry can be affected by changes in macroeconomic policy and performance at the national and the international level are recommended to read this publication.

2 Demand and Supply

INTRODUCTION

This chapter introduces its readers to two terms that are fundamental to microeconomic analysis: *demand* and *supply*. They refer to the *willingness and ability* of householders, firms, local authorities, the government or any other economic agent to buy (in the case of demand) or sell (in the case of supply) goods and services over a predefined period of time. In stressing willingness and ability, we are emphasising two points. First, a decision to demand or supply a particular commodity is made in the absence of coercion. Second, when economists refer to demand or supply, they are interested in *real* quantities rather than aspirations that may or may not be fulfilled. This is not an unreasonable stance to take. For example, firms cannot afford to be interested in what consumers would *like* to buy *if* they had the means (for example a six-bedroom house with a swimming pool and adjoining squash and tennis courts), but what they are *able* to buy with the resources at their disposal. Similarly, in the case of supply, analysis should focus on what goods and services firms are capable of producing rather than what they would prefer to supply to a market in an ideal world.

Central to much of the introductory economics you will encounter is the assumption that economic agents make decisions in a *rational* way. This means that individuals are in possession of all the information they need to enable them to make an informed choice. Furthermore, when making decisions individuals are also assumed to aim to maximise *utility* in the case of consumers, and *profit* in the case of producers. Although most readers will be familiar with the concept of profit as the difference between what a producer receives in payment for a commodity and the cost he or she incurs in making it, the term utility is used less widely. Put simply, economists use the term utility when referring to the *pleasure* or *satisfaction* individuals receive from consuming a good or service. When spending their money and/or devoting time to a particular pursuit, individuals are assumed to be aiming to obtain as much satisfaction or utility as they possibly can from the choices available to them. In the case of governments or local authorities, it is assumed that public spending reflects some notion of collective utility, though, as we hear frequently, the way in which scarce resources are used by government at all levels cannot be guaranteed to please everyone.

21

The focus of the forthcoming analysis of demand and supply will be one particular sector of the housing market, namely the owner-occupied sector. In considering the factors that can influence the demand for and supply of owner-occupied dwellings, it will be stressed that account must also be taken of changes affecting other sectors of the housing market, namely private rented, local authority and housing association properties. To provide a backdrop for the discussion to follow, let us first briefly consider some of the trends that have affected the residential housing market in Britain over recent years.

BACKGROUND DETAIL: THE BRITISH RESIDENTIAL HOUSING MARKET

Official figures show that there are over 24 million dwellings in Britain (*Social Trends*, 1995). For most of the post Second World War period, owner occupation has been the dominant form of home ownership, increasing rapidly from under 30 per cent to 67 per cent of dwellings (4.1 million in 1950 to 16 million in 1993; *Social Trends*, 1995). For much of the same period, local authority provision also experienced growth, measured both in absolute and percentage terms. From 1979, however, it started to decline. In 1951 around 18 per cent of dwellings fell into the local authority category (2.5 million dwellings), rising to 32 per cent (6.8 million dwellings) by the end of the 1970s and then falling to below a quarter of the total stock by 1993. The private rented sector has experienced a significant reduction in its relative importance in the housing market, both in terms of the total number of dwellings available and its share of the total market. Indeed, at the beginning of the period under consideration it was the dominant form of housing tenure, with 52 per cent of the total (7.5 million dwellings). From the mid 1960s it increasingly became the least popular form of tenureship, a trend that continues today, settling at around 10 per cent share of the total market. The factors that contributed to this decline will be considered in more detail in Chapter 3.

Straddling the dichotomy of private sector provision and public sector provision identified so far are properties provided by housing associations. Housing associations are non-profit-making voluntary organisations that aim to provide housing services for people on low incomes or in need. Although housing association properties only contribute around 2.5 per cent of Britain's total housing stock, their importance as a source of housing to low income groups can be seen in terms of the fact that housing associations have initiated new building which is equivalent to one half of the properties built since 1980 within the public sector. Readers wishing to gain more insight into the grow-

ing contribution of the housing association movement should consult
Cope (1990).

Although the total number of houses has continued to increase, these
figures hide an another important trend: a rise in the level of home-
lessness, particularly over the last decade and a half. Indeed, even
between 1986 and 1992 the number of households in local authority
temporary accommodation (bed and breakfast establishments, hostels,
short-term tenancies and other accommodation) trebled from 23 000
to 67 600 before falling to 58 400 in 1993 (*Social Trends*, 1995).

DEMAND AND SUPPLY

The demand function

When economists use the term *quantity demanded* they are referring
to the amount of a commodity that economic agents are willing and
able to buy over a given period of time. It is conventional for economists to identify the different variables that are likely to influence the
demand for a particular good or service within a *demand function*.
This demand function may be specified as an exact mathematical relationship between the amount demanded and a set of variables deemed
to be significant, or alternatively as a simple list of relevant variables
that leaves the relationship undefined.

The simplest relationship is one in which only one variable is assumed to influence the amount of a commodity demanded. For example, let us consider the most frequently cited relationship, namely that
between the quantity demanded and the price of a particular product.
If the exact relationship is left unspecified, we may simply write:

$$Q_d = f(P) \qquad\qquad (2.1)$$

where: Q_d denotes quantity demanded; f means 'is a function of' (or
depends upon) and P denotes the product price. The relationship is
assumed to work from right to left. In other words the quantity demanded is determined by the price, rather than the other way round.
For this reason, quantity demanded (Q_d) is known as the *dependent
variable* while price is known as the *independent variable*.

Intuitively we would expect that the higher the price of a commodity,
the lower the demand for it will be. Thus, if we were to impose a
definite relationship between the dependent variable and the independent
variable, we would expect the price variable to have a negative coefficient in the resulting equation:

$$Q_d = 1250 - 2.5P \tag{2.2}$$

Thus in the case of Equation 2.2, we know that if the price is £50, the quantity demanded will be 1125 units.

However price is not the only independent variable that can exert an influence on the amount of a good or service we demand. As a result, Equations 2.1 and 2.2 only provide a very limited insight into the demand process. For example a price tag of £50 may not seem significant to some people. However to individuals on significantly lower incomes £50 may seem a relatively high price to pay and may therefore discourage them from demanding the good. In other words, the way a price is perceived by a person varies according to the level of money he or she has at a particular point in time. If a person's income falls, he or she may choose to reduce his or her demand, even though the price of the good or service has not actually changed. Thus another variable we may wish to include in a demand function is *income*. Hence our demand function now contains two independent variables, specifically price (P) and income, which is usually denoted by Y:

$$Q_d = f(P, Y) \tag{2.3}$$

For simplicity, no precise relationship has been establised between either of the independent variables and the dependent variable.

In a similar way, it is possible to think of other independent variables that might be expected to exert an influence on the amount of a good or service demanded. For example weather (W) is often an important factor in deciding whether or not we eat ice cream; current fashion (F) frequently determines the composition of our wardrobe at a given point in time (or at least the parts we will own up to!); and changes in the price of other goods and services, P_0, may also cause us to reconsider how much of a given commodity we buy. Through the application of common sense and research, it is possible to identify the types of variable that are likely to influence the demand for a given product. Thus Equation 2.4 identifies five independent variables the demand function.

$$Q_d = f(P, Y, W, F, P_0) \tag{2.4}$$

In reality the precise relationship between the independent variables in the demand function and quantity demanded is changing all the time. It was noted in Chapter 1 that the economic environment is dynamic and hence the economist cannot rely on the demand function in one year to be the same as that in previous years. Nevertheless, when economists want to consider the relationship between one particular independent variable and the demand for a commodity, they assume that the values of all the other independent variables remain unchanged. This assumption is known as the *ceteris paribus assumption*. *Ceteris paribus* translates roughly from the Latin as meaning 'everything else held constant'. By employing it, it is possible to prevent the relationship between the dependent variable and any one of the independent variables from being obscured by changes in any of the other independent variables.

Factors affecting the demand for housing in general

Having established what economists mean by the term 'demand function', and identified the relationship between the dependent variable and the independent variables that can affect it, we are now in a position to apply the concept to the specific example of housing demand and in particular the demand for owner-occupied housing.

Our demand for a dwelling, regardless of whether it is owned or rented, stems from a basic need to be protected from the extremes of the weather and to secure our possessions. Once these objectives have been achieved, individuals are in a position to consider the other attributes of a house: its structural attributes, such as it size and age; whether it has a garden and central heating; and any locational advantages it may have with respect to its proximity to workplaces, schools, leisure amenities and bus services. Since we are all motivated by different factors and therefore ascribe different amounts of utility to each of these characteristics, the following discussion can only proceed with the acknowledgement that without precise data we can only identify relevant independent variables rather than infer any sort of precise relationship between them.

A demand function for owner-occupied housing

In putting together a demand function for owner-occupied housing, seven variables will be identified: price of owner-occupied housing, income, the price of other types of housing, advertising, government policy, spatial factors and demographic factors.

The price of owner-occupied housing

A glance in any estate agent's window soon reveals that houses are extremely expensive commodities: in 1993 the average cost of a house in Britain was over £64 000 (*Social Trends*, 1995). Not surprisingly, few people can afford to buy a house outright from accrued savings, particularly their first house. Thus most house buyers purchase their property with the help of a *mortgage loan*, usually borrowed from a bank or building society. Mortgages take two basic forms. The first is known as a *repayment mortgage*. Under this scheme the borrower pays back the loan (known as the *principal*) and the interest accruing on that loan over a fixed number of years. In the early stages of the mortgage the borrower may find that he or she is paying off the interest component and making little incursion into the principal. Over time however, repayments gradually account for greater amounts of the principal until the sum is repaid fully.

The second type of mortgage is known as an *endowment mortgage*. Under this scheme the borrower pays back the interest to the lender but in addition takes out an endowment assurance policy into which money is also paid. When the assurance policy matures, a lump sum is then available to pay off the principal of the loan. The size of mortgage that a lending institution is prepared to make available to an individual depends on a number of factors, including the size of his or her income, the amount of money he or she is prepared to deposit, the stability of the job he or she has and the type of property the individual wishes to buy.

For reasons that will be explored in more detail later in this book, the interest rate a borrower pays can fluctuate widely over the duration of the mortgage, depending on the macroeconomic policy being pursued by the government of the time. If the interest rate varies, so does the implicit 'price' of the house. Thus, although houses are advertised in terms of their full market price, it is more realistic to assume that consumers will see the price of their house in terms of the monthly repayment they have to make to a lending agency, set against their future job prospects and family responsibilities.

Income

In addition to the deposit a person commits to a house purchase, the size of the mortgage a lending institution is prepared to offer a house purchaser depends on the buyer's *permanent income*. This is the income upon which a prospective borrower can depend over the life of the mortgage. Thus, excluding the possibility of a person enjoying a large windfall gain (for example through an inheritance or a lottery win), lending organisations are most prepared to advance loans to people who are employed within highly defined career and salary structures. In contrast to permanent income, there is also the possibility of earning a *transitory income*. Transitory income refers to earnings that cannot be guaranteed over time. This may involve wages from temporary employment or even winnings from gambling. Therefore the characteristic that distinguishes transitory income from permanent income is its uncertainty. As one would expect, lending institutions are less interested in the amount of transitory income received by individuals. However, if transitory income in a particular time period is very large, it invested this may generate a stream of permanent income in future years against which a lending institution may be prepared to make an advance.

The price of other types of housing

For a consumer deciding between different types of accommodation, there are two broad categories to choose between: owner-occupied properties and rented properties. To the economist, these are a classic example of *substitute* goods. Substitute goods or substitute services are products that can be used as alternatives for each other: bus travel and train travel, tea and coffee, and timber construction and brick construction also fall under this heading. In each of these cases the consumer has to choose between two (or more) ways of obtaining the same basic outcome, namely a journey, a hot drink or a mode of construction.

By definition, owner-occupied accommodation and rented accommodation can be viewed as alternatives to each other, since for any given type of property they offer the householder the same basic attributes: warmth, shelter, a garden and so on. Economic theory suggests that if the price of one substitute good changes (*ceteris paribus*), consumers may be expected to change their product allegiance and buy a relatively cheaper alternative. Thus a rise in the price of rented accommodation relative to that of owner-occupied accommodation with similar characteristics would lead to an increase in the demand for the latter. Similarly, if the relative price of rented properties were to fall, the demand for owner-occupied accommodation may also be expected to fall. However, whereas short-run price fluctuations may have a rapid effect on the relative demands for breakfast cereals or fruit and vegetables, it is unlikely that short-run fluctuations in relative house prices will have the same effect.

Three points may be cited. First, a fall in the relative price of one type of accommodation may only be perceived as a temporary phenomenon. Second, and following on from this point, the average cost of moving house can be extremely high, both in financial terms (for example solicitors' fees and general removal expenses) and in non-financial terms (for example the need to find new schools for children and an increase in the general level of stress). Hence a change in relative prices may need to be large if it is to prompt consumers to change their mode of house tenure. Third, many people view owner occupation as part of a long-term investment strategy. Thus although it may be possible to rent an equivalent house at a lower price than the current rate of mortgage repayment, consumers may still opt for owner occupation. This strategy may be encouraged further by government policy aimed at promoting home ownership. However the rapid fall in house prices since the late 1980s has given rise to the concept of 'negative equity', a situation where home owners find themselves paying off mortgages that exceed the current market value of their property.

Advertising

Advertising can play an important role in determining what goods and services consumers buy, even if they do not intend this to be the case. In the case of owner-occupied housing, we may divide advertising into two basic categories: that for existing properties and that for brand-new properties. In the case of existing properties, it is an individual vendor who is informing others of an intention to sell. Details of the size and style of rooms, locational advantages and of course the price are usually re-enforced by a well-chosen photograph. Such information is normally disseminated through estate agents, newspapers or even word of mouth. In the case of new properties, the construction company may choose to invest part of its budget in a series of adverts on local television and radio, an option that is likely to be outside the means of the average private vendor. It would be reasonable to assume that the more people who are made aware of the property in question, the more likely it is that the vendor will be able to make contact with a person who is willing and able to meet his or her asking price.

Government policy and 'feel-good' factors

The purchase of a house is often the most significant outlay a person will make over his or her lifetime. The very size of the expenditure and the long-term commitment that is required outweighs that associated with most other purchases. The government bears some of this cost by offering home owners tax advantages through mortgage interest relief at source (MIRAS). However, the size of this concession has been cut in recent years. All other things being equal, however, consumers need to be confident about a prospective house purchase. If there is a high level of uncertainty about the government's commitment to home owners, for example the future of MIRAS, then marginal purchasers may choose to continue to rent a property. Similarly buyers also need to be confident about the government's ability to manage the economy successfully. For example, if it appears that an imminent economic recession is unavoidable, and that this may call into question a housebuyer's future job prospects, then he or she may not wish to be committed to such a purchase. Conversely if the prospects for the economy are good and real incomes are rising, a 'feel-good' factor may draw marginal purchasers into a purchase they might not otherwise have made.

Spatial factors

If we visit a chain of supermarkets we expect to pay a similar price for a basket of groceries, regardless of each individual supermarket's location. A local corner shop may charge more than a supermarket, but in general the price charged by outlets in different parts of the country does not vary significantly. However this need not necessarily be the case with the housing market, and seemingly identical houses may trade at widely differing prices. This phenomenon is not only observable at the national level, where on average houses in the south-east of England are more expensive than in the north of England (for example figures in the 1994 edition of *Regional Trends* indicate that the average price of a dwelling in the north of England was £75 700 in 1989, whereas in the south east it was £94 300), but also within highly localised areas in the same town or city.

Such disparities reflect the desirability of the *location* of the house rather than the attributes of the house *per se*. Locational characteristics that can add a 'premium' to the price of a given type of property include its proximity to schools with a good reputation, the quality of nearby facilities (for example shops, libraries, leisure centres), the reliability and frequency of the bus service, relative crime rates, the level of pollution and the general 'image' of the area. If we extend this argument to encompass a regional or national dimension, it would be reasonable to argue that houses located in areas of relative prosperity and steady employment opportunities are more likely to trade at a higher price than identical dwellings situated in areas of economic disadvantage with high rates of unemployment and limited prospects for growth in the future. These differences are reflected in the land prices construction firms have to pay before they start to build. Again using the north of England and the south-east of England as examples, the cost of buying house land per hectare in 1989 was £284 800 and £895 000 respectively (*Regional Trends*, 1994).

Demographic factors

The age and composition of households within an economy often play an important role in determining the relative price of different types of property, and indeed the types of property built. For example young people are more likely to demand low-cost 'starter homes' than five-bedroomed houses with a large garden. If construction companies are not aware of the socioeconomic composition of demand, then house prices will become distorted and there will be knock-on effects on other sectors of the housing market. Of course changes in the demographic structure of a population can be observed easily. There is an obviously a large gap between a child being born and his or her decision to enter the housing market. The main problem faced by building firms and vendors, therefore, is determining how each socioeconomic cohort will react to the numerous economic and social pressures they are exposed to.

THE EFFECT OF INCOME AND OWN PRICE UPON QUANTITY DEMANDED

Using the example of owner-occupied housing, the analysis has focused on some of the variables that are likely to exert an influence on the goods and services consumers are willing and able to buy. The aim of the next section of this chapter is to focus specifically on two of these variables – own price and income – and to introduce a simple framework with which economists can analyse their effects. The first variable we shall consider is income.

The relationship between quantity demanded and income

When economists wish to summarise the relationship between income and consumption of different commodities over a given time period, they often make a distinction between *normal goods*, whose demand rises as income rises, and *inferior goods*, whose demand is negatively correlated with income. However, it is not appropriate to pigeonhole commodities as being either normal or inferior. Our perceptions of what we would like to buy more of and what we would buy less of as our income rises depends on personal taste. Indeed most products are likely to exhibit the properties of a normal good at low levels of income but become inferior at higher-levels of income as higher-quality alternatives become increasingly affordable.

Thus a change in income may simply prompt a switch in product quality rather than a change in the number of units consumed *per se*. The classic example is that of housing – as a person's real income rises she or he is much more likely to move to a larger house with extra rooms and garden space rather than buy more houses. (Though we may ultimately aspire to a second property in a sunny clime!)

In practice economists and policymakers refer more frequently to the relationship between income and broader categories of goods, rather than that between income and single commodity items. For example, general categories in the *Family Expenditure Survey* include housing; fuel, light and power; clothing and footwear; food and so on. The relationship between such commodity categories and income can be identified with reference to an Engel expenditure curve.[1]

The Engel expenditure curve

As its name suggests, the Engel expenditure curve is used to identify changes in the level of *expenditure* on a commodity, or group of commodities, as income changes. In Figure 2.1, the horizontal axis is calibrated in terms of income, while the vertical axis measures changes in consumer expenditure. Although a commodity group is likely to include one or more inferior goods, we would expect that, on balance, normal goods will dominate, thus a positively sloped Engel expenditure curve should result. Thus, assuming that an inferior group of commodities is a trivial outcome, a number of distinctive outcomes can arise from a positively sloped Engel expenditure curve. These can be made clearer by inserting an additional line on the graph, known as a 45° line. Assuming that the vertical and horizontal axes are calibrated to the same scale (for example pound for pound, dollar for dollar), any point on a 45° line emanating from the origin will depict points on the graph where income equals expenditure. Thus, if an Engel expenditure curve coincides with this 45° line, then it means that all of a consumer's income is being absorbed by one product or commodity group. In reality this is extremely unlikely. We would expect consumers to allocate their income across a variety of commodity groups: food, shelter, clothing, travel, relaxation and so on. It would therefore be more reasonable to expect Engel expenditure curves to lie *below* the 45° line. Two possible outcomes are outlined in Figure 2.1.

It can be seen that Engel expenditure curve EEC_1 deviates away from the 45° line. This means that the commodity group in question is absorbing an increasingly smaller proportion of the consumer's income. In contrast, EEC_2 is bending towards the 45° line. This means that expenditure on the commodity group is not only growing but also becoming a relatively more important component of that individual's expenditure. Thus, whereas expenditure on fuel, light and power is likely to fall into the first category, expenditure on leisure goods and services is more likely to fall into the latter.

In practice people do not like to reveal how much they earn. Thus 'total expenditure' is often used as a proxy variable for income. An insight into the proportion of total expenditure that is allocated to different categories of commodity can be drawn directly from such

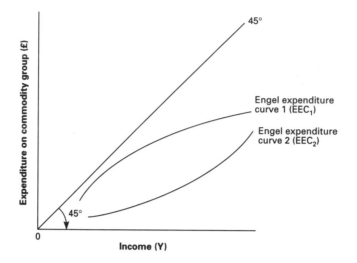

Figure 2.1   The Engel expenditure curve

publications as the *Family Expenditure Survey* and *Social Trends*. For example in 1993 household expenditure on housing was 15.7 per cent, whereas for 'food', 'transport and communication', and 'recreation, entertainment and education' the figures were 11.6 per cent, 17.5 per cent and 10.2 per cent respectively (*Social Trends*, 1995). These figures vary over time and according to the socioeconomic profile of the household. For example in 1971 the corresponding proportions of total expenditure directed towards housing and food were 12.4 per cent and 20.1 per cent respectively.

When making comparisons between different households, it must be remembered that differences exist not only between the absolute amounts spent each week but also between the relative percentages of expenditure directed towards defined categories of commodity. For example, for households headed by a 'professional', a 'skilled manual' or someone 'retired and unoccupied', average *total* weekly expenditure in 1993 was £457.78, £297.94 and £175.64 respectively. Of these totals, expenditure on housing by professional households was 17.6 per cent, by skilled manual households 16.1 per cent and by retired and unoccupied households 13.4 per cent (all figures are from *Social Trends*, 1995).

The relationship between quantity demanded and price

The demand curve

A *demand curve* is a line that measures the number of units of a good or service demanded within a defined period of time as price changes. It is assumed that all the independent variables in the demand function are held constant, with the exception of that in which we are interested, in this case price. Demand curves can be drawn to depict the behaviour of single individuals or larger groups of people within a specified region or country.

When drawing a demand curve it is conventional to measure changes in price along the vertical axis of the graph and changes in quantity along the horizontal axis. The calibration of the graph should reflect the characteristics of the commodity being analysed. Thus in the case of units measured along the horizontal axis we may be referring to weight (for example kilogram of cement), numbers (for example bricks or houses) or volume (for example litres of creosote). The range of prices measured along the vertical axis will also be commodity-specific. For example, in the case of houses we may be concerned with unit price changes of £1000, whereas for bags of cement much smaller unit price changes are more appropriate.

For the overwhelming majority of goods and services a basic law of demand applies: as the price of a product decreases, the demand for it will increase.[2] Hence the relationship between price and quantity is negative, and therefore the demand curve will be a negatively sloped line. This is demonstrated in Figure 2.2, where a fall in the price of paint from P_1 to P_0 increases the number of tins bought from Q_1 to Q_0.

Individual and market demand

When economists speak of market demand they are referring to the total demand of all those who are willing and able to buy a good or service. Thus the market demand for a particular product can be derived by adding together all the individual demands that exist for it. Put simply, if the market is only made up of two people, A and B, who are willing and able to buy a product, then the market demand curve will simply be the sum of their two individual demand schedules (d_A and d_B). Thus in Figure 2.3 it can be seen that at a price of £50, person A demands 20 units and person B 60 units, and hence the market demand is 80 units. It can also be seen that at some prices only one consumer is willing and able to buy the product in question, and hence only his or her demand is included on the market demand curve (*D*).

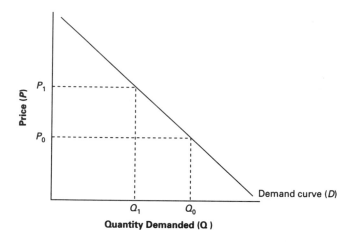

Figure 2.2   The demand curve

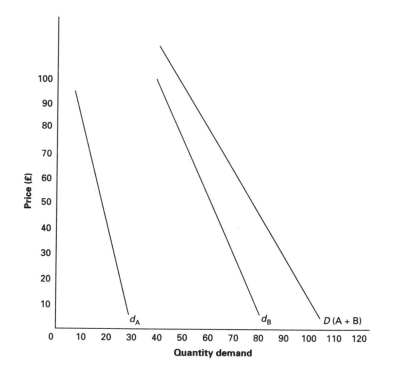

Figure 2.3   The market demand curve as a sum of two individual demand curves

In real situations the slope of the market demand curve appears flatter than any given individual demand curve. This reflects the fact that, for a given price change, hundreds of thousands or millions of individuals alter their demand by a relatively small amount, whereas overall the change in demand equals the sum of all these individual changes. Economists often refer to the market demand curve as being the *horizontal sum* of all the individual demands. This is because we are adding up the *quantities* individuals are demanding at each price.

Shifts in the demand curve

As we have already seen, demand curves are drawn under the assumption that all the other independent variables in the demand function are held constant. Thus the demand curve depicts a two-dimensional relationship between quantity demanded and price. However a wide range of other factors can exert an influence on what consumers buy, for example income, fashion, the weather and so on. A change in any *one* independent variable (other than price) *ceteris paribus* will cause the demand curve to *shift*, to the left or the right. For example, let us assume that a firm chooses to advertise its range of varnishes on television, emphasising such things as its price, relative to that of its competitors, and its durability in extremes of weather. If people respond positively to this advertising then they buy more units of the product at any given price. This is reflected in a rightward shift of the demand curve, depicted in Figure 2.4 as a shift from D_1 to D_2. If in contrast there is a bad summer, there may be a reduction in the demand for varnish even though its price has not changed. This is depicted by a shift in the demand curve from D_1 to D_0.

The direction and magnitude of a given demand curve shift will depend on the characteristics of the commodity in question. For example an increase in income will bring about a rightward shift in the demand curve of a normal good yet produce a leftward shift for that of an inferior good. Furthermore it should be recognised that the demand for products can be interrelated. For example a successful advertising campaign pursued by one firm (which will produce an outward shift in the demand curve for its product) will have the reverse effect on the demand curve of each of its competitors if the total demand for the product is static. Similarly, the same advertising campaign by a firm may also generate a rightward shift in the demand curve of its competitors if more people are encouraged to buy the type of product in question. For example the advertising campaign by the firm producing varnish may encourage consumers to treat their doors and window frames, but with a different brand of varnish.

Thus, to sum up this section it should be noted that a change in the

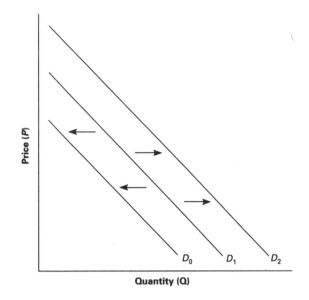

Figure 2.4   Shifts in the demand curve

price an individual can afford to pay for a commodity will lead to a movement *along* the demand curve whereas a change in any other variable in the demand function will cause the overall demand curve to *shift* to the right or left.

SUPPLY

Supply refers to the amount of a good or service that one or more producers plan to sell during a given time period. As we have seen in the case of demand, it is also possible to identify a set of independent variables that in combination influence a producer's decision of whether or not to supply a good or service. These can be set out within the producer's *supply function*.

The supply function and the supply curve

Apart from a slight change in notation and differences in some of the independent variables, we may write down a supply function in exactly the same way as a demand function, specifically:

$$Q_s = f \text{ (independent variables)}$$

where Q_s denotes 'quantity supplied' and, as before, f means 'is a function of'. As before, Q_s is referred to as the *dependent variable*. The *independent variables* are those factors identified by the economist as being likely to influence any production decision. The following discussion identifies a number of important independent variables: the price of the product in question; the price of other goods produced by the firm; the price of the factors of production used in the production process; the state of technology, the number of producers within the industry in question; the objectives of the firm's owners; the degree to which an entrepreneur speculates about the future with respect to production; and the impact of weather on a firm's ability to produce. Let us begin by considering the price of the product in question.

The price of the product

The basic law of supply postulates that the higher the price of a commodity, the greater the incentive for a producer (or group of producers) to supply it, *ceteris paribus*. This is a rational response: assuming that the unit cost of producing a good or service remains the same, an increase in a product's market price will increase the revenue that the supplier receives for each unit sold. The relationship between the amount of a commodity that is supplied within a given period of time and its price can be depicted graphically by a *supply curve*. This is denoted by S in Figure 2.5.

The position of the supply curve in the diagram should be noted carefully. The fact that it intersects the vertical axis at a point above the origin implies that the firm in question is unwilling to supply the commodity in question at or below a price of P_1. Had the supply curve cut through the origin of the graph, it is implied that as soon as the price exceeds zero, one or more firms will begin to supply the good or service.

For some goods and services it is possible to change the level of supply rapidly in response to a price change, as in the case of highly standardised items manufactured on a production line. For other products, supply may be significantly less responsive to a price change. Such cases abound within the construction industry since building projects take a long time to reach fruition. In the case of products whose output cannot be changed rapidly, it is helpful to distinguish between supply in the short term and supply in the long term. For example, let us consider the case of a particular type of house. If we were to use the same set of axis variables we would expect the short-run supply curve to be steep or than the long-run supply curve. This can be seen in Figure 2.6.

In the case of the price increase from P_0 to P_1, it can be seen that it is not possible for builders to respond quickly to a price rise in the

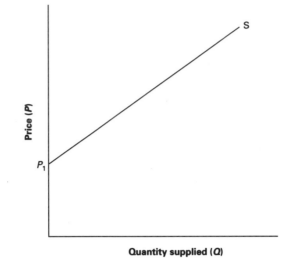

Figure 2.5   The supply curve

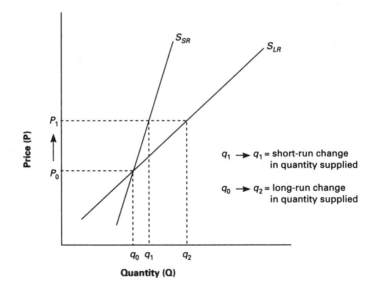

Figure 2.6   Short-run and long-run effects of a change in price on supply

short term, though it may be possible for a small number of houses to be released onto the housing market, namely q_0 to q_1 (see the section below on speculative building). In the longer term, however, it is possible to build additional properties in response to the price change, hence the overall increase from q_0 to q_2.

At this stage of the discussion it is appropriate to stress a very important point about making comparisons of supply curves (or demand curves, or indeed any other sort of curve) according to their relative gradient. Specifically, the supply curves in question should not only measure the same quantity and price changes but should also be depicted on graphs whose axes are calibrated to the same scale.

Thus, to conclude this section, it can be stated that the effect of a change in the price of a product can be measured with reference to a movement *along* the supply curve. As we have also seen, the degree to which supply responds to a given price change may vary according to the time period of the analysis. However, as we have seen in the case of the demand curve, there is also a set of independent variables within the supply function that can affect the position of the supply curve and hence cause it to *shift*. It is these variables to which the analysis now turns.

The prices of other goods

When a firm can produce more than one product, then the supply of one output may be influenced by price changes affecting another product it manufactures. There are two possibilities. The first arises when two or more products are *substitutes in production*, while the second emerges when the products in question are *complements in production*. Using the example of a firm that makes prefabricated wooden inputs for the building process (for example window frames, door frames, joists and so on), let us begin by considering an example where products are substitutes in production. Given that the basic equipment and labour skills needed for this type of work are broadly similar, the output mix of the firm will vary according to the relative price of and demand for each product. For example, if there is a surplus of window frames in the industry such that they command a low price relative to the other types of wooden building input, then their manufacture may be reduced in order to increase output of more profitable items. However, there is also a scenario whereby the production of one commodity simultaneously provides the opportunity to produce another commodity. This relates to the second of our two scenarios – when products are complements in production. For example, an increase in the price of prefabricated wooden building inputs may lead to the production of more woodshavings, which can be sold to pet shops.

The prices of factors of production

As we shall consider in more detail in Chapter 5, businesses require *factors of production* in order to produce goods and services. These are usually subdivided into three basic categories: land, labour and capital. *Land* refers to natural resources that are used in the production process, including coal and oil as well as the land upon which a factory is located. By definition, *labour* is concerned with the human dimension of the production process, ranging from the workers needed to carry out managerial tasks to the people needed to undertake less skilled activities. *Capital* on the other hand refers to the buildings, equipment and vehicles used during the production of a good or service. Output that uses a large amount of labour relative to capital, for example building a wall or designing a new housing development, is said to be *labour intensive*, whereas activities that use relatively large amounts of capital are referred to as being *capital intensive*, for example space exploration. The degree to which production is labour/capital intensive depends on two things: the technological opportunities that exist at a given point in time, and the relative price of capital and labour. Thus if wage rates are relatively high and technology permits, it is more likely that producers will adopt capital-intensive processes. Furthermore, if the price of one or more factors of production becomes too high, producers may be deterred from supplying goods and services altogether, though this will depend on the price a particular good or service can command in the marketplace.

Technological factors

Changes in the state of technology can play an important role in the degree to which an industry can supply a particular market. In industries driven by computer-aided equipment, adopting new technology can be vital to obtaining an advantage over rival producers. In the building industry, the level of technological development has not been particularly rapid, an issue we shall discuss in more detail in Chapter 6. Generally, the rise in scientific and public concern about the interface between industry and the environment, and the response of governments to this pressure in the form of legal and regulatory constraints governing the behaviour of firms with respect to the environment, has proved to be an important driving force behind innovatory change.

The number of producers within an industry

The amount of a good or service that is supplied at a given price can also depend upon the number of individual suppliers operating in the market. As we shall see in Chapter 6, the *structure* of an industry plays an important role in determining the way in which firms behave with respect to their pricing and output behaviour. Intuitively, we might expect that industries characterised by a few large firms with established brand names (which provide a potentially costly entry barrier for new firms) will be less competitive than industries containing a large number of small firms with a limited opportunity to differentiate their product from that of their competitors. Although the construction industry includes some very well-known household names, for example the Bryant Group, Blue Circle Industries and Tarmac. it continues to be dominated by a large number of relatively small firms. However, the nature of building work means that, despite being small, many construction firms can enjoy some degree of spatial monopoly. This arises from differences in regional demand characteristics, the non-transportability of the product and the fact that much construction activity is provided by specialist companies who undertake subcontract work, for example plumbers, painters, scaffolding specialists, demolition contractors, glaziers, roofers and plant hirers.

The objectives of producers

The standard assumption economists make with respect to a firm's objectives is that it seeks to maximise profit. This assumption is analagous to the assumption employed in consumer theory that individuals seek to maximise utility. However, in a business environment that is characterised by indecision, lack of knowledge and random events rather than certain outcomes, luck is probably the most important factor in maximising profits a given time period. In reality, firms are more likely to judge their performance against a target rate of profit that takes into account the uncertainties that exist in any given time period.

The weather

The weather can play an important role in determining the supply of certain products. Obvious examples include agricultural products and the level of building activity that can take place.

Business confidence

Business confidence can be an important factor in determining how much of a good or service is supplied. This is reflected by an entrepreneur's perception of the future prospects of the economy and his or her belief in the ability of the government to manage the economy effectively. For example, producers of intermediate goods for the building process will not be confident about the future if they expect that an impending economic downturn will prompt the government and local authorities to cut back their public works programmes and house-builders to reduce their output of dwellings. An indicator of improved business confidence in the construction sector is building firms embarking on *speculative building* or accumulating 'land banks' in anticipation of an increase in demand. The initial stage is to buy up plots of land, perhaps in competition with other builders, and then, if conditions appear favourable, build properties in the hope of exploiting a buoyant market in the future. Success therefore depends on the degree to which the builder has anticipated future prices, the price he has to pay for the land and the selling price of the buildings erected on it.

Shifts in the supply curve

Changes affecting one of the independent variables in the supply function, *other than own price*, can lead to a shift in the supply curve. The rationale underpinning this statement is identical to that employed when considering the factors that prompt a shift in the demand curve. The *direction and magnitude* of a supply curve shift depend on the independent variable. For example, if there is a general reduction in the price of capital, firms are able to supply more units of a good or service at any given price since one of their inputs is now cheaper. This is reflected by a rightward shift in the supply curve from S_1 to S_2 in Figure 2.7. However, as we shall see, the degree to which this reduction in costs prompts a shift in the supply curce depends on the degree of competition within the industry. A rightward shift of a supply curve may also result from an increase in business confidence, a cost-saving improvement in the technology available to firms or a decision to engage in specualtive building activity. In contrast, a deterioration in the weather, an increase in input costs or a reduction in business confidence may prompt the opposite effect, namely a shift of the supply curve to the left. In the case of Figure 2.7, this would mean a move from S_1 to S_0.

ELASTICITY

Economists are often interested in the *degree* to which demand or supply responds to changes in one of the independent variables contained in the demand or supply function. The term they use is *elasticity*. Although elasticity calculations can be undertaken for any variable, three dominate in the case of demand: own price, income and cross-price (the responsiveness of good A to a change in the price of good B). In

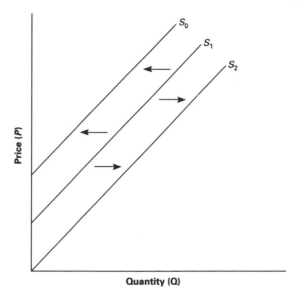

Figure 2.7 Shifts in the supply curve

the case of supply, calculations are usually based on own price. Since elasticity calculations can be undertaken with respect to a number of independent variables, it is important that the term elasticity is pre-fixed accurately. For example many students produce ambiguous essay answers when they refer to 'elasticity of demand' rather than, say, 'price elasticity of demand'.

The next stage of the analysis is to consider the first of these elasticity measures in detail. Since the principles underpinning elasticity calculations are broadly similar, only brief insights will be provided for the remainder.

Price elasticity of demand (η_p)

The term *price elasticity of demand* refers to the *responsiveness* of demand to price changes and hence refers to movements *along* the demand curve. The simplest formulation of the price elasticity of demand is:

$$\eta_p = \frac{\text{percentage or proportionate change in quantity demanded}}{\text{percentage or proportionate change in price}} \quad (2.5)$$

Three basic points should be noted before we proceed further.

First, since Equation 2.5 is defined in terms of a percentage or a proportionate change in both the denominator and the numerator, rather than actual quantities, there are no units. This means that economists can compare the price elasticities of different commodities directly, regardless of whether they are consumed by weight, volume or time.

Second, because elasticities reflect proportionate changes, outcomes are commodity specific. For example a £1 change in the price of beer will be more significant than a £1 change in the price of a house.

Third, in most cases, the relationship between quantity demanded and price is a negative one. Thus the outcome of the vast majority of price elasticity calculations is, by definition, negative. Although textbooks acknowledge this, some professional economists omit the negative sign.

In terms of equation 2.5, the majority of studies that refer to price elasticity identify one or more of the following three outcomes.

First demand is *price elastic* when the percentage or proportionate change in quantity demanded exceeds the proportionate (but opposite) change in price. In this case the number generated *exceeds (minus) one*.

Second, demand is *price inelastic* when the percentage change in quantity demanded is less than the proportionate (but opposite) change in price. By definition, price inelasticity produces outcomes of *less than (minus) one*.

Third demand has *unitary* price elasticity when the percentage change in quantity demanded is equal to the proportionate change in price. As its name suggests, a figure of *(minus) one* (or unity) results.

To illustrate the basic mechanics of undertaking a price elasticity calculation, let us consider a simple example. Two pieces of information are needed: the quantity demanded at the original price and the quantity demanded after the change in price. This information can then be substituted into the basic price elasticity of demand equation (2.5), which can be redefined as Equation 2.6.

$$\eta_p = \frac{\Delta Q/Q \ (\times \ 100\%)}{\Delta P/P \ (\times \ 100\%)} \qquad (2.6)$$

In this formulation, ΔQ and ΔP denote the change in quantity and price respectively, while Q and P signify the original quantity and price (and hence define the proportionality of the identified quantity and price changes). The percentage signs simply cancel out. As an example, let us assume that the price of a litre of paint increases from £10 to £13. It will be assumed that prior to the price change 500 litres are demanded per week, and after it the figure falls to 400. The proportionate change in demand is (minus) 100/500 whereas the proportionate change in price is 3/10. Substituting these figures into Equation 2.6 we get:

$$\eta_p = \frac{100/500}{3/10} = 0.2/0.3 = (-)0.66$$

In this case the demand for paint is price inelastic. In other words, the rise in price prompted a less than proportionate change in quantity demanded.

Factors affecting the price elasticity of demand for a product

Four factors are likely to exert an influence on a product's price elasticity, though it should be emphasised that these have not been scientifically defined.

The number of substitutes

It would be reasonable to expect that the greater the number of substitutes for a product, the greater its price elasticity of demand. Thus a product's price elasticity depends on how it is defined – the broader the definition, the less likely it is that substitutes will exist for it. For example, if we talk in terms of the product 'house' then the alternatives are extremely limited: caves, houseboats, tents and caravans spring to mind. In these circumstances the price elasticity of demand for houses is likely to be extremely low. In contrast, if we refer specifically to semidetached houses, then the alternatives become more numerous, ranging from flats and maisonettes all the way through to detached properties. Thus the price elasticity of demand for one type of house is likely to be sensitive to the existence of other types of property. Hence the broader the definition of a commodity, the more price inelastic its demand is likely to be.

The 'luxury' status of the commodity

Price elasticity of demand can depend on whether a commodity is perceived to be a necessity or a luxury. Necessities are products that individuals need for basic survival, whereas luxuries are products that are not strictly essential but nonetheless, improve the general quality of life. Thus it would be reasonable to expect that demand for necessities would be more price inelastic than demand for luxuries. However it should be recognised that which goods and services are viewed as 'necessities' and which are deemed to be 'luxuries' is a matter of personal preference.

The price of a commodity

It is often argued that low-priced goods are associated with lower price elasticities than high-priced goods. For example a doubling of the price of a box of matches would make a very small incursion into our budget whereas a doubling of the price of cars would be extremely significant for many people. Thus, whereas few people would change their demand for matches, many would be forced to readjust their demand for a car.

The time horizon

Under this heading it is postulated that demand over relatively short periods of time is more likely to be price inelastic than demand in the longer term. The classic example is the oil price increases engineered by the oil producers' cartel OPEC (Organisation for Petroleum Export-ing Countries) after the Arab–Israeli War of 1973. Although the price of oil quadrupled, the immediate demand for oil fell by only 5 per cent because oil users were already tied to using oil-intensive technol-ogies. However, in the longer term the effect of the oil-price shock was to encourage people to look towards technologies that are less oil-intensive, thereby increasing oil's price elasticity.

The relationship between price elasticity and the demand curve

The final stage of our analysis of price elasticity of demand aims to identify the relationship between price elasticity of demand and the demand curve. To facilitate this, we shall consider a reformulation of the basic price elasticity of demand equation. Equation 2.6 took the form:

$$\eta_p = \frac{\Delta Q/Q}{\Delta P/P}$$

This may be restated as:[3]

$$\eta_p = \frac{\Delta Q}{\Delta P} \times \frac{P}{Q} \tag{2.7}$$

Equation 2.7 is a useful restatement of the price elasticity equation. It is made up of two basic components. The ratio $\Delta Q/\Delta P$ can be inter-preted as the gradient (slope) of a given demand curve whereas P/Q can be used to define specific points on the demand curve at which a price elasticity can be calculated. Thus, if we have the equation for a demand curve, it is possible to estimate the price elasticity of demand at any point on that curve.

To illustrate, let us consider a simple straight-line demand curve with the equation:

$$Q_d = 25 - 2P \qquad\qquad (2.8)$$

In this case, the gradient of the demand curve is -2. If we want to calculate the elasticity of demand when the price equals 5, we know from the equation that the quantity demanded is 15 units. Substituting these figures into Equation 2.7 we get:

$$\eta_p = -2 \times (5/15) = -10/15 = -0.66$$

Thus, at that specific point on the demand curve, demand is price inelastic. By repeating the calculation for each price and quantity combination along the demand curve, it is possible to show that price elasticity varies along a straight-line demand curve in a very predictable way. This is illustrated in Table 2.1. The first two columns of the table identify the price – quantity combinations along the entire length of the demand curve (2.8). The third column measures total consumer expenditure (and hence total revenue to the producer) by multiplying together each price–quantity combination. Column four identifies the price elasticity of demand at each point along the demand curve.

The figures in Table 2.1 show that this demand curve, in common with any other straight-line demand curve, is associated with a complete range of price elasticities along its length, ranging from zero (completely inelastic) to infinity (totally elastic). Referring specifically to columns three and four of Table 2.1 it is possible to show that:

- along the price inelastic section of the demand curve, an increase (decrease) in price will produce an increase (decrease) in consumer expenditure (or revenue to the producer), whereas a reduction (rise) in price leads to a fall (rise) in consumer expenditure;
- along the price elastic section of the demand curve, the reverse is true: an increase (decrease) in price leads to a fall (rise) in consumer expenditure whereas a fall (rise) in price leads to an increase (decrease) in consumer expenditure;
- consumer expenditure is maximised at the point where price elasticity of demand equals unity.

These points are illustrated graphically in Figure 2.8, which identifies the price elastic and price inelastic sections of the demand curve, together with the change in consumer expenditure associated with a given price rise.

Table 2.1   Changes in price elasticity and consumer expenditure along a straight line demand curve with the equation $Q_d = 25 - 2P$

Price	Quantity	Consumer exp. $(P \times Q)$	Price Elasticity $(-2 \times P/Q)$
12.50	0.0	0.00	infinity
12.00	1.0	12.00	−24.00
11.00	3.0	33.00	−7.33
10.00	5.0	50.00	−4.00
9.00	7.0	63.00	−2.57
8.00	9.0	72.00	−1.77
7.00	11.0	77.00	−1.27
6.25	12.5	78.12	−1.00
6.00	13.0	78.00	−0.92
5.00	15.0	75.00	−0.66
4.00	17.0	68.00	−0.47
3.00	19.0	57.00	−0.31
2.00	21.0	42.00	−0.19
1.00	23.0	23.00	−0.08
0.00	25.0	0.00	0.00

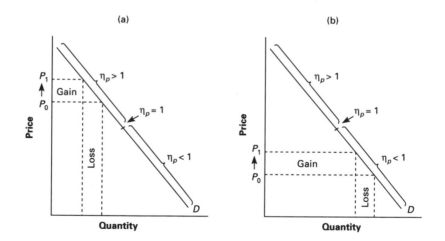

Figure 2.8   Changes in consumer expenditure (or producer's revenue) according to the price elasticity of demand

In Figure 2.8a the extra expenditure by those who continue to use the product after the price increase fails to compensate for the reduced expenditure of those who have stopped buying the product. In Figure 2.8b, the extra money paid by existing users outweighs the expenditure of people who have been deterred from consuming the product by the higher price.

At this stage it is important to highlight an ambiguity that often emerges in students' essays. Frequently, a single demand curve with a shallow slope is drawn and is labelled an 'elastic demand curve'. Alternatively a single, steeply sloped demand curve is drawn and is labelled 'an inelastic demand curve'. Two interrelated issues should be understood. First, as we have already seen, both demand curves will be associated with a range of price elasticities ranging from zero to infinity. Hence the degree of price elasticity depends on the exact point on the demand curve to which we are referring. Second, the flatter demand curve is only more price elastic *relative* to a steeper demand curve, *not* as a demand curve in its own right. In this respect we can see that the former is relatively more price elastic than the latter *at each given price.* .

Income elasticity of demand (n_y)

The theory that underpins income elasticity calculations is broadly similar to that considered already. In this case the most basic income elasticity of demand equation is:

$$\eta_y = \frac{\text{percentage or proportionate change in quantity demanded}}{\text{percentage or proportionate change in income}} \qquad 2.9$$

In contrast to price elasticity calculations, it is important to make clear whether the outcome is positive or negative. Recall that commodities fall into two general categories: those consumers buy more of as their incomes rise and those consumers buy less of as their incomes rise. These were referred to as normal goods and inferior goods, respectively, and as a result it is important not to omit the sign when reporting income elasticity figures. There are three basic outcomes of an income elasticity of demand calculation:

- *Income elastic demand*: this results when the percentage change in quantity demanded exceeds the percentage change in income. This produces a figure in excess of unity (normal goods) or in excess of minus unity (inferior goods).
- *Income inelastic demand*: the opposite outcome arises when the percentage change in quantity demanded is less than the percentage change in income. In the case of a normal good, a figure greater than zero but less than unity emerges, whereas in the case of inferior goods the result will be a non-positive figure between zero and minus one.

- *Unitary income elasticity*: this arises when the percentage change in quantity demanded exactly equals the percentage change in income. By definition, such a situation produces an income elasticity figure equal to 1 or -1, depending upon whether the good in question is normal or inferior, respectively.

As with the price elasticity of demand equation, economists usually redefine the income elasticity equation (2.9) so that calculations can be made with direct reference to the equation of the Engel expenditure curve. Following on from previous analysis, we can therefore derive the following equation:

$$\eta_y = \frac{\Delta Q}{\Delta Y} \times \frac{Y}{Q} \qquad (2.10)$$

where $\Delta Q/\Delta Y$ refers to the slope coefficient of the Engel expenditure curve and Y/Q is the point at which a given calculation is made.

Cross-elasticity of demand (n_x)

This measure can be used to show the degree to which the demand for one product is affected by a price change for another product. It can therefore be used to determine whether commodities are consumed as *complements* (cars and petrol, bricks and mortar), *substitutes* (tea or coffee, wood or PVC window frames) or *unrelated* (goldfish food, beer). The relevant equation takes the following form:

$$\eta_x = \frac{\text{percentage or proportionate change in the quantity demanded of product 1}}{\text{percentage or proportionate change in the quantity demanded of product 2}} \qquad (12.11)$$

If a calculation produces a positive figure, then goods 1 and 2 are substitutes since, for example, an increase in the price of product 2 is associated with an increase in the demand for product 1. Conversely, if a figure is negative then the two products are complements. It is therefore extremely important that the sign (positive or negative) is included when results are being reported. The *degree* to which products are complements or substitutes is reflected in the magnitude of the figure produced.

Price elasticity of supply (ϵ_p)

Just as it is possible to estimate the responsiveness of demand to a change in a variable within the demand function, so it is possible to estimate elasticities that apply to the supply function. As with demand, the main variable upon which discussion tends to focus is 'own price', whereby the term price elasticity of supply refers to the responsiveness of quantity supplied to changes in the price of a good or service. The equation therefore takes the following form:

$$\epsilon_p = \frac{\text{percentage (or proportionate) change in quantity supplied}}{\text{Percentage (or proportionate) change in price}} \qquad (2.12)$$

As before, this basic elasticity equation can be rearranged to generate an expression that refers directly to the equation of the supply curve and the point at which the analysis is taking place, specifically:

$$\epsilon_p = \frac{\Delta Q_s}{\Delta P} \times \frac{P}{Q} \qquad (2.13)$$

where Q_s denotes quantity supplied. The first component relates to the (positive) slope of the supply curve, while the second relates to the point at which the calculation is being made. Since most supply curves slope upwards (from left to right), we should expect a positive answer to emerge from price elasticity calculations.

Price elastic supply occurs when the proportionate (or percentage) change in quantity demanded exceeds the proportionate (or percentage) change in price. In these circumstances the outcome exceeds unity. Furthermore we can employ a specific rule: if a straight-line supply curve passes through the vertical (price) axis, it will exhibit price elasticities of supply in excess of unity throughout, regardless of its slope. Readers should prove this for themselves by estimating supply elasticities along two hypothetical supply curves: $Q_s = 6 + P$ and $Q_s = 10 + 2.5P$.

When a change in price exceeds a less than proportionate change in quantity supplied, supply is said to be *price inelastic*. Numerically this results in a figure greater than zero but less than unity. As with supply elasticity we can apply a specific (but different) rule of thumb: if a straight-line supply curve passes through the horizontal (quantity) axis, it will have a price elasticity of supply below unity throughout its entire length. Some readers may wish to draw two such supply curves and calculate a series of price elasticities along them to prove this.

If the proportionate response of suppliers is identical to the proportionate change in price, then the price elasticity of supply is said to be *unitary*. By definition, this generates an elasticity of supply figure of 1. This outcome is true for any point along a straight-line supply curve that passes through the origin, regardless of its slope. As in the other two cases, unconvinced readers should draw two supply curves, both of which pass through the origin, and apply the supply elasticity equation to different points along each curve.

Factors affecting elasticity of supply

Two main variables influence whether the supply of a product is price elastic or price inelastic. First is the ease with each a producer can substitute the supply of one good for the supply of another. For example a carpenter would have little difficulty switching between the production of internal house doors to external house doors if market conditions so dictated. The second factor is time. As we have seen already, the nature of any major construction project means that it is difficult for suppliers to respond quickly to changes in their economic environment. Thus, although house prices may rise rapidly, the gestation period between acquiring land and completing the construction of a house can be quite significant, thereby generating a relatively steep supply curve in the short run, but a relatively flatter one in the longer run (assuming we retain the same axes on the graph). We shall look in more detail at the implications of this in the next chapter, where demand and supply are considered together in the context of market formation.

3 Markets and Market Failure

INTRODUCTION

The previous chapter analysed the concepts of demand and supply as separate entities. The discussion that follows links the two explicitly. After all, a householder's demand will not be realised if no one is willing and able to supply the desired commodity, and similarly a firm will not wish to produce a commodity unless there is some indication that there is a demand for it. When buyers and sellers are able to communicate their willingness and ability to demand or supply a good or service to each other, a *market* is formed.

The discussion in this chapter is divided into two main sections. First, using the example of housing, it analyses the way in which economic theory predicts how simple markets should operate. Second, it puts forward the contention that markets can fail in that they do not necessarily behave in the way that individuals, pressure groups and governments would like them to. Invariably this results in market intervention by a government, perhaps in terms of regulating the quantities sold in the market, the quality of the products sold or the prices charged.

Construction activity provides an almost endless stream of examples where *market failure* can occur. Acknowledgement of market failure arising from construction activity is not a new phenomenon. For example Bowyer (1993) refers to the role of Henry Fitz-Alwyn (the first mayor of London) in establishing a series of bylaws in 1189 that were intended to reduce the risk of fire by imposing a minimum distance between the upper storeys of buildings and a minimum thickness of party walls. Indeed, the Great Fire of London in 1666 prompted the introduction of a comprehensive set of building regulations in London governing minimum standards for external walls, room height, the size of supporting timbers and the proximity of timber to chimneys and flues. Over a century later, legal provisions were introduced that required district surveyors to ensure that building regulations were adhered to. Thus the regulations and standards that now influence the way in which construction markets are allowed to operate have been part of an ongoing process of change, just as tomorrow's controls and constraints on building activity will reflect those of today.

MARKETS

For many people the term 'market' conjures up a picture of people selling fruit, vegetables, clothes and household goods from wooden stalls sited in the open air. When economists refer to 'markets' they are referring to a wider concept. To them markets are created when buyers and sellers are able to make contact with each other. Hence the term does not necessarily refer to an observable geographical location where buyers and sellers meet face to face. Markets can also emerge when consumers respond to newspaper adverts, buy from a mail-order catalogue, communicate over the telephone or even get in contact through the rapidly evolving 'information superhighway'.

Price determination in a market

The theory contained in Chapter 2 provides us with much of the insight we need to understand the workings of a basic market. It has been shown that both the demand curve and the supply curve are defined initially in terms of a bivariate relationship between quantity and price. Thus it is quite reasonable to draw them both on the same graph, with price measured on the vertical axis and quantity (demanded and supplied) on the horizontal axis. This can be seen in Figure 3.1.

Assuming that neither the demand curve nor the supply curve possess an unusual shape, there is only one point at which they intersect. This is known as the *equilibrium*. At the equilibrium point, the amount consumers are willing and able to buy and the amount producers are willing and able to sell are identical. By definition, the name given to the price associated with this point is known as the *equilibrium price*, while the quantity (demanded and supplied) associated with this point is known as the equilibrium quantity. At all other prices and quantities there is a mismatch between what consumers are willing and able to buy and what producers are willing and able to sell.

The first stage of the following analysis will show that, providing no artificial constraints are imposed on a market (for example government intervention), there is a natural tendency for it to *clear*, resulting in the emergence of an equilibrium price and an equilibrium quantity. For the purpose of the following explanation, let us assume that we are analysing the market for bricks over a given period of time. For simplicity, let us assume that brick producers set their price at £1 per brick. In Figure 3.2 it can be seen that at this price producers are willing and able to supply the market with B_1 bricks. However the demand for bricks at this price is B_2. In other words, there is *excess supply*.

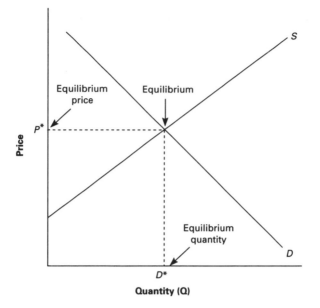

Figure 3.1   Equilibrium in the market

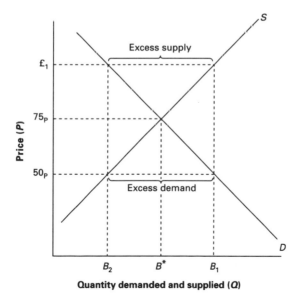

Figure 3.2   The market determination of equilibrium

Since builders and householders (the consumers) cannot be forced to buy bricks, the only way in which a producer can get rid of all B_1 bricks is to reduce their price to 50p each. If the producer chooses to reduce the price of bricks, the demand curve indicates that an increasing number of individuals will be willing and able to buy bricks. Conversely, however, if bricks command a lower market price, then the supply curve also tells us that the producer has less incentive to supply the market with bricks. Eventually the wishes of the producers and the consumers will be nudged towards equilibrium, namely a price of 75p and a quantity of B^*. As long as there are no changes in the variables that characterise the demand and supply functions of consumers and producers respectively, there is no reason why this equilibrium situation should not persist over time.

The same result emerges if the market begins in a situation of *excess demand*. Let us assume that bricks were originally priced at 50p. At this price producers were not willing to supply all the bricks that households and firms demanded. Excess demand equals the distance B_1 to B_2. In a market economy, firms cannot be told how many bricks they should or should not supply. However, in the face of the shortage that subsequently emerges, consumers are likely to bid against each other for the bricks that are produced. This increase in price will then encourage producers to increase their supply of bricks, which at the same time will discourage some consumers from demanding bricks. Eventually the market will be pushed naturally towards the equilibrium points of 75p and B^*. Again, providing that there is no change in the independent variables that characterise the demand and supply functions, there is no reason why this equilibrium should not persist over time.

Changes in the equilibrium price and quantity

So far we have seen the natural processes that prompt an unfettered market to reach an equilibrium price and quantity. However, as we saw in the previous chapter, a change in any one of the independent variables the demand or the supply function can result in a shift in the demand schedule, the supply schedule or both. In terms of the analysis contained in the previous sub-section, we should therefore expect the equilibrium price and quantity to change.

The demand for bricks is an example of a *derived demand*. In other words, bricks are not demanded because they provide pleasure in their own right but because they are inputs for construction activity. Thus the demand for bricks is derived from the demand for houses, walls, pavements and so on, and it is these structures that provide individuals with utility. With this in mind, let us assume that an increase in the demand for bricks is brought about by an increase in the demand for

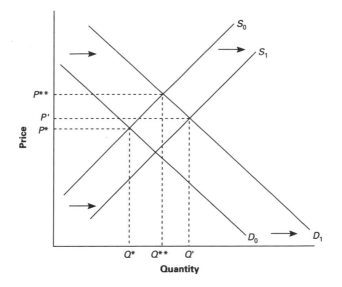

Figure 3.3   Changes in equilibrium quantity and equilibrium price

houses. If the variables that determine the slope of the supply curve for bricks remain unchanged, it can be seen in Figure 3.3 that this prompts an *increase* in the equilibrium price (from P^* to P^{**}) and an increase in the equilibrium quantity (from Q^* to Q^{**}). If, on the other hand, the supply curve was also to shift, say outwards (for example prompted by a fall in the price of the clay used to make the bricks), then a further change in the equilibrium price and quantity would be witnessed, this time from P^{**} to P' and Q^{**} to Q' respectively.

In the first case, the change in the market clearing price and quantity (from P^* to P^{**} and from Q^* to Q^{**}) was prompted by the excess demand that resulted from the outward shift in the demand curve. In the second case (P^{**} to P' and B^{**} to B'), the shift in the supply curve subsequently generated a situation of excess supply, resulting in the new equilibrium position. To demonstrate their understanding of the theory considered so far, readers may wish to consider graphically the implications of an economic recession that reduces the demand for houses, and hence bricks.

The shifts in the demand and supply schedules highlighted so far have assumed a single, 'one-off' change. In a dynamic world we should expect simultaneous fluctuations in most of the parameters that contribute to the shape and position of market demand and supply curves. If researchers are unaware of this problem and assume that the demand curve is static over time, then they may be confronted with what economists refer to as an *identification problem*, a situation that emerges

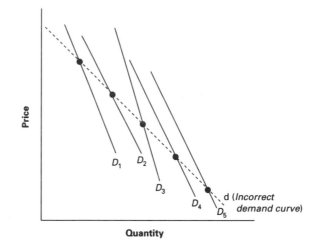

Figure 3.4   The identification problem

when the equilibrium moves over time. This is best understood with reference to Figure 3.4.

Assume that a study has been undertaken using observations over a five-year period. This period was characterised by five demand curves, D_1 to D_5, and five equilibrium points. If a researcher is not aware of this she or he may simply fit a line to these points and assume that this 'demand curve' (drawn as a dotted line and labelled 'd' identifies the price–quantity-demanded relationship during those five years. On the basis of this incorrect 'demand curve' a firm may pursue an inappropriate pricing strategy, given that it should really be concerned with the most recent demand curve, namely D_5. It is possible to take account of the identification problem during the estimation process, however such techniques are beyond the scope of this book.

Consumer surplus and producer surplus

During the discussion of price elasticity of demand in the previous chapter, it was noted that the total revenue (price multiplied by quantity sold) that accrues to a producer changes as we move up and down a straight-line demand curve. It was seen that the area of the total revenue rectangle is maximised at a point where the price elasticity of demand equals unity. Having established in this chapter the basic processes that underpin a market, it is possible to identify two other areas of interest to economists. The first is known as *consumer surplus*, the other as *producer surplus*.

To explain the theory that underpins each concept, let us refer back to the simple market situation used earlier, in which there exists an

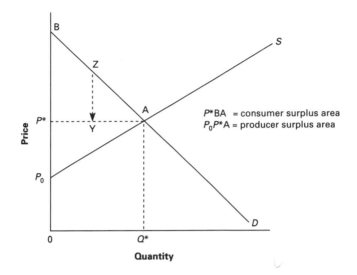

Figure 3.5   Consumer surplus and producer surplus

equilibrium price and an equilibrium quantity. This is depicted in Figure 3.5.

It can be seen that equilibrium occurs at price P^* and quantity Q^*. The amount the brick producer will receive as revenue will therefore equal P^* multiplied by Q^*, or in other words, the area $0P^*AQ^*$. However it can be seen that some consumers are willing and able to pay more than P^* for bricks. Each of these consumers will therefore feel 'better off' because the market price is lower than the price they would be prepared to pay. As a result, a *consumer surplus* is said to arise. For one hypothetical individual this is the distance between points Y and Z. The value of this gain, in terms of all the consumers in the market, can therefore be measured by the triangle P^*BA. Each individual can realise this benefit through having higher savings (added financial security) or purchasing additional goods and services in other markets.

A similar exercise can be undertaken from the point of view of the brick producer. It can be seen from the supply curve in Figure 3.5 that the producer is prepared to supply quantities between 0 and Q^* minus 1 at a price *below* the equilibrium price of P^*. In other words, for each of these units she or he is receiving P^* for each brick, even though she or he would be willing and able to supply them at a lower price than P^*. This difference is known as *producer surplus* and can be calculated by estimating the area of the triangle P_0P^*A (where P_0 is the price at which the producer is encouraged initially to start producing bricks).

Two things should be noted at this point. First, the value of producer surplus is included in the total revenue received. Second, the fact that a firm is accumulating producer surplus does not necessarily mean that profits are being earned. This can only be determined when information is available about the costs incurred by the producer as output changes, an issue that will be addressed in Chapter 5.

Taking account of time: the 'cobweb' model

It should already be clear that a characteristic that distinguishes the construction of residential or commercial property from the production of such items as chocolate bars, televisions or sweaters is the significant time lag between the start and completion of a house or factory. For example, for Britain as a whole the average lead time for dwellings for owner occupation in 1994 was 16.5 months. The corresponding figure for public sector housing (for example local authority or new town) was longer, averaging 23.8 months (*Housing and Construction Statistics*, December 1994). Thus the supply of houses at any given time depends on decisions made in the past. An attempt has already been made to 'capture' this feature of construction activity when reference was made to short-run and long-run supply curves. In Chapter 2 it was shown that, in the short run, the supply of houses is broadly unresponsive to price changes due to this time lag, and therefore the resulting supply schedule will have a relatively 'steep' slope. If we take a longer time horizon when defining a supply curve, it is more likely that construction firms can respond more readily to fluctuations in price, thereby generating a supply curve that is 'flatter' than its short-run counterpart.

There is an alternative and more illuminating way of introducing a time dimension into a market model. For reasons that will become clear shortly, the resulting framework has become known as the *cobweb model*. Economists classify cobweb models within a more general category of economic models known as *dynamic models*. These explicitly include some notion of *time* within their specification, and in this respect they contrast with the *static models* we have considered so far. Dynamic models are used by economists in order to gain insights into microeconomic and macroeconomic issues. Although dynamic models are discussed in detail in more advanced economics textbooks, it is possible to consider a relatively simple framework here in order to provide an explanation of why prices in property markets can fluctuate over time,[1] rather than achieving the single, clear-cut equilibrium usually assumed in elementary demand and supply models.

If our intention is to capture the existence of a time lag between the decision to supply and the decision to demand, we need to recognise the fact that the current supply curve of a construction firm reflects what has been planned in *previous* periods. Thus it is not unreasonable to refer to the supply curve as a *planned* supply curve, whose position and slope are determined by the relationship between the independent variables in the supply function in past periods. In contrast the position and slope of the demand curve are determined by factors influencing the *current* relationship between the independent variables in the demand function. As was noted in the previous paragraph, the implication of incorporating these assumptions into a market model is that the market need not clear over time. Indeed prices and quantities may oscillate over long periods of time without equilibrium ever being reached. It can be shown that the precise form of this oscillation and whether prices and quantities do adjust towards equilibrium depends the relative slope of the (planned) supply and demand curves.

To illustrate the implications of the cobweb model we shall use the example of the housing market. The first scenario to be considered is one in which there is a tendency over time for equilibrium price and quantity to emerge. This is depicted in Figure 3.6, where the demand curve is labelled D_t to indicate that it is demand that is revealed in the current time period (t) whereas the supply curve is labelled S_{t-n} to reflect the fact that the decision to supply houses was actually made in n time periods prior to t.

Let us assume that the initial (disequilibrium) price is P_1. It can be seen from Figure 3.6 that, at that price, firms planned to supply Q_1 housing units. However, when these houses finally reached the market they could only be sold if the price was reduced to P_2. Confronted with this lower price, construction firms planned to supply just Q_2 units in the future. However, when these Q_2 properties were finally supplied to the market, the demand for them was such that they could command a price of P_3. Construction firms then based their future supply on the new prevailing price of P_3, leading to Q_3 being built. It can be seen from Figure 3.6 that the path of price and quantity adjustment tends towards the equilibrium price and equilibrium quantity of P^* and Q^* respectively. Thus it can be seen that it is the shape of this path that gives the cobweb model its name.

However the adjustment path need not necessarily move towards equilibrium price and equilibrium quantity. In the case of Figure 3.7, the path is shifting further away from equilibrium. The mechanics of the process are the same as before, where the initial starting price of P_1 leads to Q_1 units being supplied. However Q_1 housing units can only be shifted at a price of P_2. This new (lower) price leads construction firms to plan to supply a smaller number of houses, namely Q_2. When Q_2 houses actually reach the market there are prospective purchasers who are willing and able to pay at least P_3 for them. It can

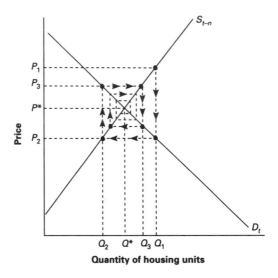

Figure 3.6   A   converging   cobweb   model

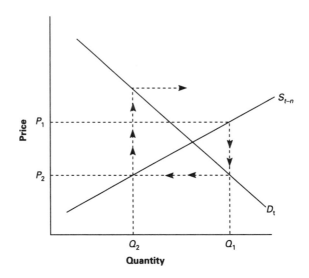

Figure 3.7   A diverging cobweb

now be seen that, instead of generating an adjustment path towards equilibrium, prices and quantities are shifting more and more wildly, such that equilibrium is never reached.

The situation depicted in Figure 3.6 is known as a *convergent cobweb* whereas that shown in Figure 3.7 is referred to as an *explosive* or *divergent cobweb*. Some readers may already have noticed that the

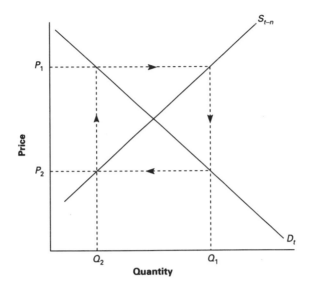

Figure 3.8 An oscillating cobweb

direction of the adjustment path depends on the relative slopes of the demand and the (planned) supply curves. If the (upward) slope of the supply curve is relatively steeper than the (downward) slope of the demand curve, then a convergent cobweb will emerge. Conversely, if the (downward) slope of the demand curve is relatively steeper than the (upward) slope of the supply curve, then the adjustment path will move away from equilibrium and a divergent cobweb will emerge. By analogy, if the demand and supply curves have the same slope (albeit in the opposite direction), the adjustment path will oscillate around a continuous loop. This is illustrated in Figure 3.8.

The explanations underpinning each of the three cobweb diagrams have made a number of implicit assumptions that should now be made explicit. First, it has been assumed that demand and supply curves remain static. In the real world we may expect the position and slope of each to change over time, so the cobweb may not have such a 'neat' shape as that depicted here or in other textbooks. For example consumers may change the weighting they give to the different independent variables as government policy changes, whereas changes in weather conditions and the availability of raw materials and labour may mean that builders cannot meet their planned output. Second, simplistic assumptions have been made about how producers behave. In reality construction firms may have access to detailed information that may allow them to predict the likely price of properties in future time periods. For example, if a general downswing in economic activity

is expected for a particular region or even the whole economy, builders may be aware that consumers will be less willing and able to move
house, and as a result they slow down the rate of house completion
until economic prospects appear more buoyant. Firms may also respond to downturns in economic activity by adding to their stocks of
land while land prices are relatively low.

MARKET FAILURE

Government intervention in the housing market

For over a century the government has actively intervened in the housing market. This intervention has not only benefited people on very
low incomes, who may otherwise have been precluded from purchasing houses of an acceptable standard, but also relatively well-off individuals, who have been offered further incentives to enter the owner-occupied
sector.

*Government intervention through a price ceiling: the case of rent
control*

Rent control is a means of protecting tenants from the high rents that
can emerge during periods of housing shortage. For such control to be
meaningful, the rent must be held below its market price so that the
tenant receives a subsidy equal to the difference between the two. In
order to protect tenants from unscrupulous landlords, governments must
also be prepared to guarantee them security of tenure. Although rent
control has been part of the British government's housing policy since
the middle of the First World War, the nature of the measures used
has changed over the years in response to the implications the policy
has had for the housing market. In this section we shall consider briefly
the history of rent control in Britain and then use a simple market
model to explain why rent control, although laudable as a redistributive
policy, has brought its own problems for the private rented sector.
    Before the First World War nine out of ten people in Britain lived in
private rented accommodation. However the onset of war destabilised
this sector of the housing market. Upward pressure began to be placed
on rents as interest rates and taxes were increased to help finance the
war effort, war production led to shortages of building materials for
domestic purposes, thereby increasing their cost, and changes in the
distribution of the population arose as workers moved to towns and
cities where essential war production was taking place. Rent increases
in areas of high housing demand led to a growing number of evictions

as tenants were unable to meet the higher costs, and this in turn led to a rise in civil unrest. Such discontent was likely to undermine the war effort and therefore the government decided to peg rents at their prewar levels.[2] Although this was seen at the time as a temporary measure that would be revoked some time after the end of hostilities, it was seen to be politically expedient to persist with rent control, albeit in a modified form. For example during the 1920s controlled rents ceased to apply when tenancies became vacant. However, fearing civil unrest, rent control was reintroduced before the onset of the Second World War, the maximum rent being set at the 1914 level plus 40 per cent.

Despite the Housing (Repairs and Rent) Act of 1954, which allowed landlords to undertake limited rent increases if repairs on properties had been undertaken, widespread rent control continued until 1957, when the Rent Act removed the rent ceilings from higher-value properties. Furthermore, the maximum rent set for lower-value properties was raised significantly, affecting around five million properties, and security of tenure was reduced. However, complaints that landlords were taking advantage of their strengthened position led to a new Rent Act in 1965. This resulted in furnished and unfurnished accommodation being treated differently. Furnished properties were left more or less uncontrolled. It was unfurnished properties within the rented sector that were the target for the legislation. Specifically, properties with a rateable value of £400 or less in Greater London or £200 or less elsewhere in the country (which were not already controlled under the 1957 Act) were accorded full security of tenure and rents were set according to 'fair rent' criteria. These rents, which were assumed to be what would emerge anyway in a completely competitive free market, were fixed by rent officers for a period of three years. Service provisions were also assessed and had to be maintained over the three-year period.

This situation continued until the 1974 Rent Act, which attempted to redress the problems faced by many private tenants in poor-quality furnished accommodation who, without the protection offered to people in unfurnished accommodation, faced artificially high rents. The 1974 Act made furnished accommodation subject to full security of tenure and the fair rent criteria.

The 1980s saw the emergence of three Acts that reflected the policy of the Conservative government to deregulate and create incentives within markets, which were perceived to have been made inflexible by public intervention (the processes that fuelled this belief will be explored in Chapter 8). The Housing Act (1980) is perhaps most associated with 'kick-starting' a programme that allowed sitting tenants to become owner-occupiers and buy their council houses at a substantial discount.[3] However, from the point of view of the private rented sector, it also removed rent controls on newly built properties let out by approved landlords in the first significant attempt to draw a halt to the ongoing decline in the size of the private rented sector.

This policy of decontrol was extended by the Housing and Planning Act (1986) to include refurbished properties, and finally in the Housing Act (1988) to all new lettings. In order to avoid the problems associated with unscrupulous landlords, which had prompted the introduction of rent control in the first place, rents become subject to 'fair rent' criteria, operated by the rent officer service, and tenants were given the right to security of tenure. Another feature of the 1988 Housing Act was the introduction of 'assured shortholds', which allow landlords to repossess rented accommodation at the end of an agreed term. The aim here was to provide landlords with a greater feeling of flexibility with respect to the properties they own. However, with house prices being depressed generally, it is not possible to determine whether all these measures are having an impact or whether owners of rented accommodation are simply unable to dispose of their property at a competitive price. Any response by existing and prospective landlords is a long-term issue, rather than something that can be evaluated over a short period of time.

The implications of rent control are best seen in terms of the simple model depicted in Figure 3.9. It is assumed that all properties in the private rented sector are homogeneous in every respect. Two supply curves are identified for rented accommodation. The first, S_{SR}, represents supply in the short run. It is assumed to be vertical in slope since over short time periods the quantity of rented accommodation is unlikely to alter significantly. The relatively flatter (positive) slope of the long-run supply curve, S_{LR}, reflects the possibility that, over time, profit-seeking landlords will change the supply of rented accommodation in response to the price signals they receive. The demand for rented accommodation is represented by line D.

Without government intervention the equilibrium quantity of rented accommodation is Q^* and the equilibrium rent is R^*. If it is now assumed that the government deems this rent to be too high, it may choose, as part of its welfare policy, to impose a rent ceiling of R_1. Since this is below the equilibrium price, there is a short-term shortage of properties, equal to the distance between Q^* and Q_1. In this case the people who are already renting accommodation are receiving a subsidy equal to R^* minus R_1. However those who are willing and able to rent accommodation at this new lower price do not receive the subsidy and need to look for accommodation elsewhere. The repercussions over the long term are more serious since landlords have more time to respond to the smaller profit margins that arise from the implementation of the rent ceiling. Specifically, there are two potential outcomes:

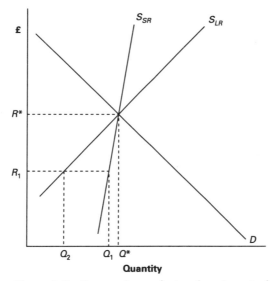

Figure 3.9   Economic analysis of rent control

- The quality of the private rented stock of accommodation will deteriorate as landlords are forced to economise on maintenance costs. Indeed some properties become uninhabitable due to a lack of general repair.
- Lower profit margins may encourage landlords to sell their properties to the owner-occupied sector. This outcome can be seen in Figure 3.9, where the long-run reduction in the private rented stock is represented by the distance Q^* minus Q_2. The overall deficit of private rented houses is Q_1 minus Q_2.

These outcomes have been be magnified by a general trend of individuals seeking to buy their own property, an aspiration encouraged by the preferential measures offered by governments of all persuasions to home owners (for example tax relief on mortgages), and the availability of subsidised rents for tenants of local authority rented accommodation.

As stated above, at the beginning of the First World War almost nine out of ten properties in Britain were rented. By the mid 1960s this figure had fallen to one in four and by the early 1980s, one in ten. Currently 1.93 million households rent from the private sector (Carey, 1995). This reflects the fact that the dice are loaded against the private landlord. Although rent control was initially introduced to counter war profiteering, limited financial returns and the general feeling of uncertainty about what the government may or may not do in the future, for example with respect to statutes affecting security of tenure, it has done nothing to promote stability in the private rented sector of the housing market, nor to encourage new lettings. Furthermore, the fact that the stock of private rented accommodation, albeit subsidised, has diminished rapidly implies that rent controls cannot be viewed as a universal antipoverty measure.

Externalities

So far, our perception of the market is one in which self-interested individuals interact with each other in a way that leads to resources being put to their most profitable use. By definition, this outcome is assumed to be the most desirable for society as a whole. However, there are many circumstances in which the actions of consumers and producers operating in a market situation impinge on what we might term 'innocent bystanders', in other words people who played no part in arriving at the original decision. In some cases this knock-on effect may be desirable for an affected third party, whereas in others it may be detrimental. Both situations, whether desirable or undesirable, are referred to by economists as *externalities* and these usually necessitate some form of government action. The aim of this section is to look more precisely at what economists mean when they refer to externalities and to assess the role of government in externality situations.

When discussing externalities, economists refer to two types of cost and benefit. The cost of an action undertaken by a particular decision maker is known as a *private cost*. When a person buys a good or service the private cost is the price of the commodity in question, together with any associated expenses incurred while the product is being used. By definition, an individual will only contemplate buying a good or service if its cost is less than or equal to the value of the utility he or she ascribes to it. In contrast the cost incurred by everyone else in society from that person's decision to consume the good or service is referred to as the *social cost*. Since, by definition, the decision maker is also part of society, his or her private costs are also included in any calculation of social costs.

It should be recognised that the magnitude of any social costs that may arise from an individual's action are not simply a function of the number of people affected. For example, if someone in a hurry drives recklessly and knocks over a pedestrian, then the (social) cost could be very high for the injured person and his or her immediate family and friends. In contrast a noisy personal stereo being played on a bus may affect many more people but the cost, in terms of their discomfort, is significantly lower than that of the accident victim.

The activities in which we engage can also generate utility or benefits. Benefits that accrue directly to the individual are known as *pri-*

vate benefits whereas those that are also enjoyed by society as a whole (including the individual decision maker) are known as *social benefits*.

When externalities arise from the activities of individuals or households they are usually referred to as *external economies of consumption* or *external diseconomies of consumption*, depending on whether the outcomes are desirable or undesirable, respectively, for the rest of society. Similarly, when externality situations arise from the activities of firms, the terms used by economists are *external economies of production* (when society also benefits from a firm's actions) and *external diseconomies of production* (when society incurs a cost from a firm's actions). Let us consider some examples of each type of externality, commencing with those that arise from individual consumption.

Housing markets provide a number of examples by which we can illustrate the externality principal. Many people, particularly those who are owner-occupiers, choose to keep their houses in good repair. After all, if they are allowed to deteriorate they will command a lower market price when the time comes to sell. Thus the benefit from such action accrues directly to the householders in question. However, everyone else on the street will also benefit indirectly from such behaviour since the neighbourhood as a whole will have a general look of being in a good state of repair and visually pleasing. Thus each person's individual actions help to maintain property values collectively as well. This is an example of an external economy of consumption. The same argument can be put forward in the case of people who choose to keep their gardens weed-free. Although the most immediate benefit of a well-kept garden is experienced by the householder, others benefit too, perhaps in terms of the effort needed to keep down the weeds in their own gardens or, where fences permit, the opportunity to see a visually pleasing garden when walking buy.

However individual actions can have a detrimental effect on others. Take the example of a vandal. The monetary cost of his or her destructive behaviour may be quite small – the price of a can of spray-paint, a hammer or a screwdriver – while the personal benefits he or she derives may be significant, whether in terms of enjoying the act of destruction or defying the authorities, and therefore it is a rational activity from the point of view of that person. However a potentially large social cost may be borne by others, for example an increase in local taxation, a decline in property values, a reduction in the quality of civic amenities and even an increase in fear if the vandal also gains a reputation for violence.

As we have already noted, externalities also arise from the everyday activities of firms or industries. External economies of production can arise if firms provide a general training programme for their employees. Although the company providing the training receives the immediate (private) benefit of its employees having the necessary skills to carry out their jobs properly, others stand to gain as well. First, the newly trained worker is now more occupationally mobile and therefore feels more secure. Second, other companies benefit if these trained workers move on to take up jobs with them. Although some of the skills may be specific to the firm in question, for example those relating to established work practices, others may be more transferable. Where general skills are required for a job – for example bricklaying, plastering or being licenced to drive a heavy goods vehicle – firms may not be willing to provide training unless the worker makes a financial contribution. This may be in terms of some sort of apprenticeship scheme, where the apprentice receives very little remuneration during a prescribed period of training in a particular firm, or in terms of the worker incurring the full costs of acquiring a particular set of skills through an outside institution before he or she can apply for a particular job. Indeed some firms may find that they do not need to have a comprehensive training programme and can operate quite successfully by advertising for the skills they need or even 'head-hunting' particular workers.

On the other hand firms are often guilty of generating significant social costs in excess of the private costs they generate. The most obvious example is pollution. Very few weeks go by without the media informing us of instances of firms discharging toxic substances into lakes, rivers and streams and hence reducing their recreational value. Similarly the emission into the atmosphere of sulphur dioxide (SO_2) and nitrogen dioxide (NO_2) following some industrial processes can eventually resulting acid rain falling on forests and into lakes, leading to the death of trees, fish and other aquatic organisms, as well as the chemical erosion of buildings, statues and other monuments.

In the absence of a mechanism to encourage economic agents to take full account of the social costs or benefits that emerge from their activities, any decisions they make are likely to reflect only their private costs and benefits. We would therefore expect that consumption or production behaviour that generates desirable externalties will be in short supply from a social point of view while activities that lead to undesirable externalties will abound. This proposition, together with an alternative perspective of the externality concept, is set out in Figures 3.10 and 3.11. The discussion here is set in the context of a firm's activities, though the analysis can be applied equally to the case of an individual or household.

Figure 3.10 defines a desirable externality situation. In each diagram, the horizontal (x) axis measures units of the firm's output whereas the vertical (y) axis is calibrated in pounds sterling. It can be seen that three lines have been drawn. The first, denoted MPB, represents the marginal private benefits the firm accrues as its output increases, that

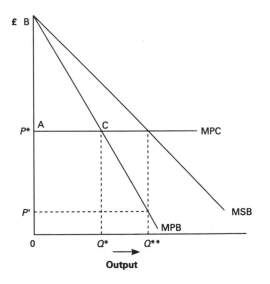

Figure 3.10 A desirable externality

is, the revenue it can obtain from selling successive units to the market. The second line, labelled MPC, measures the marginal private cost the firm incurs as successive units of production take place. For simplicity it is assumed that this cost is constant. The final line, denoted MSB, measures the social benefits that accrue from the firm's activities. Since we are analysing a situation of a desirable externality, the MSB curve lies outside and to the right of the MPB curve. In other words, for each unit of output the social benefits exceed the private benefits.

If the firm only takes its own (private) costs and benefits into account and its objective is to maximise profits, then the rational level of output is where the MPB and MPC curves intersect, namely at Q^*. For units of output between 0 and Q^*, benefits (revenue) are in excess of cost and therefore their production is desirable. For output beyond Q^* the marginal cost of output exceeds the private benefit received. In other words, the firm incurs a loss on each unit of output beyond Q^*. The value of the profit (revenue minus costs) the firm receives from producing Q^* units is equal to the triangle ABC. However the MSB curve tells us that the firm's activities also have a social desirable implication. Ignoring the possibility of social costs for the time being, it can be seen that the socially desirable stopping point for the firm in question would be Q^{**}. This is where the marginal social benefit curve intersects the marginal private cost curve. However, as we have already seen, there is no incentive for the firm to produce output beyond Q^*, even though a net social benefit will emerge for outputs up to the point Q^{**}.

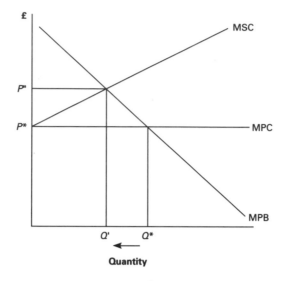

Figure 3.11   An undesirable externality

A similar but opposite argument can be put forward in the case of the undesirable externality. This is depicted in Figure 3.11. The MPC and MPB lines play the same role as they did in Figure 3.10, measuring the private costs and benefits for a firm as its output changes. However in Figure 3.11 a social cost curve (MSC) replaces the MSB curve. This has been drawn to represent an assumption that for each unit of output a social cost is imposed in excess of the private cost incurred by the firm. In this example it has been assumed that this social cost increases with output. As before, the profit maximising firm, taking its own benefits and costs into account, will produce output up to the point Q^*. However at this point the costs to society exceed the private cost. From society's point of view it would be desirable for the firm to curtail its output from Q^* to Q', the point at which marginal private benefits are equal to marginal social costs. As before, however, there is no reason why this should happen.

This analysis suggests that if the market is unable to generate socially desirable outcomes, then some form of government intervention is needed. Three basic options exist: *regulation, subsidy or taxation* and *education.* The viability of each of these measures depends on whether we are dealing with a desirable or an undesirable externality situation. Regulation is normally associated with the latter, in other words firms or individuals are forced to reduce the social cost of their activities. There are numerous examples of this type of approach. The need to obtain planning permission before building work can start is an obvious example. This applies equally to householders wishing to extend their properties, and firms, wishing to build new housing estates, factories or office blocks. Indeed without such regulations the skylines of villages, towns and cities would be determined by the profit-seeking activities of firms.

Regulations are also employed to protect existing buildings. When buildings are of historical interest, either because of their age or some unique feature of their construction, they are 'listed' according to their significance and are given a 'preservation order'. This means that features of the property can only be changed after consultation with the Department of National Heritage. In economics terms, this regulation maintains a desirable externality, where the building generates social benefits in excess of private benefits.

Regulations may also force firms to change their manner of production. For example, if regulations are set to limit the amount of toxic discharge into the atmosphere or waterways then firms may be forced to adopt 'cleaner technology'. This would not only alter the position of the marginal social cost curve, assuming that production now has a smaller impact on the environment, but also the position of the marginal private cost curve since the new technology is likely to impose a different cost structure upon the firm. The important feature of any regulations that the government or local authorities choose to introduce is that they must be enforceable. Usually this means that such regulations have the backing of the law, whereby economic agents who contravene them can be taken to court and, if found guilty, be fined or even imprisoned.

The second approach that the government may choose to adopt in the face of externalities is the use of taxes or subsidies. Where the externality generates a social benefit in excess of the private one, a subsidy is required such that the unit cost of consumption is reduced. Through the reduction in price, the firm or individual is encouraged to expand its activities or consumption to the socially optimal level. In the case of the situation depicted in Figure 3.10 the subsidy needs to be equal to the difference between P^* and P'. When the externality generates a social cost in excess of the private costs then the policy option is to levy a tax in order to raise the price of consumption or the price of the activity in question. If we use Figure 3.11 as our example, the level of the tax would need to be equal to the difference between P'' and P^*. The main problem with the subsidy/tax solution is that it assumes that the authorities in question are aware of the precise position of the marginal private benefit or marginal private cost curves. If their understanding is incorrect, then a socially optimal level of activity or consumption will not result.

Historically, governments have preferred to use regulation as a means of correcting externality situations as opposed to the taxation/subsidy option. An example of the latter approach is the tax levied on petrol and cigarettes. In the former case, different rates are levied in order to encourage motorists to use unleaded petrol rather than the less environmentally friendly leaded alternative. However, in the smoking case sceptics would argue that the full cost of the externality is not taken account of, due to the contribution cigarette sales make to government revenue. It might also be argued that the preferential tax treatment and subsidies afforded to firms that are prepared to set up in areas of high unemployment is also an example of the government responding to an externality situation. In this case the externality arises from the fact that the firm's decision to locate itself in a 'depressed area' will help to reduce unemployment, increase incomes within the locality and ultimately encourage further investment in the area.

The third and final option the authorities can adopt is to 'educate' economic agents about the desirability of taking greater account of the social implications of their activities. If totally successful this would result in the marginal private cost or benefit curves coinciding with their social counterparts. An example of such an approach is that taken by the Health Education Authority, which tries to encourage us to take more exercise and put more thought into the type of food we eat. Of course the main problem with this is that many people are set in their ways and do not respond to such information. As a consequence the authorities have had to supplement this approach with a subsidy system that allows people to exercise at their local sports centre at a subsidised price.

The analysis to date has identified externality situations in terms of clear-cut outcomes: either good or bad. In reality economic activity can simultaneously generate both social costs and social benefits. In other words, the technology that is used to produce a particular output of a firm may be costly from an environmental point of view (a social cost) yet the product may be highly desirable to its consumers (a social benefit). In such circumstances we may define the socially optimal point in terms of the intersection point between the marginal social cost curve and the marginal social benefit curve. This is illustrated in Figure 3.12. The notation used is identical to that adopted in the previous two figures.

If the decision to produce had been defined purely in terms of a firm's private costs and benefits, output would be at Q^*. However it can be seen that there is both a social cost and a social benefit, that the MSC and MSB curves intersect at an output greater than Q^*, namely Q'. In such a case the role of government is to encourage production, perhaps through some form of subsidy. However, had the production process generated relatively higher social costs due to its impact on the environment, then the government would need to intervene in or-

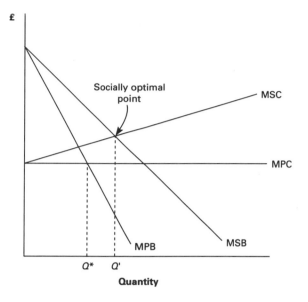

Figure 3.12 Socially optimal output

der to curtail output or force the firm to adopt an alternative technology with lower social costs.

Land use: the case for market intervention

Traditionally, building and construction activity has been subject to a high degree of market intervention, reflecting the belief that an unbridled market may result in undesirable outcomes. The supply of land is not infinite and this scarce resource is subject to a variety of competing demands: housing, business, schools, agriculture, roads/rail, leisure and so on. In order to coordinate these competing demands, land use is subject to a comprehensive system of tiered controls. National and regional guidance is provided by the Department of the Environment (England), The Scottish Office, The Welsh Office and the Department of the Environment for Northern Ireland. Below this, responsibility is devolved to county councils (or regional councils in Scotland), which produce 'structure plans' that define broad policies for land use within their area, and district councils, which produce more detailed development plans within the context of the relevant structure plan. In metropolitan areas, 'unitary development plans' are established for each administrative area by the borough and district councils. A proposed development that is consistent with existing plans is given 'planning permission'.

The advantages of imposing such regulations relate to one or both of two basic arguments. The first relates to the need to protect society from the activities of opportunistic firms and individuals. The second reason is paternalistic in nature and reflects the belief that people are not necessarily the best judges of their own welfare. In contrast, the main economic arguments against planning controls revolves around the degree to which they inhibit progress and curb enterprise. Specifically, if it is accepted that some sort of planning system is necessary, then a trade-off situation emerges. If plans and standards are enforced rigidly, there is a danger that they may not be appropriate in individual cases and therefore the system becomes perceived as inflexible. In contrast, if it is accepted that developments are individual in nature and merit case-by-case evaluation with respect to their wider implications, then the planning process becomes cumbersome and developers become frustrated by delays. This may be further exacerbated if a public inquiry is called to debate the implications of draft plans and resolve any objections that have arisen. In Britain the latter approach is favoured. Despite the inevitable delays a planning system causes, the following points can be made.

First, the need for developers to submit plans in advance ensures that the activities of individual operators can be coordinated and evaluated in the context of each other so that development is balanced according to the needs of the population.

Second, the existence of planning regulations and building standards ensures that the welfare of society is not put at risk for the sake of a quick profit. For example, such standards ensure that buildings are properly ventilated and safe to use. Furthermore, they ensure that the character of historic properties/sites is not destroyed through 'unsympathetic' development. Historic buildings are 'listed' according to their perceived significance.

Third, unbridled market activity may lead to a contraction in the amount of 'green space' and other amenities that are available to the general public, or to the decline of a particular location for both present and future generations. Planning permission may only be given if it is agreed that certain amenities will be provided, for example parkland, access roads, community centres and so on. Indeed proposals that are likely to have spillover effects on the environment must be accompanied by an environmental impact assessment (see Chapter 4). This document not only has to identify the likely environmental effects of the proposal but also the measures that will be taken to counteract them. Copies are sent to the Countryside Commission and English Nature for comment.

Fourth, incomplete information may prevent consumers from making rational choices. As we have already seen, the amount of knowledge consumers bring to a marketplace depends in part on the experiences they have. In the case of buying everyday household items, many of us may be considered 'experts', particularly in terms of what is a 'good buy' and what is not. However, when buying a house our knowledge is very limited due the infrequency with which we enter the market. Thus a company may be prevented from building cheap residential properties near a wasteland site because its potential clientele are likely to underestimate the future cost of the nuisance associated with the adjoining land.

Finally, there is a need to define the extent to which people have rights over land and property, otherwise it will be possible for individuals or groups of individuals to benefit greatly at the expense of the rest of society. For example, a person may decide to erect an unsightly extension to his or her property. Although this will generate private benefits and add to the value of the property, its existence will detract from the value of everyone else's property. In such cases consumers are bound by a whole range of standards, ranging from the size of the extension, to its position and the materials used to construct it. Another scenario is that ownership of a particular piece of land or property may enable individuals to exploit monopolistic power and hold society to ransom. For example a particular council may decided that it is socially desirable for a particular facility to be built. If an individual owns the land that would provide access to it, then she or he could extract a large sum of money from the local authority or even prevent the work from taking place. In this case the local authority can place a compulsory purchase order on the affected land, whereby the owner is paid a 'fair' market price rather than a price that reflects a large 'monopoly profit'.

A related issue – the existence of merit goods and merit bads

Nowadays a complex set of rules and regulations exist to ensure that the products we buy are of merchantable quality and that the customer is not misled about a product's qualities. Indeed a good reputation is essential if a firm is to survive in a highly competitive market. Nevertheless, when entering the market the rule of the game is *caveat emptor*. In other words, despite the existence of safeguards it is up to the individual to weigh up the pros and cons associated with buying or selling a particular commodity. Indeed, as we have already seen, elementary demand theory assumes that individuals are sufficiently rational to be able to make highly informed purchasing decisions. However it is all too apparent that, in real life, individuals accumulate a limited amount of knowledge about the consequences of certain actions. Furthermore they are likely to place an inappropriate degree of emphasis on the *relative importance* of the information at their disposal. The market system will not be perceived as 'failing' in the economic sense even if we consistently make injudicious purchases, for example spend too much on fatty foods and consume insufficient amounts of dietary fibre. However the government, in its paternalistic role, does take an interest in the consumption of some goods and services. Indeed it may even modify our behaviour by force. The need for intervention can arise for two reasons. Firstly, many people take no heed of any warnings issued. For example many children would not engage in active exercise unless they were forced to at school, preferring to watch TV or play video games. Secondly, individuals may under-consume certain commodities because they have insufficient income to purchase what is deemed to be the appropriate amount of a good or service. Examples of this type of commodity abound in the social policy literature and include health care, education and pension provision. Collectively these items are known as *merit goods*. Which goods and services fall explicitly into this category depends ultimately on the paternalistic opinion of others. It should be noted that there also exist a set of products known as *merit bads*, whose consumption is discouraged or even prohibited by the authorities. An example of the former is cigarettes and of the latter, illegal drugs.

It should already be clear that merit goods and merit bads are also commodities that form the basis of the general externality literature. For example education is cited frequently by commentators as an example of a commodity that generates both private and social benefits since it not only enhances the individual but also contributes directly to the performance of the economy. Thus parents are required by law to send their children to school between the ages of five and sixteen and students are subsequently encouraged to obtain further qualifications, either academic or practical. Hence the need for market intervention in the case of merit goods (or merit bads) can be analysed formally in terms of the externality diagrams identified earlier.

Private goods and public goods

Our discussion of externalities argued a case for the authorities to play a role in deciding individual and overall consumption of goods and services that can result in uncompensated spillover effects. On one hand, the consumption of goods and services that are deemed to be socially desirable should be promoted through rule of law, price subsidy or public education. When the effects of consumption are seen to be predominantly adverse, the authorities will feel justified in discouraging or even prohibiting consumption. The aim of this section is to consider a special type of product that generates desirable effects. This is known as the *public good*. Strictly speaking, public goods are commodities whose consumption by one person does not detract from the quality of consumption by anyone else. Public goods can be contrasted with *private goods*, whose consumption is person specific and can be denied to others. However, for reasons that will be discussed below, while the characteristics of private goods enables them to be bought and sold within the market (though private goods may lead to externality situations), the production of public goods does not. As a result, public goods are usually supplied by government and financed out of taxation. The aim of this sub-section is to look more closely at the concept of the public good as a generator of a special type of externality effect. To begin, the analysis will draw a more specific distinction between private goods and public goods.

Private goods

Private goods are assumed to possess two main characteristics, *rivalry* and *excludability*. Rivalry means that for any given unit of a commodity, one person's consumption is at the expense of another person. For example two people cannot consume the exactly the same pint of beer or use the same shovel at exactly the same time. Excludability means that if a person owns a particular commodity, he or she has the right to prevent any other person from using it. As we have already seen, all goods and services are scarce to varying degrees and hence rationed by price. For commodities that command a relatively low price, rivalry and excludability is not a problem since there is usually enough to go round. However when products are highly desirable and carry a high price, rivalry and excludability become more noticeable. In some cases this may simply generate envy and may even result in theft. More seriously, in the case of a major famine, one person's consumption may well condemn another to death.

Examples of private goods produced by the construction industry include the building, repair and maintenance of houses, both private and public sector, together with construction work associated with industrial and commercial activity.

Public goods

Basically the characteristics of public goods are opposite to those of private goods, namely *non-rivalry* and *non-excludability*. Non-rivalry means that one person's consumption of a good or service does not prevent someone else from consuming it. Non-excludability means that one person cannot prevent another from consuming the product in question. For example we may define a nice piece of scenery as a non-excludable public good. One person's appreciation of it does not prevent another person's enjoyment. If a commodity is able to meet all the criteria of non-rivalry and non-excludability, it may be defined as a *pure* public good. However, as readers may have already realised, it is difficult to think of examples of pure public goods. Strictly speaking, many examples of public goods are in fact *quasi public goods*. Returning to the example of a person appreciating the scenery, as long as there are few onlookers the problem of rivalry is unlikely to be significant. However, if too many people view the scene simultaneously, then crowding may lead to one person's enjoyment of the view detracting from that of others around him or her.

A similar issue arises in the case of access to the emergency services. Although these have clear public good attributes, for example the peace of mind they provide to a great many people and the fact that no one is denied the opportunity to receive these services, geographical location means that individuals are bound to receive a slightly different service. Furthermore, during periods of high demand there is the possibility of rivalry if the resources of one or more of the emergency services are already being used by other people.

The demand for public goods

That public goods and quasi public goods are able to provide simultaneous benefits to a large number of individuals brings about a problem. Specifically, if people who pay to consume the good or service are unable to exclude others from consuming it, there is an incentive to *free ride*. At the extreme, if *everyone* who values the public good in question decides to wait for someone else to buy it, it will never be bought despite the fact that the public good is valued by the abstainers. This *free rider problem* is the reason why there needs to be collective provision, financed through taxation. This will prevent the undersupply of a good that is socially desirable. To illustrate these points, let us use the example of streetlighting, a service that is characterised by collective provision.

Streetlighting generates a number of benefits. The most obvious are the added visibility it provides to pedestrians and motorists, and the security that well-lit areas provide to local residents. For any given road the people who place the highest value on the lighting are those who use that road the most, for example the local residents. People who use a road or network of roads infrequently will place a lower value on the existence of lights in that locality. For example a person living and working in a city may only place a value on streetlighting in a nearby village if he or she is going to pass through it. This scenario is depicted in Figure 3.13.

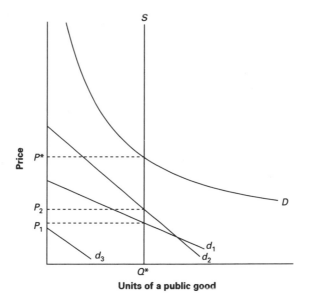

Figure 3.13   Demand for a public good

In Figure 3.13, demand curves d_1 and d_2 denote the demand for streetlighting by two different householders in the village (of course there may be tens, hundreds or thousands of these demand curves, but we shall just consider two for simplicity). It can be seen that householders characterised by d_1 have different preferences with respect to streetlighting than householders depicted by d_2. Demand curve d_3 on the other hand depicts the demand for streetlighting by someone who lives nearby but passes infrequently through the village. If streetlighting was a private good, we could calculate the market demand curve by summing horizontally the three individual demand curves such that the quantity demanded at any given price would increase as more people decided to consume the product. However streetlighting is a public good whose attributes, with respect to visibility, are not diminished as more people use the road. Thus we are interested in the total amount of money consumers are willing to pay for each unit of the service. This can be determined by summing the demand curves *vertically* rather than horizontally. This overall demand curve intersects with the supply curve at P^* Q^*. In other words, total willingness to pay for Q^* units of street lighting is P^* (the sum of p_1 and p_2). It should be noted that the individual characterised by demand curve d_3 is not willing to pay for this level of service. Nevertheless, through collective responsibility, everyone who benefits directly from the commodity in question makes some contribution towards its provision. Equity considerations may result in low-income households making a smaller contribution to the service than higher-income households.

At this point it should be noted that not all infrastructure spending is concerned with the provision of (quasi) public goods, according to the economist's strict definition of the term. For example construction activity relating to such infrastructure items as railways, harbours, the national grid, airports, communications and water supply relates directly to the provision of private goods since it is possible for individuals to be denied the opportunity to consume the product in question. Infrastructure spending directed towards the development and upkeep of the road network does however fall into the public good category (though, should tolls ever be introduced, for revenue reasons or in order to compensate for the negative environmental externalities that arise from car travel, many major roads will also assume the characteristics of a private good). Nevertheless rivalry can still emerge when cars are competing for space at peak periods of the day/week/year, hence even roads are quasi public goods rather than pure public goods.

In 1993 expenditure on roads amounted to £1951 million, having peaked in 1991 at £2102 million. Since 1983 expenditure on roads as a percentage of all new work has risen, from 6.9 per cent to 8.3 per cent. However, as a percentage of all new infrastructure expenditure the figure has fallen from 44 per cent to 35.9 per cent (*Housing and Construction Statistics*, 1983–93, p. 27).

With the economy as well as the building industry experiencing recession during the 1990s, the government has attempted to use road building as a means of providing a stimulus to the construction industry, as well as its more publicised aim of removing heavy traffic from minor roads. However the construction industry should not see such expenditure as a panacea for the problems it now faces. Not only are these monies sensitive to government attempts to contain public expenditure, but they will also be a pawn in the run-up to the next general election. Major road widening schemes, such as those proposed for the M25, may be incompatible with the government's desire to compete on a the 'green ticket' and may even be overturned should a change of government occur.

4 The Economic Evaluation of Construction Projects

INTRODUCTION

A central theme explored in Chapter 3 was the possibility that without government intervention, some markets may not function properly with respect to certain qualitative and quantitative criteria. Many of these market failures were seen to emerge for two basic reasons: (1) because many individuals do not always have all the information they need to make a rational decision, and (2) economic agents are more likely to calculate private costs and benefits when considering a particular action, rather than the wider social costs and benefits that may arise. It is usually expected that public bodies such as government departments or local authorities will take a broader perspective when committing themselves to a spending programme so as to ensure that public resources are directed towards investments that generate the largest net gain in social benefit. One appraisal method that provides a broad insight into the social gains and losses that could arise from particular projects is what economists refer to as *cost–benefit analysis*.

Cost–benefit analysis (CBA) is one of a number of techniques that provide a framework within which decision makers can evaluate the implications of a particular project. The aim of the approach is, where possible, to put a monetary value on the benefits expected to arise over the lifetime of a given programme of spending and to compare this with the costs that are expected to be incurred. If expected benefits exceed expected costs, then there is economic justification for the programme to go ahead, assuming there are sufficient funds to finance it and there are no competing projects with which it compares less favourably. An important feature of any cost–benefit study should be an explicit appraisal of 'doing nothing', that is, an estimation of the costs and benefits that will continue to arise if the status quo is maintained and the project in question is not carried out. As we shall see shortly, one of the main criticisms of CBA is that it often calls upon the economist or other professional to 'quantify the unquantifiable', in other words to put into monetary terms the value of *all* the inputs and outputs of a given project, even if they are not traded explicitly in a market.

The aim of this chapter is to identify and analyse some of the main problems that can arise when a CBA is undertaken, focusing in particular on the economic implications of road building. Indeed an appraisal of the proposed M1 link between London and Birmingham was the first major example of a CBA being used to evaluate a public investment programme in the UK,[1] though in fact the study was too late to influence the decision to build the motorway. The government continues to see road building and road maintenance as an important means of promoting economic growth and prosperity. Indeed the country's trunk road and motorway network is currently being expanded in order to keep pace with the rapid growth in journeys taken in motorised transport. However, although this activity has provided a welcome boost to a recession-hit construction industry, it has also made the industry vulnerable to policy U-turns, for example when the government made expenditure cuts in 1994–5.

The discussion is to be organised as follows. First, following a brief overview of the history of CBA, we shall identify a subset of other evaluation techniques that fall under the general umbrella of CBA. Second, the analysis will consider how economists and surveyors, amongst others, use a process known as *discounting* to take account of the fact that the costs and benefits of a given project usually accrue over a period of time, rather than at a single, distinct point in time. The third stage of the discussion will consider how the results of a CBA can be presented. Finally, having considered these general issues, the discussion will focus explicitly on how the government evaluates the costs and benefits that accrue from road building. This is not only relevant to many readers of this book, but also provides an opportunity to discuss more fully some of the problems the economist has to confront in transport-based appraisals as well as in many other CBAs, the most contentious of which is the valuation of life itself.

COST–BENEFIT ANALYSIS

Much of the theory that underpins CBA dates back to the nineteenth century (for example Dupuit, 1844). However its practical implications only became obvious when governments began to play an active role in the resource allocation process during the latter half of the twentieth century. Whereas attempts to use cost–benefit criteria can be identified in US water legislation during the 1930s, it took until the 1960s for the technique to become widely accepted in Britain.[2] As CBA became more popular and was applied to an ever-increasing variety of situations, the controversy surrounding it increased, particularly when it required researchers to place values on unpriced commodities.

CBA has tended to be used when conducting major appraisals, such as for a new motorway, rather than for individual building projects.

Exceptions are those undertaken by the Department of the Environment: first in 1971 within an evaluation of the costs and benefits associated with air-conditioned open-plan offices and with traditional cellular offices without air conditioning (see Seeley, 1983, pp. 285–6), and second in 1978 when it put forward a CBA framework to assist local authorities in their evaluation of alternative housing renewal schemes. Perhaps the most contentious area of cost–benefit study has been the evaluation of surgical procedures and health-care policies. As cost–benefit techniques have been applied to an ever-widening set of circumstances, so too have the categories of economic evaluation that can be identified. Three of the most common are discussed briefly below.

Cost-effectiveness analysis (CEA)

This is a technique that can be used when decision makers have already accepted the need for a particular objective but remain uncertain as to the best way of achieving it. For example it may agreed that a bridge needs to be built, but the question remains of the economic implications of the most appropriate bridge design. It is therefore a less stringent form of appraisal since, unlike a full CBA, it does not require all costs and benefits to be put into monetary terms. Furthermore, since the policy objective has already been accepted, there is less need to evaluate the 'do nothing' option. Classic CEAs are found in the controversial field of medical appraisal, where doubt often rests on the most cost-effective way of treating a particular illness rather than on whether it should be treated at all. For example, in the case of renal failure, CEA can be used to identify how scarce resources should be allocated between dialysis facilities (home and hospital) and transplants. These are substitute as well as complementary treatments since people waiting for a transplant will, by definition, need dialysis while waiting for a donor organ.

Risk–benefit analysis (RBA)

As its name suggests, RBA is used when a project is associated with a 'risky' outcome. The framework differs from that of a CEA since the approach explicitly considers the costs and benefits of 'doing nothing'. For example an RBA could be undertaken to consider the implications of not building a road to bypass a village that is increasingly being used as a through-route by heavy goods vehicles. The benefits of 'doing nothing' are the costs that are not incurred if the road building is not undertaken. In contrast the risks, and hence potential costs, are the accidents that are likely to result from an increasing number of heavy vehicles using a narrow stretch of road. This may be in terms of costs to property, together with any injuries or loss of life that may occur (how economists have confronted questions appertaining to injury and the loss of life is treated as a separate topic in this chapter). Some outcomes can be ascribed feasible probabilities when sufficient evidence is available. However, if we were to undertake an RBA of British nuclear power stations, this approach would be less easy to justify due to the vast cost that could arise from an accident and the mathematically small probability of an accident taking place.

Environmental impact assessment (EIA)

The aim of an EIA is to identify the environmental implications of a particular policy action or spending programme, both desirable and undesirable. The environmental implications of 'doing nothing' and the different ways of achieving a particular policy objective may then be compared, either directly or through some sort of ranking system. However, since it may not be possible to put a monetary value on certain environmental impacts, it becomes difficult to compare them with variables that can be quantified explicitly in monetary terms. As a result, its policy-making value may be limited.

UNDERTAKING A COST–BENEFIT ANALYSIS

For the remainder of this chapter the discussion will focus on the broader issues that arise when undertaking a CBA. However, questions that arise when considering more specific forms of economic appraisal, such as the CEA, will also be addressed.

Discounting

One of the problems economists face when carrying out an economic appraisal, either within the private sector or within the public domain, is the fact that the costs and benefits associated with a project rarely occur within a short, discrete time period. More realistically, we would expect that not only will a stream of costs and benefits emerge over a number of years, but also that they will be unevenly distributed over this period. The problem exists because most economic agents, whether householders or captains of industry, exhibit a *time preference* for the costs they incur and the benefits they receive. In particular it is reasonable to expect that a typical individual will prefer to receive a sum of money today rather than tomorrow, whereas he or she would rather delay making a payment for as long as possible. This behaviour arises because of the possibility of investing money in interest-bearing bank or building society accounts. For example, the longer a payment can be delayed, the more the interest that will accrue from that sum of money. Thus it may be argued that a CBA should incorporate this possibility when costs and benefits are being compared. The best way of demonstrating how economists can circumvent this problem is to consider the scenario of an individual being paid interest on a bank deposit.

For simplicity, let us assume that a person has £100 and that all financial institutions offer investors a basic interest rate of 10 per cent. This means that if the £100 is invested for one year, £10 interest will paid and the individual will have £110 at the end of the year. If the £110 were to be invested for a further year at the same rate of interest, then a further £11 would accrue (10 per cent of £110) and the individual would have £121 at his or her disposal at the end of the two-year period. Thus if the person in question was offered £100 now or £100 in two years' time, he or she would be expected to prefer the former to the latter since the money could be invested and a further £21 earned in interest. In contrast, were the offer to be £100 now or £150 in two years' time, then the latter would be the more attractive option. The formula used to calculate the future value (F) of a present sum of money (P) is as follows:

$$F = P(1 + r)^n \tag{4.1}$$

where r denotes the prevailing rate of interest and n measures the number of periods under consideration (years in this case).

Taking our previous example of £100 invested for one year at an interest rate of 10 per cent (thus $r = 0.1$ and $n = 1$), we may substitute into Equation 4.1 the following values:

$$F = £100(1 + 0.1)^1 = £100(1.1) = £110$$

Similarly, £100 invested over a two-year period would be:

$$F = £100(1 + 0.1)^2 = £100(1.1)^2 = £100(1.21) = £121$$

Indeed using this formula, we can calculate the future value of any sum of money at any rate of interest we choose. To illustrate, let us assume that we have been asked to estimate the value of £250 in eight years' time at a fixed interest rate of 7 per cent. Substituting this information into Equation 4.1 we have:

$$F = £250(1 + 0.07)^8 = £250(1.718) = £429.50$$

Readers may wish to attempt the following calculations to demonstrate to themselves that the principle has been understood fully:

- the value of £150 in three years' time at an interest rate of 3 per cent;
- the value of £900 in 50 years' time at an interest rate of 6 per cent (the answers are £163.80 and £16 578 respectively).

Having established the basic premise that individuals cannot be expected to be indifferent between the same sum of money offered in two different time periods, we are now in a position to restate the time problem in a slightly different way so that it applies directly to the question of carrying out an economic appraisal.

It has already been noted that we should expect the costs of and benefits from a given investment to occur over a number of time periods. Let us assume we are comparing two projects, A and B, whose costs (and timing) are identical in every respect. Let us also assume that the nominal value of the benefits that arise are also identical, other than the fact that they arise in different time periods: under project A they occur within one year whereas for project B they emerge in ten years. Intuitively we could argue that project A is the more desirable of the two given that it exhibits a return much more quickly. However, we need a way of demonstrating this so that a more explicit comparison can be made. The process economists use for this is known as *discounting*. It is an analogous but opposite approach to that used when calculating compound interest. In essence the question the discounting process answers is 'what is the present value of a future sum of money?' In this case the equation we use is:

$$P = F / (1 + d)^n \qquad\qquad (4.2)$$

where *d* is the rate of discount. If the calculation is being undertaken from the point of view of a private sector firm, *d* will reflect the alternative investment opportunities open to the company in question, reflected in the market rate of interest. However, if the appraisal is of a public sector investment, then an alternative rate of discount may be chosen that reflects a broader set of considerations. This issue will be considered shortly.

In order to illustrate the basic principle of discounting we shall assume that *d* is equal to the market rate of interest, and for simplicity, that this is 10 per cent. Let us also assume that the monetary value of the benefits arising from a given investment equal £20 000 and they will all emerge in one year's time. If we wish to calculate their present value, this figure simply needs to be substituted into Equation 4.2:

$$P = £20\,000/(1 + 0.1) = £20,000/1.1 = £18\,181$$

In other words, the present value of £20 000 made available in one year is £18 181. If in contrast the project were to yield the £20 000 worth of benefits in year two, then we get:

$$P = £20\,000/(1.1)^2 = £20\,000/1.21 = £16\,528$$

Thus, for the second project, the present value of the benefits is lower, even though in nominal terms the two projects are the same. Readers wishing to test whether they have fully understood the discounting principle may wish to estimate the present value of a £35 000 cost occurring in seven years' time (assume $d = 10$ per cent). (The answer obtained should be £17 967.)

It should be clear by now that the relationship between a sum of money in a future time period and its present-day value is totally dependent on the rate of discount used. In financial appraisals, private sector attitudes to time preference are indicated by the market rate of interest. If an investment must be committed for a large period of time, investors will demand a higher rate of interest than if the investment was over a short period. Thus investors will choose between long-term and short-term investments according to the relative rates of interest they will receive.

However, in the case of public sector investments there is a strong possibility that the costs and benefits are likely to emerge over very much longer periods of time, and indeed may even have an intergenerational dimension. In other words, public policy makers may not only be making choices between the present and future consumption of the present population but also between that of present and future (unborn) generations. This raises the question of whether the discount rate used in public sector appraisals should be the same as that used for private sector decision making. If it is felt that the current generation should be prepared to make provision for future generations, then the discount rate used in public sector appraisals should be lower than that used in private sector investments.

It can also be argued that because a portfolio of public sector investments carries less risk than individual private sector investments, the former should be associated with a lower rate of discount. This has two interrelated implications. First, if the public sector discount rate is 'too low', then it may result in too high a rate of public sector investment, an outcome that may be politically undesirable. Second, assuming that there is a limit to the amount of funds available for investment generally, then this increase in public sector investment would have to be at the expense of private sector investment. This may well result in a sectoral misallocation of resources and a reduction in societal welfare.

Thus, based on this opportunity cost argument, public sector projects should be evaluated in terms of a *test discount rate*, which, at the margin, ensures equivalence with private sector investment decisions. Such a test discount rate (or tdr) would also measure the marginal opportunity cost of capital within different sectors of the public sector, for example between health and transport programmes.

The idea that the opportunity cost of public sector investment should be seen in terms of the private sector investment precluded by it forms the basis of the Treasury's calculations of test discount rates. During the 1960s these ranged between 8 per cent and 10 per cent. However the decline in the profit rates of private sector firms has reduced the rate of return sought by the private sector and, by definition, reduced the opportunity cost of capital. At the time of writing the test discount rate stands at 5 per cent.

Presenting results

There are a number of different ways in which the results of a CBA can be presented. The two simplest approaches will be highlighted here. The most frequently cited method is known as the *benefit–cost ratio* (BCR). As its name suggests, it requires the sum of discounted benefits and discounted costs to be expressed as a ratio of present values, specifically:

$$\text{BCR} = \frac{\Sigma \text{ present value of total future benefits}}{\Sigma \text{ present value of total future costs}} \qquad (4.3)$$

where Σ means 'the sum of'. By this criterion, it would not be rational to proceed with a project if the BCR assumes a value below unity since the discounted benefits will be less than the discounted costs incurred. If we are only interested in the outcome of a single project as an 'all or nothing' choice, then the cost–benefit ratio is a quick way of presenting the outcome of a CBA. However, if a choice is being made between several projects, then a simple ranking exercise according to the relative size of the associated benefit–cost ratio may lead to the wrong selection being made. The reason for this will be considered shortly. For the time being we shall turn our attention to an alternative selection procedure that is more suited to making unambiguous comparisons between different projects. We shall then turn to the question of why it is superior to the benefit–cost ratio.

An alternative to the benefit–cost ratio is the *net present value* (NPV) approach. In this case we subtract the sum of discounted costs from

Table 4.1   The hypothetical values of costs and benefits arising from five different projects

	PV benefits (£m)	PV costs (£m)	B/C ratio	PV net benefits (£m)
Project V	100	50	2.0	50
Project W	200	80	2.5	120
Project X	300	100	3.0	200
Project Y	400	120	3.3	280
Project Z	480	150	3.2	330

the sum of discounted benefits and select the project that generates the largest net benefit. However, as was hinted in the previous paragraph, the BCR and the NPV methods need not imply the same ranking of choice outcomes. To illustrate this point, let us consider an example based on the costs and benefits associated with five projects, labelled V to Z. The implications of each, with respect to the two decision rules identified, namely the benefit–cost ratio and the net present value method, are set out in Table 4.1.

It can be seen that in all five cases the present value of benefits is in excess of discounted costs and hence all the projects are potentially viable. If they are compared in terms of the BCR (column three), then project Y appears to be the most desirable. However, when the projects are compared in terms of their net benefits (column four), project Z generates the highest figure. In other words, for an additional £30 million a further £50 million worth of benefits can be generated. Thus, if our aim was to generate the highest net benefits then project Z would be the most desirable option. However the preceding statement assumes that the extra £30 million can be afforded by the public body in question. This raises the general question of the best strategy to adopt when the decision maker is constrained to a particular budget, which can also be considered using the example outlined in Table 4.1.

Let us assume that a public body is restricted to a budget of £200 million. This means that six affordable combinations exist: V plus W, V plus X, V plus Y, V plus Z, W plus X and W plus Y. From Table 4.1 it can be seen that the net benefits from each of these combinations are £170, £250, £330, £380, £320 and £400 millions respectively. This suggests that a package incorporating projects W and Y is the most desirable since it will generate the greatest net benefits, subject to the constraint imposed. Some readers may be wondering whether the same outcome could have been obtained by adding the cost–benefit ratios associated with each element of the packages and then comparing them with the sum of cost–benefit ratios associated with other packages of projects. In this case, the answer is yes. However this is simply a mathematical quirk. A decision rule that involves selecting the package of projects that together generate the largest cost–benefit ratio should be avoided since it can lead to the wrong choice being made.

To illustrate, let us assume that a further £200 million has been made available such that a choice also needs to be made between the packages V plus Y and V plus Z. Using column three of Table 4.1 it can be seen that the sum of the cost–benefit ratios associated with the two packages is 5.3 (2 + 3.3) and 5.2 (2 + 3.2) respectively. By this (incorrect) criterion one would select the former since the sum of cost–benefit ratios is higher. However, as we have already seen, V plus Z generates the larger net benefits (£380 as opposed to £330) at the same cost and hence is the superior of the two remaining options.

The application of cost–benefit techniques to the construction of roads

The demand for roads (or indeed any transport system), whether it arises from householders or firms, is *derived*. That is, roads are not demanded for their own intrinsic value but to facilitate the achievement of other objectives, for example our need/desire to go on holiday, go to work, or deliver goods and services to other firms, retail outlets or households. In theory the benefits of a new network of roads will be reflected in the prices and quantities of goods and services produced in an economy. For example if a new road increases the speed at which commodities can be delivered to markets, then any reduction in transport costs can be passed on to consumers in the form of lower prices. However the process of estimating these changes is extremely complicated. Thus cost–benefit studies typically adopt a less ambitious agenda that focuses specifically on the journeys that would be undertaken on the road, for example the value of time savings that would enjoyed by road users, rather than the knock-on effects on prices throughout the economy.

The computer programme that has been used for over twenty years to evaluate the costs and benefits of new road schemes is known as COBA. Using traffic forecasts supplied by the Department of Transport, the COBA procedure identifies the main benefits of a new road development in terms of users' time savings and the value of reduced accidents. These are compared with the construction and maintenance (for example, resurfacing) costs associated with the road, based on the assumption of an 8 per cent discount rate and an estimated road life of 30 years. Consideration is also given to the 'do-nothing' option. If a scheme passes the COBA test by producing a cost–benefit ratio in excess of unity and there is sufficient money to go ahead with the programme, consideration is then given to the precise route it should take, a process that is usually accompanied by a public enquiry.

One of the main criticisms of the COBA procedure, and indeed an issue to which the analysis will turn shortly, is that it does not explicitly take into account the environmental effects of the proposed road building programme. If a new road is likely to impinge on land deemed to have an environmental value, this will enter the discussion when choices are being made between alternative routes for the proposed development. However other environmental questions do not seem to be answered at any stage. For instance the eighteenth report of the Royal Commission on Environmental Pollution (1994) notes that maintaining and developing the transport system requires substantial resources. For example 120 000 tonnes of aggregates are needed to build a kilometre of motorway, and in total the construction/repair of roads uses 90 million tonnes of primary and secondary aggregates per year, one third of the total used in Britain. Although the price of these aggregates enters the cost–benefit equation through the standard market mechanism as a building input cost, the overall implications with respect to the sustainability of road construction is not considered explicitly. Issues that relate to the ways in which the Earth's resources are used for construction activity will be discussed in Chapter 8.

In making road construction the focus of this discussion, the analysis needs to consider two issues that epitomise the problem of trying to 'quantify the unquantifiable': putting a value the value on the time saved by commuters, and estimating the reduction in costs following a decline in the number and mix of fatal and non-fatal road accidents. These come under the more general heading of shadow pricing.

Shadow pricing

The most accessible source of information about the cost of production of a good or service as well as the marginal valuation of it by consumers is its market price. Specifically, where markets are frictionless, the equilibrium price is a measure of opportunity cost. However markets can be subject to a variety of distortions. As we have already seen, governments recognise the need to intervene in markets, for example in the case of housing, education and health care, but government intervention in markets is not restricted to the goods and services that form part of its social policy. For example a government may impose tariffs on certain imported goods and services as part of a general policy to contain a growing balance of payments deficit.

However not all market distortions are the result of government intervention. Some goods and services are produced by firms with the power of monopoly, and hence they are able to drive up the prices of their products beyond those which would emerge under competitive conditions. There are also many occasions when externalities remain uncorrected such that market prices reflect private costs or benefits rather than social costs or benefits. Indeed explicit market prices may not emerge even though consumers would be gaining a desirable commodity. For example the sheer size of national parks has tended to preclude charges from being levied on visitors enjoying the landscape.

When markets are characterised by distortions, there is a danger that the use of market prices (if they exist) will import values into an economic evaluation that will render it of little value. For example, where government subsidies depress prices or markets have not formed (such that commodities are effectively zero priced), there is a danger of underestimating the benefits accruing from the goods and services in question. Thus economists attempt to compute values that reflect marginal social costs or marginal social benefits. Put another way, in the absence of a 'true' market price the aim is to identify what individuals must give up in order to gain an extra unit of the commodity in question. The result is what is referred to as a *shadow price*.

Given the multitude of commodities for which market prices do not reflect a social opportunity cost, it is difficult to give a general rule to explain how shadow prices are calculated. Thus, by using the examples of valuing travel time and the costs of injury/death from car accidents, the following discussion aims to give the reader a flavour of the problems that can confront the economist. At a later stage of the chapter the discussion will turn to the question of valuing unpriced environmental assets, another example of shadow pricing.

The valuation of time

Faster roads offer road-users the opportunity to save time. Time savings can occur during work time or non-work (leisure) time. Economists assume that it is possible to estimate the value of time savings made during work time by direct reference to wages determined in labour markets. To this figure must be added the 'on-costs' incurred by the firm, for example National Insurance premiums, pension contributions and so on. The rationale underpinning this approach, therefore, is that at the margin the value of an additional hour's work is equal to its cost to the employer. Thus if a person costs a firm £10 per hour, made up of £7.50 in gross wages and £2.50 in on-costs, and the construction of a new road enables a person to save one hour of working time per week, then the value of the time saved is £10 per week.

Although this may seem a reasonable assumption to make, it does have shortcomings. On the one hand it assumes that this extra time can be used productively. If output can only take place when large, discrete time periods are made available, then the saving of time may not facilitate any extra production. For example, if a long-distance lorry driver saves an extra ten minutes per day, he or she will not be able to fit in another long-distance trip in the spare time that has been created. On the other hand, in non-competitive labour markets gross wages may understate the profit accruing to the firm from the increase in output that would be created. Furthermore, if a firm's employees are already working during their travelling time, as may occur on train or plane journeys, then including the value of time saved is tantamount to double counting.

In the case of leisure time savings, it is conventional to assume that units of time have a lower valuation than market wage rates. Two basic reasons for this may be put forward. First, assuming that any time saving is sufficiently large, any alternative use will be more desirable than working and hence does not need to carry the 'disutility premium' that paid employment has to include. Second, taxation and the need to pay other contributions drives a wedge between what a person earns as a gross wage and what he or she receives as 'take home pay'. In the absence of an explicit 'price' for non-work time, the Department of Transport uses figures derived from two types of study. The first is known as *revealed preference*. This requires the observation of people's travel choices and comparing actual travel times and travel costs with those associated with alternative ways of reaching the same destination. The rate at which travellers trade off time for money determines an implicit price for leisure travel The second approach, known as *stated preference*, solicits information directly by asking people questions about their preferences with regard to different journey times and journey costs relative to those they actually make. Evidence shows that no single value can be ascribed to leisure time. For example leisure time values tend to be correlated positively with household income and correlated negatively with the number of children in the household. For adults there is no obvious 'age effect' or difference between males and females, though retired people tend to value their time at a lower rate than people of working age. The 'standard' appraisal figure for non-working time is 43 per cent of average hourly earnings (Department of Transport, 1987), a figure that lies at the upper end of estimates derived elsewhere in the transport economics literature, which tend to fall between 25 per cent and 50 per cent.

The value of life and the cost of injury

Simply to say that every life has an 'infinite value' is not a constructive approach to take when we are confronted with the fact that scarce resources frequently force public decision makers to make choices between policies that can affect the likelihood of injury or death. The most obvious example occurs in the field of medicine, where a choice to allocate resources to treat one particular type of illness can mean that someone else will be denied the chance of full recovery. When confronting the economics of valuing life it is best to view the discussion in the following terms: we are not trying to place a value on the life of a particular individual, rather how we might put a value on a change in the degree to which the population as a whole is at risk of death or injury. Thus the affected people are unknown to us, though it may be possible to identify sections of the population whose risk of death or injury has changed as a result of a particular policy action. New roads have explicit life and death implications. For example the building of a motorway will not only have an effect on the number of fatalities that occur from driving but also on the severity of injuries received on these roads. To begin with we will address the question of valuing life. This discussion will then be supplemented by a brief consideration of the question of valuing injury, such as the loss of a limb.

Economists have identified a variety of approaches by which a shadow price can be ascribed to life. The first is known as the *human capital approach*. This assumes that the value of a person's premature death or temporary incapacitation can be measured in terms of the value of foregone output. If, in the case of valuing life, we are trying to estimate the value of a person's contribution to society then the calculation must also include the value of that person's expected consumption had he or she lived. To many this approach is distasteful since certain sections of the population are implied to contribute negatively to society, the most obvious examples being the elderly and the disabled.

A second approach is to use *life insurance valuations*. Although this approach has intuitive appeal, it should be rejected since it is not a direct measure of the value a person gives to his or her own life or wellbeing. Even assuming that insurance markets operate perfectly, it is a measure of the concern a person has for the future wellbeing of his or her dependants. Thus a person without a close family who chooses not to buy life insurance would, by this method, be implying that he or she does not value his or her life, a highly implausible assumption to make.

Researchers have also attempted to base life valuations on the *hedonic approach*. The aim of this technique is to identify how wages respond to the level of 'life risk' particular jobs carry. The main problem with this is that it may be difficult to disentangle the degree to which wage payments respond to the 'safety' aspects of a job and the degree to which they respond to the job's other attributes. Furthermore, it is assumed implicitly that workers are aware of the risks they face and that labour markets function freely, the latter being unlikely in the presence of strong trade unions.[3] Although it is beyond the remit of this text to outline explicitly the mechanics of undertaking such an analysis, a useful discussion can be found in the work of Marin and Psacharopoulos (1982).

Rather than focus on the amount of money workers are *willing to accept* to confront additional risk in the workplace, an alternative but linked approach is to use a hypothetical approach by trying to identify the amount of money individuals would be *willing to pay* to reduce the amount of risk they face. Economists sometimes refer to this approach as *contingent valuation*. The classic choice identified by Jones-Lee (1976) was whether to make a trip on a low-priced airline or a higher-priced airline with a better safety record. As with the hedonic method, the main problem is that people may not be able to judge, with any degree of accuracy, the value they should ascribe to seemingly minute differences in the risk they face, for example a change from one in 275 000 to one in 200 000. Given that willingness-to-pay studies are normally carried out as experimental questionnaires, there is the obvious danger that people could react completely differently if they were given the same choices in a real situation.

The final approach to note, albeit fleetingly, is one that uses implicit values derived from *past decisions*, made either politically or legally. However this approach has no explicit scientific foundation, and as a result it reflects the vagaries of political decision making or the whims of a particular judge or jury.

Not surprisingly, given the diversity of the approaches considered above, researchers have produced a wide range of life valuations and costs incurred by individuals from injury, ranging from a few hundred pounds to many millions. The life values incorporated into the COBA programme to value reductions in the level of accidents from proposed road programmes are derived from a combination of contingent valuation and hedonic studies. Using 1989 prices, the value of a fatality is £608 580, serious injury £18 450 and slight injury £380.

Road building and the environment

It was noted in the general introduction to this section that the COBA approach does not explicitly take into account the environmental implications of a proposed carriageway development, though such considerations do enter the planning process at a later stage when the decision to go ahead has already been agreed. This weakness in the basic COBA approach is recognised by the government and is discussed fully in a major report by the Department of Transport (1992) entitled *Assessing the Environmental Impact of Road Schemes*, often referred to as the SACTRA Report.[4]

The amount of land that needs to be acquired in order to build a kilometre of three-lane motorway is 6.2 hectares, which is significantly more than the area taken up by the road itself (Hanley and Spash, 1993, p. 220). Although this land may have a low market value, it will have a much higher social value if it is designated as being of special scientific interest. If, in the future, attempts are made to place a shadow price on this land, there is the question of whether just the strips of land that are actually taken for development are included or whether consideration should also be given to the land adjoining that which has been acquired. The SACRA report makes passing reference to three basic techniques that can be used to place a value on a tract of land whose market value may fall short of its social value. Two of these techniques – contingent valuation and hedonic modelling – have already been referred to in the context of valuing life and valuing time. The third approach, which derives values based on the amount that visitors expend in travel costs – not surprisingly known as the travel cost approach – will be discussed briefly below.

Contingent valuation techniques

In the absence of an explicit market price, the most obvious way of finding out how individuals value changes in their consumption of particular commodities is to ask them directly. This approach is known as *contingent valuation* and can be undertaken in two ways. The first involves asking a sample of people how much they would be *willing to pay* to have additional increments of a desirable non-marketed good or to avoid consuming more of an undesirable non-marketed commodity. The second approach is to try to determine how much consumers would be *willing to accept* in compensation to consume more of an undesirable non-marketed product or less of a desirable non-marketed product. For each basic category of contingent valuation, it is possible to solicit the appropriate information using one or more of the following approaches:

- *Bidding games*: here, a representative sample of respondents are asked to indicate whether or not they would be willing to pay or accept a certain sum of money in anticipation of a change in their consumption of a particular non-marketed commodity. For example, from a predefined starting point each consumer may be asked to reveal whether the hypothetical offer is worthwhile. If it is not, then the offer is raised or raised or lowered in successive units until the respondent declares a willingness to accept or pay the last sum of money.
- *Take it or leave it experiments*: as the term suggests, the approach involves giving each member of the sample a simple 'one-off' choice of giving/receiving a fixed sum of money *and* a predefined change

in his or her consumption of a non-marketed good/service or rejecting the offer and maintaining present consumption levels.
- *Trade-off games*: rather than getting people to reveal their preferences in terms of money, a third alternative is to ask people to rank different combinations of goods and services. The choices may include increments and/or decrements of both marketed and non-marketed goods and services.

The main problem with all these techniques is that it they do not rely on the direct observation of individual action. Thus there may be significant differences between what a person may *say* he or she is willing to pay (or accept) for a given change, and what he or she would actually pay or accept. This may reflect the basic fact that the individuals are being asked to play a 'game' with an unfamiliar set of rules. For example, few people know how to price a change in the quality of the air they breathe, a deterioration of a view due to the building of an office block, or a reduction in traffic noise. This is particularly noticeable in studies that incorporate willingness to pay and willingness to accept exercises. Typically it is found that people value the loss of something they already have more highly than the opportunity to gain something they do not already have.

A second problem with this type of study is that estimates revealed by individuals may reflect bias. This may arise because respondents feel that they may be able to influence public policy through the answers they give. This is known as *strategic bias* and may arise, for example, if it is believed that the authorities are intending to make people pay for something they are currently receiving free of charge. Bias may also arise from the way in which an interviewer explains the exercise to each respondent (*interviewer bias*) or in the case of bidding exercises, the point at which people are asked to show their preferences (*starting point bias*). In the latter case, if the starting point is too far away from a person's actual valuation, he or she may be led to feel that his or her valuation is too far off the mark and is therefore unwilling to reveal his or her 'true' valuation. Alternatively, it may take too long to reach the actual end point and the respondent may simply get bored. If it is felt that the study is in great danger of incorporating one or more of these biases, it may be decided to employ an alternative approach known as the *Delphi technique*. This involves canvassing the opinion of a panel of 'experts'. However this raises the further question of whether the experts' opinion is in line with that of society as a whole.

Hedonic models

The principle underlying hedonic models is that the utility an individual derives from consuming a good or service reflects the attributes inherent in the characteristics of the product. The aim is to find a *surrogate* good or service whose price can be used to measure the implicit price of the non-marketed commodity. One of the most extensive literatures on hedonic pricing uses changes in residential property values to measure the (explicitly non-priced) environmental attributes of a particular location.

House prices vary for a number of reasons: physical characteristics (for example the age and condition of the property, the number of bedrooms it has, the size of garden and so on); alternative use characteristics (whether for example it is possible to obtain planning permission to extend the property or carry out other economic activities on the land); service characteristics (such as the property's proximity to good schools, major employers, shops, leisure centres and other important facilities); and its general neighbourhood characteristics (level of traffic, degree of peace and quiet and so on). The rationale underpinning the hedonic approach is that if all the major explanatory variables that determine house prices can be controlled statistically, then any residual differences can be attributed to the environmental characteristics that exist. Clearly, this approach is information-intensive, though it has become easier since the availability of digitised maps.

In a recent paper Willis and Garrod (1991) used the hedonic approach to place a value on countryside characteristics based on a sample of over 2000 properties in central England and the Welsh borders. It was found, for example, that on average a house price is 4.9 per cent higher if the property is located near a river or canal and 7.1 per cent higher if it is located near an area with 20 per cent or more of woodland. The Garrod and Willis study also revealed how physical attributes can affect the value of a property: having more than one bathroom can raise the price of the property by 14.8 per cent compared with single-bathroom properties; central heating adds 6.5 per cent to a house's value; while a single garage produces a 6.9 per cent differential over houses without that facility.

As with all attempts to derive shadow values, a number of caveats must be recognised beforehand if a hedonic study is to be undertaken. First, the method assumes that markets function properly. In the case of housing markets, few buyers are fully informed about the attributes of properties, even if professional surveyors and solicitors are employed to ascertain their structural quality and legal rights. Second, the price of a property will in part reflect expectations for the future. However the hedonic method is concerned explicitly with the pricing of current environmental conditions. Third, house buyers and sellers are unlikely to understand fully the environmental attributes of individual properties. Thus although it may be possible to measure non-marketed characteristics such as noise (in decibels), individuals are likely to be unaware of their precise values, and even if they were informed they would be uncertain about how to respond to them. Finally, the impact of some non-marketed variables cannot be measured precisely, for example smell or taste. This will therefore import further uncertainty into any values that are estimated.

The travel cost method

This approach is used mainly in studies attempting to place a value on rural sites, such as a national park, a reservoir or even a nice view. As its name suggests, the approach rests on the assumption that the value a person places on a location can be inferred from the travel and time costs he or she is prepared to incur in order to experience it. The technique is most effective when the site entrance fee is low, relative to the travel costs incurred, or preferably zero. In its simplest form, site visitors are allocated to one of a number of origin zones. The travel costs associated with each origin zone and the rate of visitation (based on the overall population of each origin zone) are then calculated. From upon this information a (travel cost) demand curve can be extrapolated.

The basic logic is as follows. Assume that it costs £10 for a person from origin zone A to visit a zero-priced site, whereas for people from origin zones B and C the costs are £15 and £20 respectively. Also assume that the population of each zone is 12 000, 16 000 and 7000 respectively and that the visitation rate per 1000 is 19, 16 and 10 respectively. Thus in a given period the total number of visits from each zone (A, B and C) will be 228 (19 x 12), 256 (16 x 16) and 70 (10 x 7), a total of 554. From this information we may infer that when the entrance fee of the site is zero there are 554 visitors, a figure that can be observed.

Although this is only one point on the demand curve for the site in question, namely the point at which it intersects the quantity axis, from the information we have it is possible to calculate other points for a (hypothetical) travel cost demand curve. For example, what if the owners of the site were to choose to levy an entrance fee of £5? The rationale underpinning the travel cost approach assumes that people in zone A, whose total costs would now be £15 (£10 travel costs and £5 entrance fee), would react to the new charge as zone B people had done when confronted with a travel cost of £15 and a zero entrance fee (again an overall total of £15). Specifically, zone A people would assume zone

B's visitation rate of 16 per thousand. Applying this new rate to zone A's population, we get a figure of 192. Similarly, if the entrance fee was raised to £5, visitors from zone B, now facing a total cost of £20, would exhibit the same visitation rate as zone C people had done with £20 travel costs and a zero entrance fee, namely 10 per thousand. Thus we would expect a total of 160 visits (10 x 16). This process can be replicated for successive increments in a hypothetical entrance fee in order to derive further points and hence the whole 'demand curve' for the site. The final point would be that at which the demand for the site equals zero.

The main advantage of this technique is that it is based on observed demand, namely that of visitors to the site when the entrance fee is zero, and hence avoids the biases that are likely to be incorporated into a contingent valuation study. Predictably however, it does have its limitations, the most important of which are as follows.

First, it is assumed that consumers in each origin zone have the same socioeconomic characteristics. Otherwise visitation rates could not be transferred between origin zones.

Second, some trips involve multiple objectives such that the visit to the site in question need not be the primary objective of the journey. Thus although it is possible to use questionnaires to ascertain the proportion of visitors that fall into this category, researchers have yet to come up with a satisfactory means of accommodating such information into a single model.

Third, the approach does not address the question of existence values and option values (see below) since it focuses only on site users.

Fourth, the technique is not particularly useful for evaluations that involve urban sites. The main problem arises because the travel costs are typically low relative to the entrance fees. An attempt to overcome this problem can be seen in Cooke (1993).

Finally, results will be sensitive to the assumed price of the time visitors expend during their journey. As we shall see below, leisure time is a classic variable for which a shadow price has to be ascribed.

Despite these problems, the travel cost approach has been central to the environmental economics literature since its popularisation by Clawson (1959) and Clawson and Knetsch (1966). Since then the technique has been refined significantly in order to circumvent the statistical and economic biases that can arise. On concluding this subsection it should be recognised that *indirect approaches* such as hedonic modelling and contingent valuation, and *direct approaches* such as the travel cost approach should, where possible, be seen as complementary techniques by which the economist can estimate the value consumers place on commodities for which there is limited or no market information, and hence maximise the information used as a basis for decision making.

Option value, existence value and total economic value

The utility that contributes to the social benefits derived from a piece of countryside can in fact be divided into three. The first is the most tangible as a concept, namely that derived by people who actually use a particular resource. For example a person who travels regularly between two cities may well be able to decide whether or not he or she would rather spend less time travelling by using a proposed motorway extension, or continue to use the slower route, which allows him or her to enjoy a view of some ancient woodland. However, problems can emerge when people place a value on resources they may never use. The other two facets of utility relate to the demand of individuals for resources they will never use. Each of these terms will be explained in turn.

As we have already seen, option demand for a good or service arises from people who do not use it at present but would like the *option* of using it sometime in the future. Although we have only considered option values as a positive addition to overall benefits, it should be recognised that they may also be negative. This can occur when a person expects *not* to use a particular facility in the future.

Existence value is a term economists use when referring to the possibility that individuals also value things which they may never use or even see. For example the number of people who are willing openly to express their opinion about the need to preserve woodlands that are 'standing in the way of progress', ancient monuments, works of art, historic buildings or endangered species of animals is far in excess of those who are ever likely to see them. In effect their concern is for the potential lost consumption opportunity for future generations. In many cases there is the question of *irreversibility*, such that once a particular action has been undertaken it would be prohibitively expensive or even impossible to retrieve the situation.

If we add up total user benefits, option values and existence values we have what is known as *total economic value*. The main problem is that although it may be possible to estimate the benefits that would accrue to the direct users of a particular facility, it is more difficult to ascertain the benefits derived by people who do not use the site. One approach is to use contingent valuation, a technique described earlier in this chapter. However this requires people to place a value on consumption behaviour they may never exhibit and upon items they may never have experienced directly, other than perhaps through television documentaries. Nevertheless any economic evaluation should demonstrate an awareness of the implications of a particular project if it is likely to lead to costs (lost benefits) being imposed on present and future generations, for example if a valley is flooded to create a reservoir or a major trunk road is built across ecologically valuable countryside.

Other cost–benefit issues

The above analysis has focused explicitly on roads building in order to demonstrate the problems economists can face when undertaking an economic evaluation. The remainder of this chapter will identify two final issues of which readers should be aware.

Distributional questions

Some projects lead to a redistribution of resources from one part of society to another. In pure accounting terms, these should be ignored in a CBA. Let us continue to use the example of a new motorway. If petrol stations are built along the route of the new road we should not include the profits they subsequently make from selling petrol and other goods. In part this is a *redistribution* of profits from non-motorway to motorway petrol stations. Society as a whole does not gain, though some people will be made better off and others worse off. In societal terms, the two cancel out.[5] However it is important to identify how resources are being redistributed. For example it may not be deemed desirable for the interests of higher socioeconomic groups to be met at the expense of poorer sections of society, unless adequate compensation can be paid.

The implications of risk and uncertainty

So far the analysis has assumed that the costs and benefits that are expected to emerge from a particular investment are assured. However, it is unlikely that everything will go to plan, and indeed no one can *guarantee* that their predictions will be accurate, particularly if a project has a long time horizon. Economists use two terms to encapsulate this problem: *risk* and *uncertainty*. Frequently these terms are used interchangeably, though to the economist the terms have very distinct meanings.

A risky situation arises when, although we are unsure of the future outcome, there is sufficient statistical evidence to make it possible to attach probabilities to that outcome. For example, if we were to gamble on the probability of a tossed coin falling tail upwards, then we know that the probability is 0.5 (if the range of probabilities is between zero and one), 50 per cent or one in two (the possibility of a coin landing on its edge is so remote that it can be ignored as a probability). Similarly, the probability of correctly guessing the face value of a playing card pulled from a full deck would be 0.019, 1.92 per cent or one in fifty two. Economic agents are not just interested in the probability of different outcomes so that they can play games of chance.

Insurance firms use information based on previous claims in order to determine their premium prices. Thus although two people may own an identical car, one may pay a significantly higher premium if he or she parks the car on the road rather than in a garage and lives in an area where car crime is high.

In contrast, uncertainty arises when there is no reliable information upon which an individual can base his or her decision. For example the effect that global warming is likely to have on future crop yields and sea levels can only be expressed as an informed guess since scientists have only limited information about the implications of rises in global temperatures.

Having briefly considered what economists mean by the terms risk and uncertainty, we may formally define a risky project as one in which the costs and benefits vary according to the current state of the world. There are a number of ways in which an economic appraisal can respond to the problem.

In situations of risk it is possible to ascribe probabilities to different events occurring, and from this information calculate an expected value for a cost or benefit. For example, if the profits from an amusement park are particularly sensitive to changes in the weather, then from past records it may be possible to estimate that there is a 25 per cent chance of a poor summer and an expected profit of £20 000, a 60 per cent chance of an average summer and £45 000 profit or a 15 per cent chance of a hot summer and an average profit of £60 000. From this information it is possible to calculate the expected profit as follows:

$$
\begin{aligned}
\text{expected profit} &= (\pounds20\,000 \times 0.25) + (\pounds45\,000 \times 0.6) + \\
&\quad (\pounds60\,000 \times 0.15) \\
&= \pounds5000 + \pounds27\,000 + \pounds9000 \\
&= \pounds41\,000
\end{aligned}
$$

Of course these probabilities are bound to contain some element of guesswork, and hence such a calculation implies a scientifically defined single outcome, which is not really justified.

If a project is characterised by complete uncertainty, then it is not possible to ascribe precise probabilities to each outcome in the manner described above. Nevertheless a similar exercise can be undertaken that generates a set of expected pay-offs. For simplicity, assume that we have to compare two projects, X and Y, both of which are associated with four uncertain outcomes (Table 4.2).

This process, known as *Bayes criterion*, assigns equal probabilities to each uncertain outcome. Thus in this example it is assumed that each of the four outcomes in Table 4.2 has a one in four or 25 per cent chance of happening. From this assumption, it is now possible to

Table 4.2   Four uncertain outcomes from two projects, x and y

	Out 1	Out 2	Out 3	Out 4
Project X	180	200	420	380
Project Y	200	160	460	200

estimate a set of expected outcomes. In the case of project x, we get:

outcome = $(180 \times 0.25) + (200 \times 0.25) + (420 \times 0.25) +$
(380×0.25)
= 45 + 50 + 105 + 95
= 295

whereas for project y we get:

outcome = $(200 \times 0.25) + (160 \times 0.25) + (460 \times 0.25) +$
(200×0.25)
= 50 + 40 + 115 + 50
= 255

Thus, using Bayes criterion, we would select project x since it offers the potentially higher outcome. However it should be made clear that decision rules such as this are dependent on the number of possible outcomes associated with each project.

Two other decision criteria can be adopted in the face of uncertainty. The first, known as *maximin*, assumes that the decision taker is extremely pessimistic and behaves in a risk-averse manner. Specifically, he or she is assumed to compare the worst possible outcomes and to adopt the project that compares most favourably. In the case of projects x and y the 'worst' outcomes are 180 and 160 respectively. Thus, using the maximin criterion, project x would be selected.

An alternative approach is to take what is known as the *minimax regret* criterion. This approach takes a general overview of the implications of making a mistake and selecting the wrong project. To illustrate how the approach operates, let us refer back to the outcomes of the example set out in Table 4.2 and compare these with the outcomes in Table 4.3. In each cell of Table 4.3 the projects are compared in terms of the best outcome. Thus in the case of outcome 1, project y would provide the highest returns and the 'cost' of selecting project x instead is 20 since a gain of 180 is obtained rather than 200. Similarly, in the case of outcome 2, project x generates the highest outcome and the cost of selecting project y is 40. The remaining cells of Table 4.3 have been completed in the same way.

Table 4.3 Outcomes using the minimax regret criterion

	Out 1	Out 2	Out 3	Out 4	Regret sum
Project X	20	0	40	0	60
Project Y	0	40	0	180	220

This time the pay-offs are measured in terms of selecting the wrong project. Hence we are seeking to select the project that minimises 'regret'. Summing horizontally, it can be seen that the regret associated with project x adds up to 60, whereas that associated with project y is 220. Thus, if we are to minimise regret we have to select Project x.

All the selection criteria outlined in this section imply a degree of scientific insight, but this this really is not the case. These are simply decision rules that an economist may or may not wish to follow. Indeed the outcomes of projects may be such that one project may be desirable under one decision rule yet be rejected under another, a problem we have already encountered when discussing the cost–benefit ratio. In the light of this situation, the economist may prefer to show that there is an element of doubt surrounding any estimates and therefore include a range of estimates within the study. For example the economist may choose to complement his or her estimates of the value of a particular outcome with some upper and lower bounds, what we might term 'optimistic' and 'pessimistic' outcomes or 'high' and 'low' outcomes. This approach is known as *sensitivity analysis*. Although the presentation of the final results from a CBA may appear less scientific in nature, since several potential outcomes are listed, the sensitivity analysis does ensure that a particular project is characterised by a certain degree of risk and uncertainty. As more information becomes available over time, the range of estimates to be included in similar analyses could be reevaluated.

Less informed commentators sometimes suggest a third way in which risk and uncertainty can be acknowledged within a CBA. This involves adding a 'risk premium' to the discount rates employed in the economic appraisal such that a range of discount rates are used within a study. Thus, where estimates of costs and benefits are highly subjective, a higher discount rate will cause them to decay more quickly over time, thereby generating lower estimates of present values than if the risk premium was not employed. This approach is inappropriate for two reasons. First, the costs and benefits associated with a project will be characterised by levels of risk and uncertainty. Hence one or more arbitrary risk premiums would continue to cloud the figures and therefore not assist the decision maker's choice between a risky and a less risky project. Second, and more serious, varying the discount rate confuses two different problems: time preference and uncertainty. Both these issues need to be acknowledged separately within an appraisal so that rational choices can be made between projects carrying different degrees of risk.

This section has identified risk and uncertainty as problems that can cast serious doubt on the reliability of a cost–benefit study. Where high levels of risk or uncertainty do exist, this may well be the case. However it should be recognised that many economic evaluations have the advantage of being able to use data based on past experience. Thus although the economist may still prefer to include some form of sensitivity analysis within his or her appraisal, relatively simple decision making rules, such as the net present value method, may still be the most appropriate.

5 The Theory of Costs

INTRODUCTION

The aim of this and the following chapter is to look specifically at the behaviour of firms. The analysis outlined in this chapter is concerned mainly with identifying the relationship between a firm's inputs and outputs, together with the approach used by economists to analyse the costs a firm incurs and the revenue it receives from engaging in a productive activity. Drawing on this material, Chapter 6 focuses on the importance of market structure as a determinant of producer behaviour, with direct reference to the construction industry.

FACTORS OF PRODUCTION

Economists group the inputs used in the productive process into three main categories: *labour*, which encompasses all working people, ranging from the most unskilled worker to the most highly trained surgeon; *capital*, which includes all the manufactured inputs into the production process, such as machinery, partly finished goods and factories; and *land*, which encompasses all the natural resources used in production, including non-renewable resources such as coal or oil, renewable resources such as trees or fish stocks, and of course land itself. Collectively, these elements are known as *factors of production*. Some economists add a fourth element to this list, namely *entrepreneurship*, which, as an input, adds an organisational dimension to the production process. As noted in Chapter 1, entrepreneurs are individuals who are prepared to take risks, and as a result they are treated as a separate category of labour input. The role of entrepreneurs as promoters of economic change is exemplified by their contribution to the industrialisation of Europe in the eighteenth and nineteenth centuries.

The value of land and the concept of economic rent

When deriving models that identify the relationship between a firm's costs, introductory economics textbooks tend to focus their attention on the analysis of two factors of production, namely labour and capital. Although capital and labour are clearly important inputs for construction firms, and indeed will form the centrepiece of much of the analysis to follow, it is important, within the context of this book, to set aside some time to consider some of the attributes of land, given that it plays a significant role in determining the ultimate price of construction output. In the previous section it was noted that the economist's definition of 'land' is extremely broad, extending beyond the more familiar meaning used in everyday language. Although this is an economics text, the following discussion refers explicitly to the latter.

In common with the demand for all factors of production, the demand for land is a derived demand. Unlike other factors of production, however, land is not transportable. Thus its value is determined by the competing demand for that location and the supply of other plots with similar attributes, for example in terms of their geological characteristics. In a global sense, land is fixed in supply. However it is not fixed in terms of the uses to which it can be put. First, technology enables a given plot of land to be used more intensively. For example, in agriculture, scientific advance has allowed farmers not only to increase their crop yields but also to produce a wider range of output. Similarly, advances in materials technology and building technique have provided the opportunity for construction firms to build taller structures and hence increase population densities. Second, where there is no government intervention, we would expect the market mechanism to allow land that is used for one activity to be diverted to another use if a higher commercial rent or price is offered.

Thus we should expect the price of land to be a function of the price that can be obtained for the final product for which it is an input. Therefore the price of land will change when the prices of the commodities for which it is a significant input change. For example, assume that there is an economic boom, similar to that which occurred in the latter half of the 1980s. These expansionary conditions will encourage more people to enter the housing market, either as first-time buyers or as purchasers of more expensive properties. Given that the supply of houses is highly price inelastic in the short run, house prices will rise and this will provide builders with an incentive to build more houses. This will in turn increase the demand for land. If builders are to entice land owners to sell their land, they will need to offer a price in excess of that needed to keep it in its present use, thereby increasing land values. The degree to which land prices vary can be seen in the following statistics, which refer to housing land. During 1989, the year in which land prices in most areas of Britain peaked during an almost unprecedented economic boom, the price per hectare in Greater London was £3 095 772 whereas in Yorkshire and Humberside the corresponding figure was £252 798 (*Housing and Construction Statistics*, 1983–93). By 1992, when the economy was in the midst of recession and the demand for construction output had fallen rapidly, the corresponding prices had dropped to £1 562 743 and £280 222 respectively.

Writers such as Harvey (1981) refer explicitly to the *real property market*. This term simply refers to the market that brings together buyers and sellers of resources embodied in land, such as land itself, farms, and industrial and commercial properties. The real property market differs from other markets in that the commodities traded are not physically moveable before or after their sale, unlike labour, cornflakes or paint. When land or buildings are traded within the real property market, trade is also taking place in property rights. It may be recalled from Chapter 1 that property rights are legally enforceable privileges or restrictions that determine how individuals may use the resources or commodities they have bought. For example, ownership of a piece of land does not mean that a person can do as he or she pleases with it. New buildings must conform with existing planning regulations and be within the guidelines set out in health, safety and environmental regulations, even if the builder owns the land in question. Similarly the owner of a piece of land may also have to respect the property rights of adjoining land owners, for example the right of others to peace and quiet or the right of individuals to have their drains and water supply run under someone else's land without having to pay compensation. If the property rights associated with a piece of land (or a building) change, so too will the market price of that land.

This discussion of land prices provides the background to a term used frequently economists when discussing factors of production: *economic rent*. In this case, it will be applied to the specific case of case of land. So far, we have seen that the price of land as an input is determined by the price of the output produced from it, the output being determined in part by property rights enforced by the legal system. Let us assume that there exists an area of good farming land in close proximity to a major town. It will be assumed that currently the land cannot be built upon. The demand for it as farming land is mirrored by the demand curve D_f in Figure 5.1.

It can be seen that in equilibrium, the price of the land is P_f. Let us now assume that the authorities have provided planning permission for houses to built upon that land. If the profits that will accrue from that land after the houses have been built are expected to be in excess of those that would emerge if the land continued to be used in agriculture, it is reasonable to assume that the demand curve for the land as building land will lie wholly outside D_f, say at D_h. In this example the opportunity cost associated with using this land for housing development are the profits forgone had the land been used for agricultural production. Because the developer is willing and able to pay a price for the land in excess of P_f, there is said to exist an *economic rent*, an amount equal to the shaded area in Figure 5.1. Care should be taken

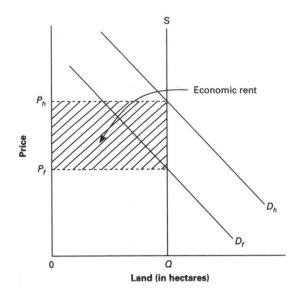

Figure 5.1   The concept of economic rent

not to misinterpret the meaning of economic rent. The strict definition of economic rent is the payment made to a factor (which in this case is land) in excess of that needed to keep it in its present use. Thus in Figure 5.1 the economic rent is the difference between P_h and P_f multiplied by the number of hectares, Q. Applying the concept hypothetically to labour, we would therefore argue that the economic rent associated with a person employed as a bricklayer would be the difference between his or her current salary and that which he or she would earn in the next highest paying occupation he or she is qualified to undertake. *Commercial rent*, on the other hand, is simply an amount of money paid by an economic agent to a landowner for the hire of land. Thus, in terms of Figure 5.1, commercial rent is the equilibrium price for the land, determined by the interaction of supply and demand, for example $0P_f$ multiplied by Q or $0P_h$ multiplied by Q.

THE PRODUCTION FUNCTION

Production is a multifaceted transformation process. It is usually associated with the creation of a brand new entity that can be used by one or more consumers, for example a bridge, road or house. However a significant amount of production is associated with the manufacture of products that are themselves inputs into other productive processes, for example quarrying, brickmaking and the prefabrication of window frames. Economists refer to such outputs as *intermediate goods*. Furthermore, production is not limited to tangible objects such as houses. It is also associated with services such as surveying, estate agency and property conveyancing.

Before any type of production can take place, firms need access to factors of production, specifically land, labour and capital, together with appropriate raw materials and/or intermediate goods. Economists identify the relationship that determines the *maximum* output that can be obtained from a given combination of inputs over a given period of time within a *production function*. In elementary economics, production function analysis may be discussed as a simple two-dimensional relationship, for example how output changes as a firm employs more and more workers. Of course such a basic framework can be expanded to incorporate multidimensional relationships involving more complex mathematical equations. However, for the purpose of this text the discussion will avoid the more esoteric digressions!

Production functions are constructed according to two basic assumptions. First, technology is constant. This means that the relationship between an array of inputs and the output that can be generated from them is fixed at any given point in time. Thus the production function identifies the constraints that confront firms on a day-to-day basis. When new technologies emerge, the relationship between the inputs and the output will also change, and by definition so too will the precise form of the production function. Second, it is assumed that inputs are used at their maximum levels of efficiency. It should be understood at this point that these assumptions do not mean that all firms are using the most up-to-date technology – they merely imply that any inputs used by a firm are put to their best use, thereby maximising output given the constraints of the technology the firm currently has at its disposal. Of course even this is a strong assumption to make. In reality many firms may not be aware that a reorganisation of the inputs at their disposal could lead to an increase in output.

Typically, production functions are expressed as follows:

$$Q = f(\text{land, labour, capital, } X_1, \ldots X_n, R) \tag{5.1}$$

where Q denotes maximum output during a given period of time; f means 'is a function of'; land, labour and capital are the factors of production used during that period; $X_1, \ldots X_n$ denotes any other inputs used per period; and R is a returns to scale parameter (this term will be explained shortly). For simplicity however, we shall express subsequent production functions in terms of either one or two inputs, namely capital and/or labour. Where both capital and labour are acknowledged, the expression compresses to:

$$Q = f(K,L) \qquad\qquad (5.2)$$

where K and L denote the respective quantities of capital and labour used in a given time period.

Production functions in the short run and the long run

Because inputs can be varied at different rates, economists frequently make a distinction between production functions in the short run and in the long run. Specifically it is assumed that *all* inputs can be varied in the long run, whereas in the short run only certain inputs can be varied. Due to the potentially long 'gestation period' associated with the buying of land, the building of factories and the purchase of machinery, economists tend to assume that only *labour* is *variable* in the short run. All other factors are therefore *fixed*. Whereas this is an extremely valid assumption to make in the case of casual labour, many skilled workers may best be viewed as *quasi-fixed* in the short run. Thus some industries may be characterised by what we might term 'disguised unemployment'. This is due to the existence of contracts, the need to engage in multistage job-selection processes, sunk training costs, potential training costs and so on. In the case of the construction industry, the casual nature of much of the work undertaken means that employment levels are extremely sensitive to the level of demand for construction work, and hence labour readily fulfils the economist's definition of a variable factor of production. For the purposes of the analysis to follow it will be assumed that all labour is variable in the short run. By definition, it is unnecessary to make a distinction between fixed and variable factors in the long run.

The next stage of the analysis is to depict production functions graphically. This will provide a frame of reference from which we will derive the cost curves that can be used to estimate a firm's price and output. We shall first consider the simplest of cases, namely a short-run production function.

Graphical representations of production functions

Short-run analysis

As we have already seen, economists frequently assume that only labour can be varied in the short run. The amount of land, factory space and machinery is assumed to be fixed. Thus, if output is to be increased, it can only take place by varying the size of the workforce. This scenario may be written in two basic ways – as a variant of equation 5.2:

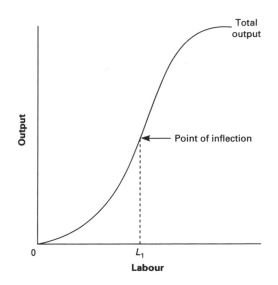

Figure 5.2   The relationship between labour and output (capital fixed)

$$Q = f(K',L) \qquad\qquad (5.3)$$

where K' denotes the fact that capital is fixed, or as:

$$Q = f(L) \qquad\qquad (5.4)$$

where K is omitted for convenience.

Let us predict the likely impact on output of adding extra units of labour to a fixed amount of capital. This relationship is expressed in Figure 5.2. It can be seen that the relationship emerges graphically as an elongated 'S' shape. Let us consider why. Assume that a building firm has been asked to build a house. If only one worker was employed, she or he would be responsible for all the jobs involved during construction, ranging from basic manual work through to more skilled tasks. Initially, as more people are hired the rate of output is likely to increase at an increasing rate as the new workers are able to collaborate in the work required. In other words, the marginal product is increasing. Eventually, however, a point will be reached (known as the point of inflection) where additional workers are unable to sustain this increase, so although they make a positive addition to output, their marginal contribution begins to fall. Indeed past a certain point, limitations of space and tasks may prevent additional workers from making any contribution at all and may even lead to a decline in output as everyone starts to get in each other's way. In terms of Figure 5.2, labour input from 0 to L_1 is said to be associated with *increasing returns* whereas beyond L_1, production is beset with *diminishing returns*. This outcome gives rise to the *law of diminishing returns,* which states that if increasing quantities of a variable factor of production are added to a given quantity of a fixed factor, the marginal product (and average product) of the variable factor will eventually decrease. Diminishing returns are therefore said to exist when marginal product begins to fall, and hence output increases at a decreasing rate.

Long-run analysis

Having considered the implications of having only one variable factor of production, namely labour, let us now move on to consider the implications for the entrepreneur with two variable factors at his or her disposal. The production function we shall use takes the following form:

$$Q = f(K,L)$$

When both factors are variable we can construct a simple analytical tool known as the *isoquant.* Isoquants depict different combinations of capital and labour that can be used to produce a fixed level of output, assuming that both inputs are combined optimally. Usually, on a graph the quantity of labour inputs is measured horizontally and the quantity of capital inputs is measured vertically. Let us assume that a firm has a variety of possible ways of producing output. At one extreme there is the possibility of using *labour-intensive* techniques, where workers perform all the major production tasks with minimal amounts of capital. At the other extreme, *capital-intensive* techniques use a relatively large amount of technology and only require a small number of workers to oversee production. Alternatively it is possible to use a combination of labour and capital that falls somewhere in between these two extremes. The exact shape of the isoquant depends on the various technologies available to the firm at a given point in time. For reasons that will be explained shortly, it will be assumed that the isoquant associated with each level of output is not only negatively sloped but also convex to the origin. Consider the hypothetical isoquants depicted in Figure 5.3, where Q_1, Q_2 and Q_3 map out the capital and labour combinations needed to produce increasingly higher levels of output.

Five alternative processes are depicted along the isoquant Q_1, labelled A to E, where A denotes a highly labour-intensive process while shifts to B, C, D and E show factor combinations of increasing capital intensity. Each combination produces Q_1 units of output. The negative slope shows that to maintain a given level of production, any reduction in labour must be met by an increase in the amount of capital

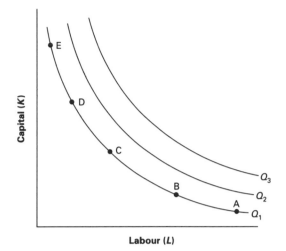

Figure 5.3   Isoquants

used. Had the isoquant been drawn as a straight line, this would have implied a fixed rate of substitution between capital and labour.

However it is more likely that the relationship between capital and labour will not be fixed but will instead reflect the impact of diminishing returns. Thus it is predicted that the greater the amount of labour (capital) used in the production process, the smaller the amount of labour (capital) that needs to be released to maintain output at the level designated by the isoquant. Any isoquant that is convex to the origin is said to display a *diminishing marginal rate of technical substitution*. Isoquants possess a number of properties, as follows.

First an isoquant can pass through every possible combination of capital and labour on the graph. In other words, each combination of capital and labour will be associated with some level of output. Thus we may draw a whole family of isoquants, which reflect increasing levels of output as they move in a north-easterly direction. Of course this property is unlikely to hold good in practice as much depends on the nature of the output under consideration.

Second, since isoquants depict the minimum input combinations that produce each level of output, it is inappropriate for isoquants to cross. If they did, this would imply that a single combination of capital and labour is able to produce two levels of output, which, by definition, is an illogical statement.

Third, isoquants are likely to be convex to the origin, reflecting a diminishing marginal rate of technical substitution.

It has already been noted that Figure 5.3 implies isoquants have a smooth curve, which in turn implies that an infinite number of capital and labour combinations are available to the producer for each given level of output. In reality most building processes can only be undertaken in a very limited number of ways. This results in the isoquant assuming a more jagged shape. At the extreme, if there is only one viable capital–labour combination at each level of output, the isoquant assumes an 'L' shape. Both possibilities are set out in Figure 5.4. In the case of the L-shaped isoquants, any addition to the optimal combination of capital and labour has no effect on the level of output, despite the additional factors of production being used. Only when labour and capital are added in the proportions dictated by existing technology can output be increased, for example from Q_2 to Q_3.

Returns to scale

At this point, we are in a position to be able to clarify what is meant by the term *returns to scale*, a term introduced earlier in the chapter when the variables that should be included in a production function were listed. Specifically, it refers to the changes in output that take place when all inputs are varied *in the same proportion*. Three possibilities are described below and depicted in Figure 5.5:

- *Increasing returns to scale*: this means that if inputs are increased by a given proportion, there is an even larger proportionate change in output, for example if the amounts of both inputs are doubled and output trebles in size.
- *Decreasing returns to scale*: this is the opposite scenario, for example when all a firm's inputs are trebled but output only doubles as a result.
- *Constant returns to scale*: following on, constant returns to scale emerge if a doubling of inputs leads to a doubling of a firm's output.

The proportionality of the changes in factor inputs is highlighted by the fact that we are focusing on the implications of combinations that lie on any straight line extending from the origin of the graph. It can be seen that the output associated with the input combination of L_1 and K_1 is 20 units (measured with reference to the isoquant passing through point A). If we then move to the input combination L_2, K_2, then increasing returns to scale would exist if the isoquant passing through point B (labelled Q) was associated with an output of greater than 40 units, for example 50 units. When returns are decreasing, isoquant Q will be associated with an output of less than 40 units whereas if returns are constant, isoquant Q will be associated with an output of exactly 40 units.

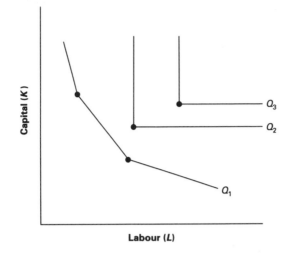

Figure 5.4   Technology and isoquants

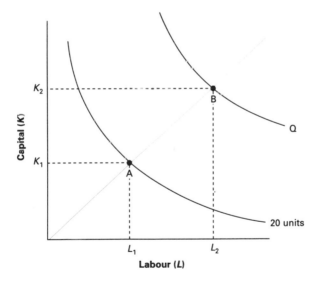

Figure 5.5   Returns to scale

Productivity in the construction industry

Improvements in productivity can arise in a variety of ways: improvements in training and working practices, and technological advancement with respect to the materials and equipment used. A useful source of basic productivity data is the *Employment Gazette* (Table 1.8), though not all of the monthly editions during a given year provide a full-scale breakdown of figures at the industry level.

Like all industries, the construction industry has benefited from the standardisation of inputs, for example factory-made roof trusses and window frames, which reduce the need for highly specialised carpenters or on-site tools. Since the manufacturers have been able to take advantage of the lower unit costs that arise from large-scale production (discussed later in this chapter), cost savings have been passed down to building firms. This raises the possibility for architects to use cheaper, standardised inputs as the basis for a plan that is acceptable to the client, rather than highly individual designs that require a greater degree of on-site input and hence are more costly.

Nevertheless the construction industry has tended to lag behind other industries with respect to productivity, despite the fact that a significantly smaller proportion of its labour is quasi fixed. Evidence from the *Employment Gazette* illustrates this. For example, in 1994 output per person in construction expressed as an index number (1990 = 100) was 109, whereas in the case of manufacturing as a whole the corresponding figure was 115.1. Indeed productivity in construction only exceeded that of two of the eight identified manufacturing sectors: 'textiles, footwear, clothing, and leather' (97.8) and 'base metals and metal products' (105.9). The highest figures in the manufacturing category were for 'solid fuels, and nuclear fuels; oil refining' (131.0) and 'chemicals and manmade fibres' (128.8). Since construction-related output has fallen dramatically since 1990, the productivity gains that have occurred have emerged from reductions in the size of the labour force. Again, using 1990 as the base year, employment in construction measured as an index number amounted to 82.8 (total employment in construction in 1994 was around 870 000 people), compared with 86.1 for manufacturing as a whole. These figures contrast significantly with those associated with the latter part of the 1980s, when the construction industry was enjoying relative prosperity. For example in 1988 productivity in construction exceeded that for manufacturing, with figures of 100.2 and 94.2 respectively. There are a number factors that may explain why the construction industry has fallen behind manufacturing with respect to its productivity.

First, the nature of the work does not always lend itself to productivity-enhancing mechanisation – around one-third of construction activity consists of repair and maintenance work, which is largely labour intensive and does not lend itself to mechanisation.

Second, the theory used by economists tends to assume that capital and labour can be easily substituted for each other. In reality, capital in the building trade is not necessarily a good substitute for labour, for example in the case of specialist electricians and bricklayers or more general labourers who may be expected to perform several distinctive tasks on site (isoquants are not smooth). In many cases, therefore, capital equipment (either hired or bought) may only be seen to be relevant for specific operations, for example digging foundations, site levelling, mixing cement and soil/material moving.

Third, the uncertainty that characterises the building industry increases the likelihood of capital equipment laying idle for long periods of time during a recession. Thus, unless a firm is large and has a number of projects running simultaneously, or projects that can be run sequentially after each other, the substitution of capital may not be a viable proposition. Problems associated with dovetailing particular activities may emerge if a firm is undertaking work on geographically dispersed sites.

Fourth, capital equipment is likely to have a high rate of depreciation if it is being used on extremely rough terrain or is exposed regularly to adverse weather conditions.

Finally, as we shall see in Chapter 6, many construction firms only take on work within a distinct geographical locality. The absence of competition may therefore not force firms to look as closely at their costs as they would if they faced extreme competition from other firms.

The cost implications of production functions

Having commented briefly on the basic tools economists use to analyse the relationship that exists between inputs and output, the next stage of the analysis is to look at how the *price* of factors of production constrains the number of choices available to the entrepreneur.

Ignoring the costs associated with hiring and maintaining a workforce, for example an employer's contribution to his or her workforce's National Insurance contributions (sometimes referred to as *on-costs*), the price of a unit of labour over a given period is the wage that he or she' paid. For simplicity it will be assumed that all workers are paid the same wage. Thus the total wage bill is simply the weekly wage of each person, multiplied by the number of employees, multiplied by 52.

The cost of capital is a little more tricky to consider. It is assumed by economists that capital goods carry an imputed *rent* over their lifetime, even if a firm buys its capital goods outright. Thus, if an excavator costs £100 000 to buy and it has a productive life of ten years, then the imputed rent is £10 000 per annum (assuming that it has no scrap value).

Having established the basic conventions economists use to value labour and capital, we shall now turn to a consideration of the average costs firms incur in the short run and the long run.

Average costs in the short run

For reasons considered earlier in this chapter, the total costs incurred by a firm are the sum of total fixed costs and total variable costs. If we divide each of these figures by the number of units produced, then we may define the average cost incurred per unit of output.

Since by definition fixed costs are constant, whatever the output, the average fixed cost of production will fall as output rises. Thus the *average fixed cost curve* slopes downwards (labelled SRAFC in Figure 5.6). The *average variable cost curve* (labelled SRAVC), which in this example reflects labour costs, can be calculated by multiplying the wage rate by the number of units of labour used to produce each level of output and dividing this figure by the level of output. In this case the curve takes a flattened 'U' shape. Indeed by comparing the average variable cost curve (labelled SRAVC) with the total output curve in Figure 5.2, it can be shown that where increasing returns exist, the average variable costs *decrease* whereas when diminishing returns set in, average variable costs *increase* again. If the average fixed cost curve and the average variable cost curve are added together we get the *average total cost curve*. This is labelled SRATC in Figure 5.6.

For reasons that will become clear shortly, an extremely important cost curve still to be derived is the *short-run marginal cost curve*. This curve identifies how costs change as output is increased or decreased by one unit. It is important to establish its exact relationship with the other three curves we have derived so far. If average costs are falling (total or variable), then marginal costs must be below the average and indeed pulling the average down. Thus the short-run marginal cost curve (labelled SRMC) will lie below curves SRAVC and SRATC. Conversely, if average costs are rising (total or variable), then marginal costs must be greater than the average and therefore the short-run marginal cost curve will lie above the average variable and total cost curves. It therefore follows that the marginal cost curve will intersect the average variable cost curve and average total cost curve at their *minimum points*. This relationship is also depicted in Figure 5.6.

Having derived the four main cost curves as they apply to the firm in the short run, let us now consider average costs as they apply to a firm in the long run when both factors of production are variable.

Average costs in the long run

With an extended time horizon there is no need to make a distinction between average variable costs and average fixed costs since both factors are variable. Hence we need simply to refer to the *long-run average cost curve*. This may be derived by extending our analysis of isoquants.

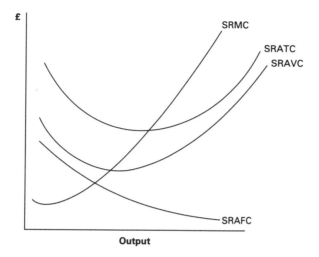

Figure 5.6   Costs in the short run

Recall that an isoquant identifies the combinations of capital and labour that can be used to produce a fixed level of output. To date, however, no mention has been made of the constraints that confront an entrepreneur in practice. The most obvious constraint is a financial one. This can be identified with reference to an *isocost line*, which is determined by the budget an entrepreneur has at his or her disposal and the relative cost of labour and capital.

Specifically, the isocost line depicts all the combinations of labour and capital that can be afforded with a fixed sum of money. For example, let us assume that in each time period an entrepreneur has £10 000 to spend on factor inputs and that the cost of each unit of labour is £100 while the rent of each unit of capital is £500. If production is completely labour intensive (that is, with no capital at all), then the largest number of workers that can be afforded is 100. In contrast if no labour is used and production is completely capital intensive, 20 units of capital could be afforded (of course both scenarios are trivial in reality). If these points are plotted on the basic isoquant graph and a line is drawn between them, then we have the set of labour/capital combinations that can be afforded by the entrepreneur. These are identified in Figure 5.7.

Algebraically the constraint facing the producer may be defined as:

$$B = wL + rK \tag{5.7}$$

where w and r denote the cost of hiring labour (L) and renting capital (K), respectively.

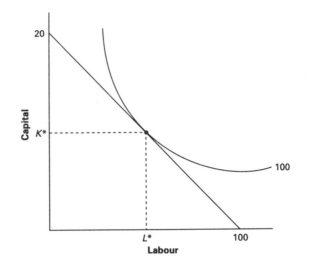

Figure 5.7   The isocost line and the least-cost production of 100 units of output

Let us now assume that a producer wishes to maximise output from a given budget. The combination of capital and labour associated with this output is the point that is just tangential to the highest possible isoquant. This is also shown in Figure 5.7. It can be seen that the largest output the firm can afford to produce is 100 units, an output that consumes L* labour and K* capital. This is the equilibrium point. On the one hand, any other affordable combination of labour and capital (either on or inside the isocost line) is associated with a lower output, whereas on the other hand the 101st unit of output cannot be afforded with the available budget. Of course, should there be a change in the relative price of labour and capital or a rise/fall in the general budget available to the producer, it is likely that there will be a new point of equilibrium. Let us briefly consider each of these scenarios in turn, initially focusing on a rise in wage rates.

A change in relative factor prices from an increase in the price of labour

In this analysis it is assumed that there will be no change in the price of capital or a change in the budget available to the entrepreneur to buy factors of production. Under these conditions, a rise in the price of labour will cause the isocost line in Figure 5.8 to pivot from AB inwards to AC. The new isocost line shows that the money released from forgoing a unit of capital buys less labour than it did before.

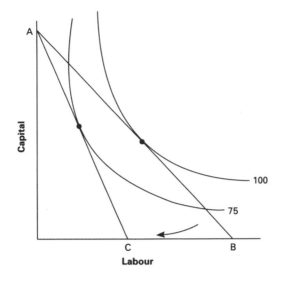

Figure 5.8　Factor price change (labour)

Thus not only has the number of affordable factor combinations of labour and capital diminished, but also the maximum output that can be produced from a given budget.

An increase in the producer's budget

The second stage of this analysis is to consider what happens when the producer has an increase in budget. Invoking the *ceteris paribus* assumption again, it follows that the effect of such an increase will be to cause a parallel shift in the budget constraint. Additional increases will precipitate further shifts. This is depicted in Figure 5.9.

These shifts in the isocost line mean that the producer has the resources to increase output, which, if maximised, is that associated with the isoquant just tangential to each isocost line. The line that joins each of these points of tangency is known as the *long-run expansion path*. If the long-run expansion path is a straight line extending from the origin of the graph, it implies that relative factor intensities are unchanged despite the increase in output. If, on the other hand, the long-run expansion path bends towards either the capital or the labour axis, then a change in factor intensity has taken place.

The long-run average cost curve

Based upon the information taken from the long-run expansion path, it is possible to derive the average cost curve for a firm in the long run.

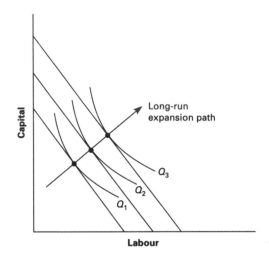

Figure 5.9   The long-run expansion path

The procedure is to take each level of output and determine the cheapest combination of factors of production (in this case, labour and capital) that can be used to produce it. By dividing the appropriate cost by the level of output, the average cost can be calculated. For example, if the isoquant associated with an output of 100 units is tangential to the isocost line associated with combinations of capital and labour whose total value is £150, then the average cost of output is £1.50. By repeating this process for each level of output, an average cost curve can be plotted.

The assumption adopted in textbooks, based on evidence from actual businesses, is that the long-run average cost curve assumes the shape of a flattened 'U'. This implies that as output initially rises, average costs fall. Eventually an output or series of outputs are reached that are associated with the lowest average cost before the average costs start to rise again. This is depicted in Figure 5.10.

When businesses enjoy cost advantages from increasing their scale of production, they are said to be exploiting *economies of size*, whereas when the average cost of production begins to rise again, *diseconomies of size* are said to prevail. Some of the reasons why economies and diseconomies of size emerge will be discussed shortly.

Readers who have already had some previous exposure to economics may be wondering if these concepts differ from the more frequently cited terms *economies of scale* and *diseconomies of scale*. The answer is yes!. The terms economies of scale and diseconomies of scale refer specifically to the effect on average costs when any inputs used in production are increased in the *same proportion*. Hence these terms

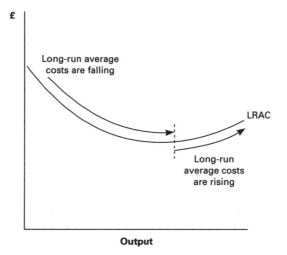

Figure 5.10   Economies of size and diseconomies of size

are much more precise in their meaning. For example economies of scale would be said to emerge if output trebles in response to a doubling of all inputs, whereas the term economies of size implies no specific constraint on the change in factor inputs, such that production may become more or less capital/labour Intensive. Both, however, imply a reduction in the average cost of production.

Economies of size and economies of scale

Having established the precise distinction between economies of size and economies of scale, the next stage of the analysis will be to consider some of the reasons why we should expect certain increases in production to be associated with falling average costs and subsequent increases to be associated with increases in average cost. The discussion of the factors that can prompt a reduction in average costs is set out under five main headings, as follows.

Specialisation

Increases in company size make it increasingly feasible to employ specialist staff. Over two hundred years ago Adam Smith wrote about the benefits of such specialisation. The example he used was that of a pin factory, in which each worker was responsible for a *specific* task within the eighteen stages of pin manufacture rather than being expected to carry out all eighteen processes. This approach, which is known as *division of labour*, not only allows workers the opportunity to become experts in the job they undertake but also reduces the amount of time lost when non-specialised workers pass from one task to the next. Examples of division of labour can be seen in everyday life, ranging from house buyers employing solicitors to see them through the legal complexities of conveyancing, to construction firms employing surveyors and subcontracting work to more specialist companies during the building process.

Indivisibilities

Indivisibilities refer to the fact that firms require a minimum quantity of certain inputs in order to remain operational, and in turn these inputs have an optimal level of usage. For example firms will require certain amounts of space to store inputs, and will own or rent machinery whose average output costs fall as the equipment is used more intensively.

Purchasing and financial advantages

We read frequently in the press that smaller firms are treated less preferentially than large firms when it comes to raising funds or purchasing inputs. Despite the frustration felt by many small-scale entrepreneurs, this is predictable. For example the need to buy in bulk often enables larger producers to secure more preferential deals than their smaller, less economically powerful counterparts. Similarly smaller firms, which often have less opportunity than larger firms to use internally generated funds for investment purposes, are confronted with the need to pay back loans over a shorter time period and/or have to pay higher rates of interest on loans because they are perceived to be at greater risk of bankruptcy. This is a particular feature of the construction industry, where smaller firms are forced to become heavily reliant on personal loans, trade credit, bank overdrafts and ploughed-back profits.

Law of large numbers

The law of large numbers is best explained by a simple example. Assume that a firm has a single production line comprising a number of individual pieces of machinery. Given that it is not desirable for production to be delayed for too long if a machine breaks down, it would be rational for the firm in question to have a maintenance engineer and a set of spare parts to cover most breakdown contingencies. However, if the firm expands and as a result buys five additional (identical) production lines, it is unlikely that they will all break down at exactly the same time or for exactly the same reason. Thus the firm is unlikely to need five extra maintenance engineers or five sets of spares in stock. Due to the fact that proportionately less expenditure is being incurred to maintain the additional production lines, average costs are by definition falling.

Minimum efficient scale

When a firm is operating at the lowest average cost it is said to be achieving productive efficiency. By definition, this will be the point at which the LRAC curve is at its lowest point. The *smallest* output level at which the least average cost is incurred is known as the *minimum efficient scale* (or mes). In Figure 5.11 it can be seen that size economies exist for all outputs from 0 to A. In this example the lowest average cost is achieved at more than one output, namely all the outputs between A and B. However, according to the above definition, the minimum efficient scale is at A. Nevertheless any point between A and B minimises average costs.

In the case of the British brick industry, Pratten (1989) found that the mes could be achieved by producing at a level that coincides with only 1 per cent of domestic output whereas, for example, in the case of cement and washing machines the corresponding figures are 10 per cent and 57 per cent respectively. Further insights can be gained by asking the question: how much would a firm's costs increase if it were to produce a level of output that is half that associated with the mes? In the case of brick production, costs would increase by 25 per cent. For cement and washing machines the corresponding figures are 26 per cent and 7.5 per cent respectively.

Diseconomies of size and diseconomies of scale

Should a firm choose to produce beyond output B (reconsider Figure 5.11), it is experiencing increases in its average costs, or *diseconomies of size*. These diseconomies may be the result of the firm becoming so large that it is more difficult to organise and coordinate its activities. Such bureaucracy may prevent a rapid response to emergent difficulties, a problem that may be exacerbated if growth has coincided with the firm becoming more geographically spread. This can be particularly important for construction firms whose activities extend to more than one site, thereby making it more difficult to supervise workers effectively. Generally it can be argued that basic economic theory would lead us to expect that the first location a firm chooses is the most desirable with respect to its production and distributional requirements. Subsequent sites may be less advantageous, thereby adding to the unit cost of production as output rises.

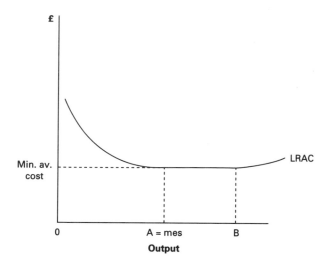

Figure 5.11   Minimum efficient scale

External economies and diseconomies of size (scale)

The factors that prompt a reduction (increase) in average cost as a firm increases its scale of production reflect the individual response and characteristics of the firm concerned. For this reason these are known as *internal (dis)economies of size*. However, there is a possibility that a reduction in unit costs may reflect general changes affecting all firms operating in that industry or even firms outside the industry. These are known as *external (dis)economies of size (scale)*. External economies of size may arise because suppliers of inputs for one or more firms are themselves able to exploit internal economies as the demand for their output increases. This reduction in the suppliers' costs may be passed on in part to all the firms who purchase goods from them, thereby reducing the purchasers' input costs. Other examples of external economies of size are the prime minister or royal family entertaining foreign governments in order to encourage the purchase of British goods and services, and improvement of a country's transport network reducing everyone's transport costs. The effect of one or all of these initiatives may extend to numerous firms, either in a specific locality or more generally throughout the country. In terms of Figure 5.11, the effect of such changes is to cause a downward shift (not necessarily a parallel one) in the LRAC curve such that any given level of output can take place at a lower average cost. This is depicted in Figure 5.12.

Of course external change is not always beneficial to industry. A deterioration in road networks due to congestion or an increase in

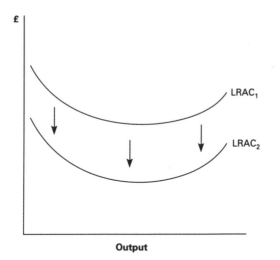

Figure 5.12 External economies and diseconomies of size

border bureaucracy may have a detrimental effect on firms in several industries rather than a single producer. In such cases the LRAC curve will shift upwards, reflecting the increase in average costs at every level of output.

The relationship between short-run and long-run average costs

The preceding discussion has treated short-run and long-run average cost curves as separate entities. However they are inextricably linked. Tangential to every point on the long-run average cost curve there is a short-run average cost curve, which indicates the short-run options available to the firm if changes its level of output. Three such cases are highlighted in Figure 5.13.

Consider the point labelled A. This is associated with a range of outputs associated with falling average unit costs. Should a decision be made to increase output from A to B in the long term then a change in both capital and labour inputs can be contemplated. However, if the increase is to take place in the short term, capital remains fixed. Thus any increase in output must arise from employing more labour and the average costs associated with such an increase can be read from the SRATC curve, which is just tangential to point A'. It can be seen that, in the short term, an increase in output from A to B results in an increase in average costs. Had the increase been to C instead, then average costs would have fallen, even in the short term. It can also be seen that if the firm in question was operating at its minimum efficient scale, for example output D, any attempt to change output in

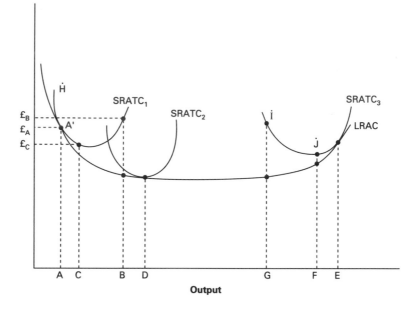

Figure 5.13   Short-run and long-run average

the short run (up or down) would lead to an increase in average costs. A similar argument can be employed with respect to production where diseconomies of size exist. By definition, reductions in output in the short run may add to or reduce average costs, though in the long run average costs will fall. Consider the average costs associated with moves from E to F and E to G respectively.

For firms to be operating at a point on their long-run average cost curve they need to be using the least-cost combination of resources associated with each level of output. In theory this a reasonable assumption to make. However in practice numerous factors prevent this from happening. For example outdated employer–worker agreements that are too costly to 'buy out', lack of access to external finance or a general lack of confidence about the future may prevent firms from adopting the new technology associated with the lowest average cost for each given output. The result is that firms may instead be operating at a point *inside* the LRAC curve, such as H, I or J in Figure 5.13. Such an outcome will however be ignored in subsequent analysis.

Having established the shape and the relationship that exists between average cost curves in the short and long run, the next stage of the analysis is to consider the problems economists and other professionals face when they try to estimate cost curves in practice. The literature on the subject highlights three basic approaches: statistical cost analysis, the engineering approach and the survivor technique.

Estimating cost curves in practice

Economists have adopted three basic approaches to derive the long-run average cost curve for firms and industries, none of which are particularly suited to an analysis of the construction industry. The first is known as *statistical cost analysis*. This involves a comparison of one or more firms, either as their level of output changes over time (time series analysis) or by comparing the costs of different sized firms (cross-section analysis). However this is unsuited to the construction industry because of differences between firms with respect to the age of the capital stock they use, the prices they pay for inputs, the types of work they undertake and the degree to which they are diversified into other industries. Attempts to standardise such differences abound in the literature, though no one approach can be said to be accepted universally.

The second technique is known as the *engineering approach*. This methodology derives its name from the fact that engineers who plan new production units and plants accumulate significant amounts of information with respect to alternative production technologies/plant layout and their associated operating costs. However, for reasons that have already been highlighted briefly above, the cost functions derived from these technical relationships may differ significantly from the costs experienced by firms in practice since they operate in different regional markets and terrains. Furthermore, managers may not know in detail the average costs associated with unfamiliar levels of output at which they do not produce, and furthermore the approach fails to yield estimates for administrative and research costs.

The final technique is an attempt to circumvent the problems encountered in the previous two approaches, namely valuation and informational difficulties respectively. It is known as the *survivor technique* and rests on the initially plausible idea that firms whose share of an industry's output grows over time are operating efficiently, whereas firms whose share falls over time are either too large or too small. However this assumption does not take into account the two-dimensional relationship between output size and cost. Rather the approach embraces a multidimensional set of interrelationships that determine the long-term performance of firms. In other words, the ability of a firm to expand its operations and 'survive' also depends upon the locality within which it operates and the mix of building work that it is capable of competing for.

Economies of size are usually associated with standardized products that allow mass production tecniques to be exploited. However, the unique nature of many building projects, the relatively small scale of individual building programmes and the general 'lumpiness' of demand

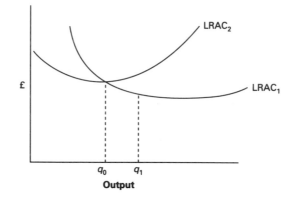

Figure 5.14   Economies of size in the construction sector

over time means that even larger firms are unlikely to be able to exploit size/scale economies to their full potential. This can be seen in Figure 5.14

In Figure 5.14, the long-run average cost curve $LRAC_1$ depicts the average costs of production if a firm is able to exploit a wide range of scale economies, including specialisation and large-scale purchasing of standardised inputs. It can be seen that the mes is at point q_1. In contrast $LRAC_2$ lies to the left of and above $LRAC_1$ and denotes the long-run average costs associated with projects with lower levels of standardisation. It can be seen that it is only when production exceeds q_0 that the firm is able to exploit size economies and experience the reductions in average unit cost associated with the outputs q_0 to q_1.

6 The Organisation of Firms

INTRODUCTION

With the specific aim of gaining an insight into the characteristics that distinguish the construction industry from other productive sectors of the economy, this chapter identifies some of the factors that determine how firms behave within markets. Much of the analysis falls under the general heading of 'industrial economics'. Not surprisingly this branch of economics continues to be a vibrant focus of research, and not surprisingly for economists(!) it can result in considerable disagreement. At one extreme is the view that firms that are able to exploit favourable market conditions will do so to the detriment of the consumer, necessitating piecemeal government intervention. This view is embodied in what economists refer to as the *structure–conduct–performance (SCP)* approach. Although this framework is now seen by some economists as somewhat limited, since it tends to imply a simple causal relationship between the structure of an industry and the way in which firms respond to it, the approach continues to provide the blueprint for investigations by the British Monopolies and Mergers Commission.

The opposite view, which superseded the SCP paradigm for a brief period a couple of decades ago, is that government intervention can be detrimental to progress and development and therefore it should restrain any interventionist tendencies it may have. Any opportunities that firms are able to exploit are simply temporary phenomena and over time will be eroded away by a process of technological advance and freedom of entry/exit to/from the market.

Current research is more biased towards the SCP approach than the anti-interventionist stance adopted by promarket economists. In particular it reflects an interest in the strategic behaviour exhibited by firms competing in industries dominated by a few large firms. This 'game-theoretic' approach emphasises the ways in which firms make decisions, bluff and respond to the decisions of competitors in order to maintain or increase their relative profitability and market share. It is beyond the scope of this text to provide a detailed analysis of these different approaches – this is the province of a mainstream book on industrial economics. The aim of this chapter is simply to provide the reader with a flavour of the terminology and approach that economists use when confronted with an analysis of market behaviour with special reference to the construction industry.

Although the SCP paradigm no longer commands a central role in

135

the current debate on industrial economics, it nevertheless provides a coherent framework within which the rest of the chapter can be organised. Thus, under the two general headings 'Structure' and 'Conduct and Performance', the following discussion provides not only a general insight into the basic terminology and assumptions economists use, but also an opportunity to analyse some of the main characteristics of the construction industry. Under the heading of 'Structure' we shall consider the way in which industries can be categorised according to the number of firms that exist within them. In the section on 'Conduct and Performance' the analysis moves on a stage to consider how different market structures determine the way in which firms behave, for example in terms of pricing policies and their willingness to merge or collude with their competitors. 'Performance' issues relate to outcomes, for example whether or not profits are made in the short term or the long term and the degree to which market structures encourage firms to use efficiently the resources at their disposal.

STRUCTURE

Standard economic theory identifies four basic market structures: perfect competition, monopoly, oligopoly and duopoly, and monopolistic competition. Their main characteristics may be outlined as follows.

Perfect competition

As its name suggests, perfect competition represents a totally competitive structure. The assumptions that underpin perfect competition often result in it being perceived as a theoretical indulgence with little opportunity for application. However perfect competition can be viewed as a benchmark against which all other market structures can be compared, and as a result it provides important insights for the economist. The main characteristics of a perfectly competitive industry are as follows:

- There is an extremely large number of buyers and sellers.
- Each buyer and seller is so small, relative to the overall amount that is traded, that the market price is completely unaffected by a change in the behaviour of any one of them. Buyers and sellers are therefore referred to as *price takers*.
- The products that are traded are completely identical (or homogeneous), regardless of who produces it. If a firm chooses to raise its price above the market price, it will lose all its customers since they will simply buy an identical product from a (cheaper) source elsewhere.

- There is no uncertainty or industrial secrecy – all economic agents, whether buyers or sellers, are assumed to be endowed with perfect information about the market.
- There are no impediments to prevent a firm from entering or exiting the industry. For example no product is afforded patent protection.

Pure monopoly

Strictly speaking, 'monopoly' refers to a situation where just one firm is operating in a particular industry. However, because the term 'monopoly' is used in policy-making circles to refer to firms that account for 25 per cent or more of the market in which they operate, the term 'pure monopoly' should be used when refering to 100 per cent dominance. The goods or services produced by the pure monopolist are assumed to have no close substitutes and are demanded by a large number of buyers who have no market power. Despite being the only producer of a given commodity, the pure monopolist does not have total power over the market. With reference to the demand curve it faces, it can choose either to restrict output and charge a relatively high price for each unit, or to increase production and charge a relatively lower price. The monopolist cannot increase profits by forcing individuals into consuming high-priced goods they are not willing and able to buy.

Oligopoly and duopoly

Oligopolistic industries are characterised by a small number of firms accounting for a large proportion (or all) of total output. In the case of *duopoly*, this is limited to two firms. Oligopolistic market structures are common throughout the developed world in industries that provide firms with the opportunity to exploit size economies. Analysis of oligopolistic industries using a game-theoretic framework is currently at the forefront of industrial economics research. A simplified insight into this approach will be considered later in this chapter.

Monopolistic competition

Monopolistic competition exists when a large number of firms are operating in a particular market but, unlike perfect competition, each producer offers the customer a slightly differentiated product. This differentiation may be explicit in the good or service; lodged in the mind of the consumer by persuasive advertising; or because the firms competing against each other are located in different geographical areas.

This means that, unlike firms in a perfectly competitive industry, it is possible for a firm increase to the price of a product without losing all its customers. The outcome of such a policy will clearly depend on the product's characteristics and the geographical location of the supplier relative to its customers. There are numerous examples of this type of market structure in the construction industry. For example, although all qualified plumbers can offer the same basic service, it is possible for a plumber based in Edinburgh to charge a higher price than a plumber in Birmingham without losing customers in Edinburgh.

The structure of the construction industry

Having outlined the four basic market structures to which most introductory textbooks refer at some stage, the aim of this section is to deal explicitly with the organisation of the construction industry. Of course few industries can be expected to fit precisely into any one of the above categories. However, as we shall see, there is strong evidence to suggest that there are examples of both oligopolistic and monopolistic competition.

Although most people will know the names of the very large firms in the construction industry, for example Wimpey, Taylor Woodrow, Tarmac and Blue Circle, they will be less aware that the industry is dominated by a large number of small firms. As we saw in the previous chapter, large-scale production has a number of advantages. Large civil engineering/building contractors involved in major construction projects, such as office blocks or road building, have the advantage of being able to utilise specialised equipment, buy in bulk, negotiate more favourable financial packages, employ their own specialist workers (for example surveyors and legal experts) and spread any risk over a large number of projects. Unlike most manufacturing operations, the construction industry is, by definition, location specific. Although the bricks, timber, tarmac, cement, window frames and other materials used may be produced at a factory some distance away, construction activity must take place on the site itself. Thus, although development within other sectors of the economy has often involved expanding the size of operations, and hence increasing the level of industrial concentration, the construction industry continues to be geographically fragmented with a large number of small firms.

The previous statement raises an important question: what is meant by small? Is it in terms of employment, turnover, market share or some wider matrix of characteristics that also captures the way in which firms behave and carry out their business? Ultimately, the definition rests with the opinion of the commentator, since there is no agreed definition within the literature. The simplest approach is to take the first of these indicators, namely employment. This provides two ways of gaining an insight into the characteristics of the construction industry. The first identifies the *number of firms* according to the size of their workforce, and the other highlights the *number of workers* employed by firms that are classified by the size of their workforce.

Time series data in the publication *Housing and Construction Statistics 1983–93* shows that the total number of private contractors in Britain rose steadily for the first eight years of this period, from 160 596 in 1983 to 209 797 in 1990. The number subsequently fell and in 1993 it stood at 195 107. Of course these are highly aggregated data. The pattern varies slightly according to the trade firms are engaged in and also by region. For example the number of building and civil engineering contractors increased throughout the period 1983–93, from 3722 to 6234; while firms engaged in such activities as glazing, demolition, scaffolding and electrical contracting all peaked in number in 1992. Similarly, the number of contractors based in Yorkshire and Humberside, the West Midlands, Wales and Scotland also peaked in 1992, rather than in 1990.

Within the overall total it is possible to calculate the relative importance of the small firm to the industry as a whole. Let us take an extremely conservative view of what is deemed to be small, namely any contractor employing up to seven people. Between 1983 and 1993 the proportion of firms falling into this category rose from 89.3 per cent to 94.3 per cent. Conversely, firms employing more than 80 people remained at less than 1 per cent of the total throughout the period.

It is possible to gain a slightly different picture by focusing on the proportion of the total workforce employed by firms of different sizes. In 1993 firms with seven workers or fewer employed just over 40 per cent of the total workforce. The corresponding figure for firms with 80 or more workers was 32 per cent. However these figures are best seen in the light of those which applied to 1983. In that year the proportion of the workforce employed by firms with seven workers or fewer was 31.1 per cent, whereas that for firms with 80 or more workers was 36.9 per cent. In other words, the importance of the small firm increased over that period rather than diminished. A further insight can be gained by comparing the 1993 figures with those for manufacturing as a whole. Unfortunately the organisation of the statistics used in *Business Monitor* does not mesh exactly with those used in the *Housing and Construction Statistics* series. Specifically, the category nearest to that used above to define 'small' relates to nine workers or fewer. Nevertheless it is possible to calculate that in 1993, only 6.5 per cent of manufacturing workers were employed by firms with nine workers or fewer, and that such firms represented 69 per cent of all legitimate manufacturing units.

These figures seem to imply that the large construction firm is relatively unimportant to the industry. However if, instead of focusing on employment, we consider the value of output, then a slightly different picture emerges. For example during the trading year 1992–93, 28.4 per cent of the 8919.4 million construction projects undertaken was by firms employing seven workers or fewer. This compares with a corresponding figure of 43.1 per cent for firms employing 80 workers or more (calculated from *Housing and Construction statistics 1983–93*). Nevertheless, although these figures show quite explicitly that the 'small' firm is extremely important to the construction sector, it should be recognised that a large firm that uses a lot of technology-intensive capital and a relatively small amount of labour may appear 'smaller' than a firm engaged in activities that require lower capital–labour ratios.

Thus the question arises as to why the small construction firm continues to be dominant, indeed increasingly dominant, within the sector. A number of reasons may be put forward:

- Small firms can offer a localised and flexible service.
- Building firms tend to grow in size when they begin to offer more and more services. When building work is taking place in localised markets, both small and large firms may prefer to subcontract rather than risk expanding if specialist services are needed, though this in itself generates transaction costs (for example coordinating several suppliers of specialist services).
- Economies of size may be small relative to the size of a localised market – building sites are invariably geographically spread. The alternative would be a series of multiplant oligopolists or monopolists which erect barriers to entry that prevent smaller, more localised competitors from tendering for work.
- Because building work is extremely seasonal and is frequently bunched into the spring and summer months, remaining small can offer a high degree of flexibility without accumulating periodically underused overheads.

Builders' merchants

The link between the manufacturer of components and the builder, particularly the small builder, is a network of builders' merchants. The builders' merchant plays an important role in the industry. First there is a potential efficiency gain. On the one hand the builders' merchant provides a central focus for the manufacturer, who does not have to deal directly with a potentially large number of builders whose demand and indeed creditworthiness may not be stable over time. On the other hand the builder will need to contact fewer outlets for his or her materials since the builders' merchant may be able to supply products from more than one manufacturer, thereby reducing negotiation and transport costs. Second, given the long-term uncertainty surrounding the precise characteristics of building contracts, builders do not have to store a large amount of inputs – the builders' merchant provides a responsive service that can be tailored to the builder's requirements.

It should be understood that many builders' merchants are themselves specialists in their own right. For example one may stock bricks, cements and aggregates whereas another may be a supplier of fittings for kitchens and bathrooms, such as baths, washbasins and showers. For the DIY enthusiast whose interest is predominantly associated with gardening, basic carpentry, painting, wallpapering and tiling, examples of builders' merchants include the familiar names of Homebase, Do It All and Great Mills.

CONDUCT AND PERFORMANCE

This section describes some of the ways in which economic theory predicts that firms will behave and the implications of that behaviour. Underpinning the most basic analysis of the firm is the assumption that owners wish to maximise profits. This assumption is perhaps most appropriate in the case of the owner-manager who has direct control of the firm, and as a consequence all profits enter the utility stream of that individual. Although the profits earned by large firms are also channelled to their owners, usually a diverse group of shareholders, the managers who are responsible for day-to-day decisions may have the opportunity to pursue policies that enhance their personal wellbeing, rather than that of the company as a whole. In this case profit maximisation may be a less justified assumption to make.

The ideas that economists put forward to explain the behaviour of firms are varied. Some can result in neat mathematical outcomes since they assume that the firm tries to maximise a specific variable (perhaps subject to certain constraints), whether it be profit, sales revenue, company growth or whatever. Alternative approaches look either to the organisation of the firm as a constraint upon its activities, for example the need for managers to maintain the status quo between potentially unstable worker coalitions, or to the need for firms to adopt strategies to outmanouvre their competitors.

Profit maximisation

The basic rule of thumb for profit maximisation is that the firm should equate its marginal revenue with its marginal costs. The principles underpining this approach are no different from those considered in Chapter 3, when the consumer was seen to select his or her optimal point of consumption with reference to the marginal cost of consumption and the marginal benefits derived from each unit of the product. To illustrate the basic implications of profit maximisation, two scenarios will be considered. The first looks at the firm operating in a perfectly competitive industry, while the second considers the firm operating in a more concentrated industry, which allows it to exhibit some degree of market power.

Profit maximisation and the perfectly competitive firm

It should be recalled that perfectly competitive industries are characterised by an atomistic structure in which small price-taking firms produce an undifferentiated product for an almost infinite number of buyers. It is also assumed that all relevant information is symmetrically distributed between buyers and sellers and that firms can enter and exit the industry costlessly. It can be seen from Figure 6.1 that, in these circumstances, each firm can be assumed to face a perfectly horizontal demand curve (d), which reflects the equilibrium price determined by the interaction between the market demand and market supply curves (D and S respectively).

In the introduction to this section it was noted that, if a firm is to maximise its profits, it must set its output at the point at which its marginal cost and marginal revenue are equal. By now, readers should be familiar with the term marginal cost, but *marginal revenue* is appearing for the first time and describes the change in the total revenue of a producer after a unit increase or decrease in output. For example, if an extra unit of production increases total revenue from £50 to £70, marginal revenue equals £20. Thus, if the marginal revenue from a unit increase in output exceeds the marginal cost, it is rational for the firm to produce that unit of output. Conversely, if the marginal cost of an extra unit of output is greater than its marginal revenue, it is inappropriate for that unit to be produced, since its cost exceeds the revenue that would be derived from it. It therefore follows that production should stop at the level of output at which marginal revenue and marginal cost are exactly equal. This decision rule is represented graphically in Figure 6.2.

Since the demand curve for a perfectly competitive firm is horizontal, its marginal revenue curve must be identical to it since the marginal revenue associated with each unit of production equals the equilibrium price, namely P^*. Superimposed on the demand/marginal revenue curve ($d = MR$) in Figure 6.2 are the firm's average total cost (ATC) curve and marginal cost (MC) curves. The total output for the

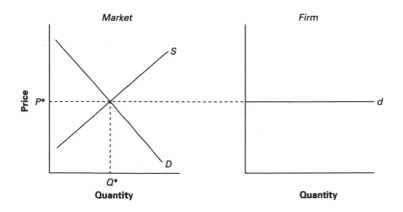

Figure 6.1   The demand curve facing a perfectly competitive firm

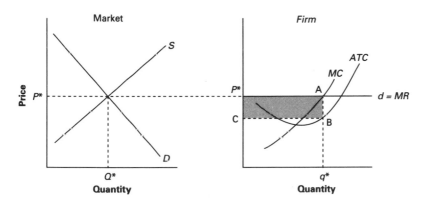

Figure 6.2   Profit maximisation and the perfectly competitive firm

industry is Q^*, of which the identified firm is predicted to contribute q^* units. All outputs below q^* are associated with marginal revenues that exceed marginal costs, whereas the reverse is true for all outputs beyond q^*. From this diagram it is also possible to depict the profit earned by the firm at this level of output. Specifically, for each unit of the output q^*, which the firm sells at a price of P^*, an average cost of C is incurred. Hence, the profit is q^* multiplied by (P^* minus C), or the shaded area, CP^*AB.

In this example the perfectly competitive firm is making a profit. Following previous assumptions we should therefore expect that new firms will be attracted into the industry. As we can see in Figure 6.3, new entrants will cause an outward shift in the industry supply curve, and hence a reduction in the market equlibrium price (from P^* to P^{**}).

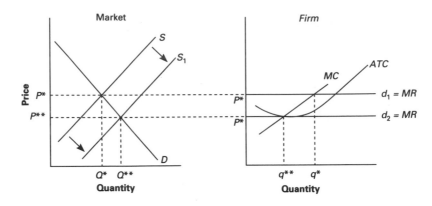

Figure 6.3   Equilibrium in a perfectly competitive industry

This reduction in the market price of the product will simultaneously cause a downward shift in the firm's (horizontal) demand curve (d_1 to d_2). Over time, any profit being earned by existing firms will be eroded away by the impact of new firms costlessly entering the industry. In the long term the firm in question only produces q^{**} and only receives sufficient profits to discourage it from leaving the industry, a return that is included nominally in the cost curves of the firm. This is depicted in Figure 6.3 and is known as *normal profit*. It therefore follows that profits in excess of normal profit can only be accumulated in the short term. These are known as *supernormal profits*. Thus in Figure 6.2, the area CP^*AB is supernormal profit. Conversely, if losses are being made, firms will costlessly leave the industry, causing the market supply curve to shift to the left. The demand curve of firms remaining within the industry will shift upwards in response to the higher equilibrium price that has resulted, ultimately allowing the firms that remain in the industry to earn normal profits. By referring to how a perfectly competitive firm's output changes with shifts in its demand curve, it can be seen that its MC curve is effectivly the firm's own supply curve, since it also identifies the amount it is willing and able to supply at different price levels. Thus the supply curve depicted in the market scenario is equivalent to the horizontal sum of all the individual firms' MC curves.

Profit maximisation when the firm faces a downward sloping demand curve

The next stage of the analysis considers the implications for profit maximisation when firms are confronted by a standard downward-sloping demand curve, rather than the horizontal schedule that underpins per-

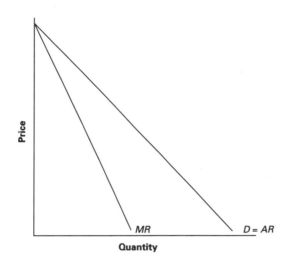

Figure 6.4 Relationship between a downward sloping demand curve and the marginal revenue curve

fect competition. The reasons why this is a more likely scenario are industry specific. As we have already seen, small building firms can enjoy significant power at the local level; in other cases, products can only be realistically produced by large firms; indeed firms may actively deter others from entering the industry by aggressive marketing and collusion. In such circumstances firms are able to exploit total or partial monopoly power. Whatever the reason for a firm's downward sloping demand curve, it follows that the demand curve and the marginal revenue curve cease to be a single entity. Let us consider why by looking at Figure 6.4.

As we have seen previously, the demand curve depicted in Figure 6.4 shows that if a firm charges a single price for its product and wishes to sell an extra unit of output, then it must charge a lower price for all the previous units of output as well. The demand curve therefore maps out the average revenue (*AR*) received by the firm as its output changes. As we saw in Chapter 3, for each price–output combination characterised by price elastic demand, any reduction in price will increase total revenue. It therefore follows that, in these circumstances, marginal revenue will be positive. Conversely, for price–output combinations on the price inelastic section of the demand curve, a reduction in price will reduce total revenue and hence marginal revenue will be negative. By definition therefore, marginal revenue will be zero at the point where total revenue is maximised, which in the case of a straight line demand curve is the mid point of the demand curve. Thus, in relation to the demand curve drawn in Figure 6.4, the

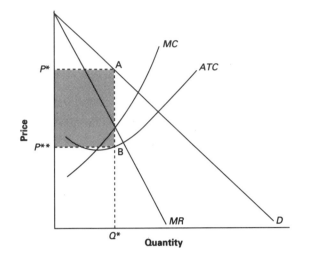

Figure 6.5   Profit maximisation in the case of a monopolised industry

marginal revenue curve is not only downward sloping but also twice as steep. As a result it intersects the x-axis (the quantity axis) exactly half-way between the origin and the output at which the demand curve intersects the x-axis.

Thus, with the demand curve mapping out average revenue at each level of output and the MR curve that is associated with it, we can now superimpose the MC and ATC curves for the firm in question. This is done in Figure 6.5. According to the basic rule of profit maximisation, optimal output occurs when marginal costs equal marginal revenue, specifically at output Q^*. Our demand curve tells us that these Q^* units of output can each be sold at a price of P^*. It can also be seen that the average total cost incurred by the producer is P^{**}. The difference between the average revenue received by the firm (P^*) and the average cost incurred during production (P^{**}) is the profit earned on each unit of output. Thus the shaded area $P^{**}P^*$AB denotes the supernormal profit enjoyed by the firm. However, unlike in the case of perfect competition, this state of affairs can persist over time since new entrants may be deterred from entering the industry.

At this point it is possible to put forward a simple case for government intervention in industries characterised by long-term supernormal profits (or monopoly profits). Specifically, these industries are associated with higher prices and lower levels of production than would occur under the perfectly competitive scenario. This is demonstrated in Figure 6.6.

Let us assume initially that an industry is perfectly competitive and in long-term equilibrium (hence no firm is earning a supernormal profit

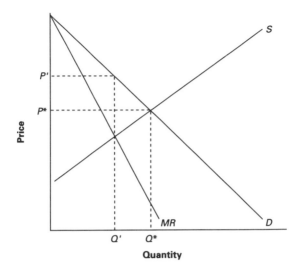

*Figure 6.6   The case for the government intervening in a monopolised
industry*

or incurring a loss). In this case the industry's output will equal Q^*
and this will be sold at a price of P^*. Each firm within the industry
will therefore contribute to the industry's output at the point where
marginal cost equals marginal revenue and hence price. If we assume
that this industry is now taken over by a profit-maximising monopoly
whose costs are identical to those of the original perfectly competitive
firms, then the monopolist's marginal cost curve will be the same as
the supply curve for the perfectly competitive industry. Thus, the profit-
maximising monopolist will equate its MC curve (by definition equivalent to the sum of the individual MC curves of the perfectly competitive
industry) with its MR curve. As a result, there will be a reduction in
the level of output (to Q') and a rise in the price charged for these
units (P').

The welfare implications of this outcome can be demonstrated in
terms of changes in consumer surplus and producer surplus, the basic
principles of which we encountered in Chapter 4. Consider Figure 6.7.
When the industry operates under perfect competition, the profit maximising price and output are P^* and Q^* respectively. This results in a
consumer surplus equal to area P^*AB and a producer surplus equal to
area P^*BC. If the industry is taken over by a single monopolist, the
price rises to P' and output falls to Q'. Under this outcome the area of
consumer surplus is reduced to the area $P'AD$. Part of this consumer
surplus is transferred over to the monopolist and becomes producer
surplus, namely the area $P^*P'DE$. The triangle EDB is the area economists

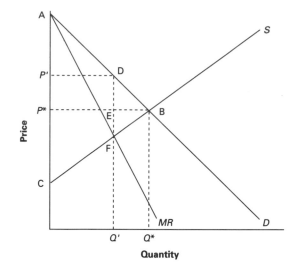

Figure 6.7   Welfare losses from a monopoly

refer to as *deadweight loss*. The term reflects the fact that it is a total loss to society since it is no longer enjoyed by consumers as consumer surplus, nor is it transferred to the monopolist, who is also part of society. Indeed the total deadweight loss is EDB + EBF, an area lost from the original producer surplus. To sum up, the effect of a perfectly competitive industry becoming monopolised is (1) part of the consumer surplus is transferred to the monopolist (though it must be stressed that, in societal terms, there is no change in overall welfare since the monopolist is part of society), and (2) a deadweight loss is created from consumer surplus and producer surplus. This deadweight loss is a societal loss arising from productive inefficiency since output is held below its efficient competitive outcome.

That the creation of a monopoly not only has distributional consequences when part of the consumer surplus is transfered to the monopolist, but also a loss in productive efficiency, provides the basic rationale for government intervention in monopolised markets in the 'public interest'. Indeed since 1948 the British government has had the power to refer monopolies to the Monopolies and Restrictive Practices Commission, which was renamed the Monopolies Commission in 1956 and the Monopolies and Mergers Commission in 1973. The current definition of a monopoly is a firm that has a market share of 25 per cent or more, or a firm that is small in national terms but has a 25 per cent share of a local market. The Monopolies and Mergers Commission (MMC) is also empowered to investigate any merger that would create a new monopoly or result in the creation of an entity with assets in excess of

£30 million. However, although the government has the power to investigate monopolised markets, the lack of resources available to the MMC means that only a very limited number of monopolies and mergers are investigated in any given year.

Students wishing to read a relevant MMC report are directed to a 1981 investigation into the supply of concrete roofing tiles in Britain. In this case two firms, Redland and Marley, were seen to dominate the market, with a 46 per cent and a 36 per cent share of the market (by value) respectively. By definition, therefore, a monopoly situation was found to exist. As a result it was recommended that both firms should inform the Director General of Fair Trading (DGFT) of any proposal to take over other manufacturers of concrete roofing tiles. Local authorities and other public bodies were asked to include a wide specification for tiles within procurement projects so as not to preclude smaller firms from submitting tenders. Furthermore, the DGFT would monitor the prices charged by Redland and Marley to ensure that they did not use 'excessive discounting' or low prices to act as an industry entry barrier or to prevent existing firms from expanding within the industry.

Other maximisation theories

The assumption of profit maximisation is perhaps most appropriate when the firm's owner(s) is (are) in direct day-to day control of the firm. However, if a firm is owned by a group of shareholders their ability to influence the individuals they delegate to manage the firm depends on the degree to which the shareholders themselves are a coherent pressure group. If a firm underperforms relative to expectations and a growing number of shareholders choose to dispose of their shareholdings (because higher returns can be earned elsewhere), the excess supply of that company's shares on the stock market will drive down the share price. If another firm believes that it can run the company more efficiently it may choose to purchase the available shares (at a low market price), and when in control impose its own management team. Thus the fear of losing control of the firm or being made redundant provides an incentive for the existing team to perform well. Alternatively, if the shareholders are a coherent group, they may simply sack the current directors and appoint a new set of directors. In either case the job security of the current management team depends in part upon the degree to which shareholders are dissatisfied with the return they are getting. If shareholders do not take an ongoing interest in the relative performance of their investment or are ill-informed about the company in question, they may have little impact on either the price of the shares (by not selling current holdings of shares) or the stability of the current directorship. Thus the aim of managers may simply be to prevent shareholders from becoming too dissatisfied. In these circumstances managers can take the opportunity to pursue their own objectives, which will be seen as a combination of prestige seeking, salary enhancement and the accumulation of perks.

Hence alternatives to profit maximisation reflect the possibility that a firm's manager(s) can pursue objectives more in keeping with their own personal utility function rather than that of the owner(s). Economists often refer to this situation as the *principal–agent* problem. The 'principal' is the person who wants a particular job to be done, for example a firm's owner(s), while the 'agent' is the person who is employed to do that job, for example the manager. This relationship manifests itself all the way down the firm's hierachy such that managers become principals who hire, on behalf of the company, agents to undertake less demanding work. Alternatives to the profit maximisation assumption fall into two categories: those which stress some other form of maximisation behaviour and those which do not. The former examples fall into a body of literature known as *managerial theories* whereas the latter are referred to as *behavioural theories*. Common to both sets of theory is the view that firms that are insulated from competition are likely not to produce at minimum cost because of the existence of *organisational slack*. This arises because payments, in cash or in kind, need to be made in order to contain any conflict that may arise from the principal–agent relationship. The difference between the perk/salary package that workers would like to receive and that which they actually receive is a measure of organisational slack. It exists because the principal does not know precisely what his/her agents will accept and the cost of finding out may be prohibitive.

At this point it is appropriate to introduce another term into the discussion. As well as experiencing organisational slack, firms may also be subject to *x-inefficiencies*. These are the technical or organisational inefficiencies that exist within production processes and prevent profits from being maximised, even in the unlikely circumstances of organisational slack being zero. Specifically, the firm is not operating at a point *on* the long run average cost curve but at a point inside it.

Managerial theories

The approaches that come under the heading of managerial theories fall into two basic categories – in one the objectives of principals and agents conflict to some degree; the other suggests that although principals and agents have different objectives, the outcome is satisfactory to both parties. In the first category are the *sales revenue maximisation* and *managerial utility* theories, whereas theories that focus on *company growth* are consistent with the latter.

Sales revenue maximisation

Under this scenario the salaries and perks of managers are seen as a function of sales revenue rather than profit. This may be particularly important in oligopolistic industries where market share can be significant in terms of the firm's image in the business sector as well as with its current and potential customers. Any decline in this variable may therefore be perceived to be an indicator of managerial failure at departmental or firm level. Since this objective may ultimately conflict with shareholders' interests, it is most likely to be pursued with reference to some minimum level of profit that provides shareholders with an 'acceptable' return from their investment.

Managerial utility

Closely related to the maximisation of sales revenues is a view that managers have their own utility function, identified by such independent variables as high salaries and bonuses, job security and professional prestige, the latter reflected in terms of the number of staff who are directly answerable to the manager, the quality of office accommodation and company car, and the 'pet projects' he or she is able to pursue. Thus shareholders' returns become a function of the degree to which a manager can maximise this utility function rather than maximise profit.

Company growth

If a company is able to maintain a high and non-fluctuating rate of growth, it is likely to be of benefit to both its managerial team and its shareholders. For managers, a growing firm is more likely to meet their utility function requirements, whereas for shareholders, long-term wealth is most likely to be maximised in a stable, high-growth firm. Central to this approach is the concept of the *retention ratio*, the ratio of retained profits to distributed profits. If managers maintain a low retention ratio and distribute the majority of profits to shareholders, the latter remain satisfied in the short term and share prices remain high enough to deter any immediate threat of takeover and the likelihood of subsequent job losses. If, on the other hand, a large proportion of profits are retained in order to stimulate company growth, for example through product diversification, shareholders may become disenchanted with the reduced dividends they receive. Although the potential for enhanced earnings and job security may emerge in the longer term, the company may become more susceptible to takeover. Thus the manager has to decide which retention ratio is consistent his or her own utility function as well as the shareholders' long-term desire to maximise their wealth by receiving high dividends.

Non-maximising theories

Central to the approaches considered so far is marginal analysis. Although economists recognise that marginal analysis is unsuited to day-to-day decision making, it nevertheless allows them to calculate expected values for a range of potential variables, and to compare these values with a firm's stated aims and subsequent performance. Economists have never purported to provide a detailed insight into what happens within firms, indeed they are often accused of employing a 'black box' approach to the analysis of firms. Insights into the ongoing relationship between the coalitions that exist within firms remains the preserve of management scientists. Central to the theories that emphasise the behaviour of such coalitions is the establishment of minimum levels of acceptable achievement. This process is known as *satisficing*. Since these are minimum levels, there is no unique value that variables such as output or profit can take. Much will depend on the economic circumstances that characterise the industry within which the firm is operating.

Pricing in the construction industry

If a person wants to buy a new car, television or piece of hi-fi he or she will contact a number of shops or showrooms in order to identify the range of prices and qualities available. Economists refer to this process as *search*. Since search can be expensive in terms of both time and money, it is likely that the intensity of search will depend on the amount of money the person intends to pay. Unfortunately, when an individual, a firm or an organisation wishes to have a particular piece of building work undertaking, the search process is more complicated since it is not possible to go window shopping or consult specialist magazines to determine which outlet is the most competitive. Instead, competition can only be created by contacting firms and asking them to provide an estimate of how much they would charge to undertake the work. Initially the client has to choose whether to drive a wedge between the specific design of the building and its subsequent construction, such that the former activity is undertaken by an architect and the latter by a construction firm, or to deal with firms that offer an integrated service from the design through to the construction stage. The following discussion identifies different ways in which search can be undertaken, ranging from *open tender* through to *management contracting*.

A *tender* is a bid submitted by a firm in response its being notified that a particular project is open to bidding. The tender may encompass a range of variables, the most important of which are the price and the time it will take to complete the work. Tenders fall into two distinct types. If the work in question is advertised openly such that any firm can put in a bid, the tender is known as an *open tender*. If, on the other hand, it is decided to invite tenders from a particular group of firms only, such as those have given good service in the past and have the appropriate resources, then the tender is known as a *selected list tender*. Whereas the latter option can reduce the time it takes to assess the viability of all tenders, it may also encourage collusion if the number of companies on the list is fixed for long periods of time.

The tendering system raises a number of important issues. First, the client needs to be sure that a bid is realistic in terms of price and time. Once the tender is accepted, both these variables become fixed and unable to respond to unforeseen difficulties. This may prompt the more opportunistic to cut corners if the contract is inadequately specified. Indeed, if a low tender price causes the contractor to experience financial difficulties such that it has to pull out of the project, then the client may have to throw itself on the mercy of one of the unsuccessful firms if it is to get the work completed on time. Second, the price of any project is likely to be biased upwards to reflect some form of risk premium. This arises because firms incur costs when putting a bid together. The price may also reflect resources expended when compiling unsuccessful bids in the past. Thus, although tendering appears to promote competition, transaction costs are incurred and these must be viewed as a resource loss. Third, periods of oscillating inflation can quickly destabilise a fixed-price contract, particularly if the work in question extends over a number of years. If safeguards are built into the contract to protect the contractor, such that any increase in the price of materials is covered by the client, it may discourage the contractor from being cost-efficient.

There are alternatives to the tendering system. Rather than having to process bids from a large number of firms, it may be decided to approach a single firm and establish a *negotiated contract* for the work required. This may be the only option if the work is highly specialised, or more generally it may reduce the costs associated with the tendering process if it is possible to deal with a contractor whose work has proved reliable in the past. Although the contractor is now in a stronger position, competitiveness can be promoted if the firm is given a guarantee that a satisfactory performance will generate additional contracts. This is known as *serial contracting*. Competition can be enhanced further by discussing plans with two or three firms at the outset.

Where there is only a limited amount of leeway with respect to the design of the building work, an alternative approach is to ask a contractor to be involved in all aspects of the construction work and in the specific design of the building. This is known as a *package deal*. Obviously the contractor must have appropriate architectural support in order for this to be a viable option. Under the package deal heading comes the *design and construct* approach, whereby the client prepares a basic specification and then requests firms to put in tenders for the exact design and the construction work associated with that design. This approach can provide time savings since a single firm is more likely to be able to dovetail sequential processes more effectively than a number of unrelated firms. Another way of reducing the coordination costs associated with a buiding project is to engage in *management contracting*. In this approach a contractor manages the project for a fixed fee. Subcontractors are either employed by the client or the management contractor, though in the latter case it is the client who directly bears the costs of the subcontractors. With the contractor in overall control of the project, unnecessary delays can be kept to a minimum.

The relationship between firms

So far the analysis has circumvented the possibility that many firms make pricing and output decisions with reference to competing firms. This is exemplified by the literature focusing on oligopolistic market structures. The aim of this section is to look at three basic issues. First, it will focus on the problems large firms face when they devise strategies to predict and counteract the actions of their competitors, a situation embodied in *game theory*. Second, the analysis identifies the implications of firms agreeing to collude with each other in order to avoid the costs and uncertainties that arise when firms compete. The final part considers the implications of firms agreeing to merge with each other, or one firm adopting a predatory strategy and taking over a company within its own industry or one in an unrelated industry.

Non-collusive behaviour – 'the prisoners' dilemma'

On commercial television we often see firms adopting aggressive advertising campaigns in order to promote their product. More often than not, such advertising is for market share and is initiated by firms operating in oligopolistic industries. Examples include washing powder, chocolate bars, soft drinks, supermarket chains and motor cars. It soon becomes clear from such advertising that competition within oligopolistic markets can be very intense and extends beyond simple price wars, for example ongoing programmes of product refinement and product repackaging aimed not only at maintaining the brand loyalty of existing customers but also at diverting demand from competing firms.

A simple exercise that reflects the uncertainty firms face in duopolisitic and oligopolistic markets is known as the *prisoners' dilemma*.[1] Assume two competing firms (A and B) are deciding whether or not to initiate a new advertising campaign and that neither firm has 'insider information' about the likely actions of the other. In Table 6.1 the *pay-off matrix* outlines the profits (in millions of pounds) that each firm will receive if (1) both choose to advertise, (2) only one firm chooses to advertise, and (3) both decide not to advertise.

It can be seen from the figures in the pay-off matrix that if neither firm advertises both will accrue profits of £20 million. However both firms know that their profits will rise to £30 million if one of them advertises and the other does not. Furthermore if, for example, firm B decides to advertise then A will be better off doing the same since it will only receive a profit of £5 million if it does not respond. Given the symmetry of the numbers in this example and the mutual lack of knowledge, the dominant strategy for both firms is to advertise. The net result is that they both receive a profit of £15 million. With knowledge of each other's actions, plus a high degree of trust, it would actually be advantageous for neither firm to advertise since profits of £20 million would then be accrued by both.

Collusive behaviour – cartels

An alternative to playing what are, in effect, strategic games, rival oligopolistic firms may choose to collude with each other in order to reduce the costs of trying constantly to outguess each other. Such agreements are known as *cartels* and in their simplest form are attempts to maximise joint profits and achieve a higher level of profit than could be achieved if the firms in question pursued independent profit maximising strategies. However a cartel cannot eliminate the uncertainties and transaction costs that characterise business activity. For example firms need to negotiate and ultimately agree on the best collective strategy. With firms using different technologies and utilising different outlets, each will have different opinions as to the best strategy to adopt collectively (obviously, self-interest will guide each firm's negotiating strategy). However, even when an agreement has been made, there remains the problem of maintaining it over time. The creation of a cartel gives members an incentive to 'cheat' by producing more than their agreed output and/or undercutting the agreed prices. The greater the number of firms operating within a cartel, the greater the likelihood that some firms will feel agrieved by the constraints they face,

Table 6.1   Payoff matrix for two firms in a Duopolistic industry

		Firm B	
		None	Adv
Firm A	None	20,20	5,30
	Adv	30,5	15,15

and hence the greater the likelihood that they will cheat. If a firm within a cartel is likely to incur losses at the agreed price/output, then it is up to the firms that are earning profits from the cartel to subsidise it or else the cartel will lose members, potentially leading to it breaking down.

Although most cartels are illegal in Britain and indeed in most developed countries, the construction industry does provide examples of collusion. For example, from 1934 until it was abandoned in 1987 the Cement Makers' Federation was allowed to operate a cartel by the Restrictive Practices Court (which was seen as allowing the industry to operate in an orderly way). For cartels to operate successfully, one firm has to be sufficiently dominant to exert control over the other signatories. Within the cement cartel the main player was Blue Circle (with 60 per cent of the market). Other important firms included Rio Tinto Zinc (22 per cent) and Rugby Portland (18 per cent). The federation divided the country into eleven regions, within each of which a common price was determined (based on the average costs of the producers) and market shares were determined on a monthly basis. The demise of the cartel reflected two factors. First, the threat of cheap imports from Eastern Europe and Greece was beginning to prompt firms to look more closely at their cost structures. Second, cement sales had begun to decline due to the discovery that the addition of pulverised fuel ash to cement not only improved its quality but also meant that less cement was required to make a given amount of concrete. As a result firms began to disregard their commitment to the cartel.

Mergers and takeovers

When two or more companies unite, they are said to *merge*. Strictly speaking, merger activity can fall into two general categories: *mergers* and *takeovers*. However in practice it may not be possible to distinguish between the two, and as a result the terms have tended to become interchangeable. A merger takes place when the owners of two firms agree to exchange their respective shareholdings for the shares of a new entity that may also bear the name of the companies concerned.

The implication is that the transaction is desired by both parties. A takeover, on the other hand, has more predatory connotations. In this case the shareholders of one firm make an offer for the shares of another firm, possibly resulting in the latter losing its corporate identity. Because, by implication, a takeover is conducted against the wishes of the shareholders of the firm to be acquired, the offer made by the acquiring firm is in excess of the market value of the firm concerned. However, since the distinction between mergers and takeovers is not fundamental to the discussion here, the general term 'merger' will be adopted throughout.

There are three basic forms of merger: *horizontal, vertical* and *conglomerate.* Horizontal mergers occur when two firms at the same stage of production combine with each other. The advantage of such a merger is that it can facilitate the exploitation of economies of size at both plant and firm level. A vertical merger occurs between firms involved with different stages of the same productive process and is invariably an attempt to gain greater control over its activities. Under this heading the merger may be 'backward', for example when a firm merges with one or more of its suppliers, or 'forward', for example when a manufacturer merges with one or more firms who act as market outlets for its finished product. A conglomerate merger takes place between two firms engaged in the production of different products. Such activity is usually prompted by a desire to spread risk between markets, though it may also be prompted by financial reasons whereby one firm is bought cheaply in a time of recession and sold at a profit at a later date.

Examples of merger activity abound in the construction industry. The Bryant Group's 100 per cent purchase of Vigobridge Ltd in May 1994 was a classic horizontal acquisition. The former's primary interests are the construction and repair of buildings, and real estate. At the time of acquisition, Vigobridge had £14 million in land holdings and £5 million of work in progress. Similarly, the purchase of John Mowlem's housebuilding operations by Beazer Homes in July 1994 was a 'pure' horizontal acquisition.

Not all mergers fall strictly within textbook definitions. Some firms in the construction industry have acquired interests that are not at the same stage of production *per se* but remain explicitly within the confines of construction-related activity. For example, in addition to its better known activity, Blue Circle Industries has acquired business interests in fans and ventilating equipment, plastic building products and real estate. Like many construction firms, John Laing not only deals in real estate but also in the hiring out of construction machinery and equipment to smaller building enterprises. Conglomerates such as Trafalgar House have acquired interests inside and outside the construction industry. For example, as well as providing steelwork for civil engineering works, Trafalgar House also owns firms involved with textile machinery, gas, water, waste, rubber, marine engines and ocean-going vessels.

In a world characterised by producer uncertainty, merger activity can in part be seen as a rational attempt by firms to counteract their inability to see a long way into the future. However, having interests in more than one market may not necessarily be seen as desirable. For example, in 1994 Taylor Woodrow, which is associated primarily with building and construction, engineering works and real estate, opted to dispose of A. and S. Andrews Ltd (cars) in an attempt to concentrate on its core business strengths.

Sources of finance for construction firms

In Britain, half of the funds used by private sector companies are internally generated, that is, derived from profits. However, this is only an average: the construction industry is so dominated by relatively small firms that 98 per cent of construction firms employ fewer than 25 people. Thus, with the exception of the very large firms, the majority of the industry is dependent on external sources to finance its activities. Furthermore, many consumers of the products of the industry, for example houses, depend on external loans to buy those products. Thus the aim of the following section is to look more closely at the relationship between the providers of finance, for example banks, and the recipients of it. The first stage of this analysis provides a general introduction to the financial services industry, and this is followed by a discussion focusing specifically on its relationship with the construction industry.

The finance industry

In many respects, financial markets are no different from any other market. Specifically they bring together economic agents who want to *borrow* money or paper assets and those who are willing and able to *lend* it. Borrowers and lenders are diverse in nature, ranging from single individuals through to larger concerns such as companies or even governments. Lenders and borrowers may deal *directly* with each other (although perhaps through the services of a broker), for example when a person buys shares in a company. In this case the person concerned bears the risk of the shares increasing or decreasing in value during the period when he or she owns them. Alternatively the lender/borrower relationship may be *indirect*, such that the lender deposits funds with a *financial intermediary*, which then decides which of the potential borrowers should be lent monies subsequently. The survival of these financial intermediaries depends on their ability to borrow money at a lower rate of interest than that at which they lend.

For most people the most common types of financial intermediary are *banks* or *building societies*, which receive deposits from individuals who do not wish to spend all their funds immediately and redirect these monies towards economic agents who wish to spend more money than they currently have at their disposal. However banks and building societies are not the only financial intermediaries that populate financial markets. There are also *discount houses*, which act as intermediaries between the Bank of England and the rest of the banking sector; *finance houses*, which arrange hire purchase agreements to enable households and firms to buy commodities such as cars or machinery; and *insurance companies* and *pension funds*, which, like banks, take monies from their customers (for example those buying a life assurance policy or contributing to a pension scheme) and lend it to borrowers.

The fact that the relationship between lender and borrower is circuitous when a financial intermediary is involved raises the question of why the system has evolved. A number of arguments can be put forward. First, financial intermediaries reduce the costs of *search*. In the case of everyday commodities, supermarkets ensure that consumers do not have to visit an individual supplier in order to buy each item on their shopping list. Similarly, financial intermediaries enable borrowers to borrow a large sum of money from one place, rather than having to visit a large number of potential investors. Second, financial intermediaries allow risks to be pooled. If lenders and borrowers transact on a one-to-one basis, the lender faces all the risk of the borrower defaulting on his or her obligation to repay. In contrast a bank or other financial intermediary spreads the risk of default across its entire customer base. Third, financial intermediaries have the resources to buy in experts who are able to assess the relative ability of economic agents to bear a loan. Since these experts are responsible for managing a large number of loans, the marginal cost of their activities is relatively low. In contrast, it would be expensive and difficult for most individual lenders to monitor the activities of the people/organisations to whom they lend. Finally, financial intermediaries 'borrow short and lend long'. This means that they are prepared to repay at short notice the monies they take from their customers (for example deposits in a bank account), yet are willing to make loans for long periods of time (for example a mortgage on a house).

Finance and the construction industry

The main source of funds for construction firms or the financing of construction projects are the clearing banks. The capital market has only a limited involvement with the construction industry. When banks are approached to provide loans for expansion, new equipment or working capital, they will take a number of factors into account when determining whether or not a company is a safe risk. Brownlie and Harris (1987) provide a basic checklist of characteristics. These include company reputation, its balance sheet, the reason for borrowing, the company's managerial quality (for example, whether it could call on a broad base of skills, for instance in finance and marketing, to ensure the maximum profitability of contracts as well as in construction *per se*), the systems that exist to monitor ongoing company performance, the extent to which its activities are diversified (and indeed the degree to which the company has the skills to be diversified), any outstanding claims and the nature of its clients. According to a survey of contractors carried out by Brownlie in 1986 and discussed subsequently in Brownlie and Harris (1987), these criteria (somewhat predictably) mean that company size is an important criterion in determining the size of the loan and the interest rate charged by banks. Furthermore it was revealed that contractors prefer clearing banks to merchant banks, mainly because the former seem able to provide the services required by contractors, making it less necessary for the latter to be contacted.

In the same study Brownlie and Harris report on the criteria used by banks to assess whether or not they should become involved with the financing of construction projects. There are three basic yardsticks against which the viability of loans are assessed. First, whether all the risks associated with the project have been identified and, where appropriate, insured against; second, whether the construction stage will be carried out by reputable contractors using appropriate technology (indeed banks may demand to be involved with contractor selection); and finally, whether there is a market for the project once its construction phase is completed. The charging of a higher rate of interest would reflect the 'premium' for any concern of the lender with respect to the fulfilment of any of these criteria. The attitude of the banks is that risks should be shared between the bank and the promoter of the project. Nevertheless the banks were found to be flexible with respect to setting loan periods and the rate at which loans are paid off. If a particular project is to take place overseas, especially in developing countries, the project promoter is expected to have the blessing of the Export Credits Guarantee Department (though this is concerned mainly with political risk). In this case the promoter negotiates an insurance deal with the ECGD, which means that the bank will be paid in the event of the borrower defaulting on its obligations. These monies may also be supplemented by loans from the host country.

Organisational structure

Most discussions on the construction industry focus on the fact that the majority of firms are small organisations that exploit localised monopolies. The aim of the final section of this chapter is to focus specifically on why some firms have been able to grow and diversify, and in doing so become household names.

In an earlier section of this chapter the discussion raised the possibility of a wedge being driven between the individuals who own a firm (namely its shareholders) and those in control of its day-to-day running. As firms grow in size in order to exploit new openings in new or growing markets, the span of control that can be exerted by owners and managers over their subordinates becomes curtailed as the number of communication channels multiply. This provides an increased opportunity for managers further down the firm's managerial hierachy to work to their own agendas. These informational problems not only relate to the ability of decision makers and managers to pass instructions down the hierachy but also their ability to receive information from the 'front line'. There are a number of ways in which the firms can organise themselves in order to confront this problem. Following Williamson (1981), three will be identified here: the unitary form; the holding company form and the multidivisional form; also known respectively in the literature as the U-form, the H-form and the M-form.

The U-form structure

In this case the firm is organised centrally in terms of a series of functional divisions, regardless of the number of product lines and product markets with which the firm is engaged. Each of these functional divisions is answerable directly to the chief executive. A classic example of this organisational form was Du Pont prior to its conversion to an M-form structure (discussed later) during the 1920s. An example of a U-form structure is set out in Figure 6.8, with the functional divisions highlighted as production, sales, marketing and research and development.

The degree to which such a system can effectively utilise generated information depends on the number of product lines that exist. Consequently the U-form as an organisational structure is most suited to firms whose activities are restricted to a limited number of closely related products.

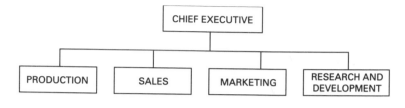

Figure 6.8   The U-form firm

The H-form structure

In complete contrast to the U-form is the holding company or H-form company, whose structure originated in the nineteenth century. The H-form is simply a decentralised collection of separate firms under common ownership, typified by General Motors prior to its becoming an M-form (see below) organisation during the 1920s. The head office of the H-form company has no strategic role and simply collects the profits of the constituent elements of the firm. According to Williamson (1981, p. 1556), the H-form company is 'little more than a corporate shell'. There is little if any common expertise and each division enjoys a high level of autonomy. As long as no significant gains can be derived from the coordination of such activities as investment or research and development, the H-form is a viable organisational structure. However, if gains can be made, then it is rational for firms to reorganise into an M-form structure.

The M-form structure

The M-form structure not only confronts the control problems experienced within the U-form company, but also the lack of coordination experienced in H-form companies. Specifically, it involves organisation on a product-by-product basis. For each product group (or division) there exists a series of individual functional departments (sales, marketing and so on) akin to the U-form structure. In order to oversee the overall performance of the company there is a general office, which is responsible for resource allocation and setting the general strategy for the firm. Indeed these are the processes from which size economies may be exploited. Thus, amongst other things, it is responsible for investing resources in each product division. In this respect it can be argued that the M-form structure allows the firm to recapture the attributes of textbook profit maximisation since the general office will allocate resources to the company's most successful divisions, and as a result will encourage divisional managers to attempt to maxi-

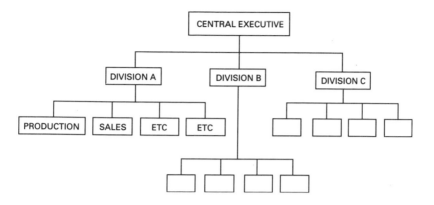

Figure 6.9   The M-form firm

mise the rate of return on resource use. This structure can be seen in Figure 6.9.

As we have already seen, there are only limited opportunities for the majority of firms to exploit economies of size and monopolistic power. However the industry is characterised by a number of very large firms that have become household names. In a recent article, Ive (1994) put forward three possible reasons why very large firms can emerge.

First, these firms have been run by senior managers and directors who have the desire and opportunity to pursue policies directed towards increasing the rate of growth of the firm, and as a result increasing their own power within the firm. Such an explanation fits neatly into our previous discussion of the managerial theories of the firm.

Second, as we have already seen, larger firms gain advantages with respect to obtaining cheaper finance (financial economies of size) and the opportunity to spread their risks across several projects rather than just one. This explanation refers to the greater likelihood that larger firms will also have interests outside the immediate construction industry, or even outside the wider built-environment sector.

Third, during boom periods, when a large amount of construction activity takes place, firms with growth potential exploit the opportunities available to them and as a result they become larger than their rivals. This growth may reflect overoptimism by the firm's managers, who are willing to obtain external finance (as we have seen, not necessarily its owners *per se*), as well as by the people who are willing and able to lend funds to them.

Ive (1994), in his attempt to analyse the main characteristics of large construction firms, uses a definition that '... remembers their origin as well as reflecting their present diversification and total group size'. (p. 352) The criteria he uses are as follows:

- a group turnover of £1 billion or more in 1989;
- at least 33 per cent of group turnover should be derived from construction activity, which is defined strictly as contracting and speculative house building;
- firms whose core activities are property development or the manufacture of building materials are ignored.

The first and second criteria were met by eleven British firms in 1989, each with a construction-related turnover of at least £333 million. These firms are listed in Table 6.2. Each of the eleven firms was assessed according to its general characteristics in terms of the following:

1. Their range of activities:
   A: mainly or only construction;
   B: across the 'built environment' sector (defined as construction plus property development and the manufacture of building materials);
   C: characteristic B plus one or two other sectors;
   D: characteristic B plus many other sectors.

These shall be referred to subsequently as 1A, 1B, 1C and 1D.

2. Their organisational control:
   A: U-form;
   B: M-form;
   C: H-form.

These shall be referred to as 2A, 2B and 2C respectively.

The eleven companies identified in the study assumed the characteristic of either 1B and 2C, or 1C and 2C, referred to by Ive as 'diversified construction groups' and 'bisectoral conglomerates' respectively (ibid., p. 353). In other words, even the largest firms have tended to concentrate their interests in sectors where they have the most expertise and the best reputation. Such diversification allows them to take advantage of the tendency for profit cycles in different sectors of the wider industry to be slightly out of phase with each other (that is, a decline in one sector can be cushioned by activities in other sectors).

The characteristics exhibited by the eleven companies are summarised by Ive as follows:

- A relatively high proportion of growth financed through external acquisition, namely merger/takeover activity ('high' relative to the construction sector rather than industry as a whole).
- A high proportion of growth financed through share issues.

Table 6.2 Characteristics and turnover of eleven major construction firms

Name of group	Characteristic	Turnover (£M 1989)
P&O	1C and 2C	4578
BICC	1C and 2C	3792
Tarmac	1B and 2C	3527
Trafalgar House	1C and 2C	3229
Wimpey	1B and 2C	2065
AMEC	1B and 2C	1993
Beazer	1B and 2C	1970
Costain	1B and 2C	1404
Laing	1B and 2C	1363
Taylor Woodrow	1B and 2C	1321
Mowlem	1B and 2C	1305

Source: Ive, 1994, Table 1, p. 352.

- A high proportion of fund transfer between divisions to promote efficiency of resource use, for example between construction divisions and speculative house-building divisions during boom periods.
- Although a large proportion of activities remain within Britain, activities are also spread to exploit markets in North America, Europe and other parts of the world.

7 Introduction to Macroeconomics

INTRODUCTION

The remainder of this book is devoted to macroeconomic issues in recognition of the fact that the behaviour exhibited by firms, regardless of their industry, reflects the characteristics of the economy within which they operate and the measures taken by the government in response to any fluctuations in the performance of that economy. This and the following chapter are policy-oriented. Chapter 7 is a facilitating chapter that identifies some of the key principles that underpin macroeconomic analysis and the relationships that exist between different macroeconomic variables. Based upon this foundation, Chapter 8 focuses explicitly on how changes in postwar government policy have affected the construction industry. It will be seen that the postwar era can be divided into two discrete periods. The first, 1945 to the mid-1970s, was a period when governments were prepared to intervene actively in their economies in order to rectify shortfalls in employment (and hence economic activity), which was deemed to be economically and politically unacceptable. The second period, which takes us to the present day, reflects a changed political and economic philosophy that has resulted in the government attempting to reduce the role of the state in the economy and correct the underlying structural deficiencies that characterise the British economy.

BACKGROUND TO POSTWAR MACROECONOMIC POLICY MAKING

During the late 1920s and throughout the 1930s the world economy was characterised by a period of high unemployment that became known as the *Great Depression*. The response of many governments to this problem was to erect trade barriers in an attempt to protect domestic jobs. However this simply pushed the world economy into further decline and caused further unemployment in countries with export-sensitive industries. Based on the work of the economist *John Maynard Keynes* (see Chapter 8), postwar governments pursued policies that had the explicit objective of promoting domestic employment. Specifically, if unemployment rose too quickly, expansionary government spending was used to create jobs and pull the economy out of recession.

At the global level, attempts were made to prevent a repetition of the mistakes that had led to the collapse of the international capital market and the emergence of international protectionism. To this end, in 1944 representatives of the United States, Britain and 42 other countries met at Bretton Woods in the United States (although the USSR participated in the negotiations, it opted ultimately to maintain its prewar isolation and to build a power base in Central and Eastern Europe). The result of the Bretton Woods conference was threefold.

- A new blueprint governing foreign exchange, in which member countries were required to maintain their currency within a band of ± 1 per cent of the currency's value against the US dollar, which in turn was linked to gold.
- The creation of the International Bank for Reconstruction and Development and the International Monetary Fund. The former was set up initially to provide a flow of soft loans (loans below the market rates of interest) to finance postwar reconstruction, while the latter was established in order to encourage international monetary cooperation, stabilise exchange rates and facilitate a multilateral payments system between member countries.
- A parallel organisation – the International Trade Organisation (ITO), which was intended to orchestrate the elimination of tariff barriers between countries – was also conceived, but for political reasons this organisation never reached fruition. Instead the promotion of orderly trading relations emerged through the less ambitious General Agreement on Tariffs and Trade (GATT). This survived for almost fifty years, but was recently replaced by the World Trade Organisation (WTO).

Thus, with institutions in place to promote world trade and an overriding desire to maintain a low level of unemployment, the governments of most industrial economies began to lead their respective countries into an era of economic prosperity.

THE BASIC PROBLEMS OF MACROECONOMIC POLICY MAKING

It was argued in Chapter 3 that there is no guarantee that the actions of economic agents will combine to generate outcomes that are economically, politically and socially desirable. Just as this is taken to be a justification for governments to exercise their power to initiate microeconomic policies aimed at specific sectors of the economy, for example health care, education and infrastructure development, so too is it a reason why governments aim to influence the overall perform-ance of their economies at the national and international levels.

When commenting on macroeconomic policy making economists often use three terms: objectives, instruments and constraints. Macroeconomic *objectives* are those things the government wishes to achieve, for exam-ple inflation below a particular rate. The policies it uses to achieve a particular objective are usually referred to as *instruments*. Policy in-struments fall into four main categories, each of which will be consid-ered below: *fiscal policy, monetary policy, exchange rate policy* and *supply side policy*. However, it should be noted that it is not possible to define unambiguously what constitutes a policy objective and what constitutes a policy instrument. For example, during the postwar era governments have identified a particular rate of exchange for their currency as a policy objective, yet on other occasions they have manipulated the exchange rate as a policy instrument to achieve other objectives, for example rectifying balance of payments difficulties. However, in formulating its objectives and deciding which instruments to use to rectify them, governments also face *constraints*. These include:

- the current level of technical knowledge, which determines how available factors of production can be used;
- the current legal framework – existing laws cannot be changed rapidly according to government whim;
- any international agreements by which a country is bound, for example members of the EU cannot take unilateral action with respect to trade policy;
- the political and social constraints that determine what a govern-ment may or may not do, for example break promises made in a manifesto or pursue policies that exacerbate existing inequalities.

OBJECTIVES OF GOVERNMENT MACROECONOMIC POLICY

Controlling the level of unemployment

Given that every postwar government has had to confront the problem of unemployment at some time during its term of office, it is surprising that there is still not a definition of unemployment that is acceptable to all commentators. This results in news bulletins featuring politicians tediously arguing the semantics of what is meant by a rise or a fall in the unemployment figures.

Clearly it is inaccurate to say that all jobless people are unemployed, since not all jobless people seek employment. Thus there is a need to recognise a desire for paid employment on the part of the individual, whether it is in terms of seeking it, being available for it or claiming benefits in lieu of it. However, numerically speaking there is a difference between, for example, the numbers who are seeking work and those who are actually drawing unemployment benefit. It is at this point where the definitional problems emerge. Since 1982 the official British unemployment figures, as reported in the media, have been derived from the number of people who are eligible for and claiming unemployment benefit. The main problem with this approach is that a change in the eligibility conditions for a particular benefit (for example unemployment benefit or income support) also changes the official level of unemployment, without a corresponding change in the underlying conditions affecting the labour market.

The existence of some unemployment within a country is inevitable while people are changing jobs and being reallocated from declining sectors of the economy to expanding ones. Unemployment emerges as an economic problem when it is caused by a downswing in economic activity at the national or local level.

The experiences of most countries during the interwar years convinced many governments that combatting unemployment should be given the highest priority after the Second World War. From 1945 until the early 1970s governments, prompted by the writings of John Maynard Keynes, intervened actively in their economies in order to contain unemployment at or below an acceptable level. However, from the late 1960s, when memories of the Great Depression were fading and governments were increasingly unable to correct the structural defects that were causing a rise in the underlying level of unemployment, economists and politicians began to turn their attention to a problem that was perceived to be the root cause of many countries' economic problems: the presence of increasing and persistent inflation.

Maintaining a low and stable level of inflation

Inflation refers to any rise in prices that reduces the purchasing power of a nominal sum of money. The inflation figures reported in the media are based on changes in the price of a weighted 'basket' of goods and services, usually over the course of a year. Until mid-1979 there was only one way in which inflation was measured, namely the *retail price index* (or RPI). Since then a second measure, known as the *tax and price index* (TPI), has also been used by the government as a more 'accurate' reflection of the level of inflation confronting economic agents. Let us consider each briefly in turn.

As we saw in Chapter 1, the rate of inflation is calculated with reference to a representative basket of goods and services that are weighted according to their relative importance in the average family's expenditure pattern. The weights are derived from the Central Statistical Office (CSO) publication, the Family Expenditure Survey (see Chapter 1). Because prices not only vary significantly between different regions but also between different outlets in the same locality, a large sample of price quotations are collected and these are then averaged. The average price for each commodity is then calculated and compared with that prevailing, say, a year before.

The TPI has been estimated since mid-1979. As we shall see, one of the objectives of the newly installed Conservative government of the time was to correct the disincentive effect that it believed to result from the relatively high rate of income deductions (specifically, income tax and National Insurance contributions). Thus the TPI identifies changes in *real* spending power, specifically, changes in the average take-home pay (earnings after income tax and National Insurance contributions have been deducted) as well as the price level. Within this alternative indicator of inflation, price changes have a weighting of three quarters, the remainder reflecting changes in the tax burden of individuals. The rationale underpinning this new measure was that if direct taxation was reduced and people were therefore made 'better off', lower pay settlements would result, which would reduce employers' wage costs and hence exert a further downward pressure on prices. For much of the time since its instigation, the TPI has indeed been below the RPI. However, since the end of 1993 the TPI has exceeded the RPI.

Economists often make a distinction between *anticipated inflation* and *unanticipated inflation*. The degree to which inflation is 'unanticipated' depends on how well economic agents predict future levels of inflation. If inflation can be anticipated completely, markets can function properly since economic agents simply include the anticipated price change(s) in their decision-making framework. In contrast, if a large proportion of inflation is unanticipated, then price signals become inconsistent and resource allocation becomes inefficient. However, the need to hold a certain amount of cash in order to finance day-to-day purchases means that no-one is exempt from the cost of inflation, even if the remainder is invested. If inflation rates are extremely high, economic agents are forced to engage in transactions or renegotiate contracts more frequently, a process that imposes additional costs upon them.

Inflation is an international problem. The fact that countries experience different levels of inflation, depending on the structure of their respective economies, means that inflation is yet another determining factor in their willingness and ability to trade with each other. *Ceteris paribus*, economies experiencing high rates of inflation are more likely to find themselves at a competitive disadvantage when trading with countries with low inflation rates. Over time, high-inflation economies are more likely to experience balance of payments difficulties as exports fall and imports rise, unless remedial action is taken.

Preventing long-term balance of payments deficits

The balance of payments account records all the transactions a country undertakes with the rest of the world over a given time period. The value of exports to other countries, dividend payments from abroad and inward investment by foreigners are entered as *credits*. Conversely, the value of imported goods and services, dividend payments made to foreigners and outward investment by home investors in other countries are entered into the account as *debits* since they represent an outflow of currency from the country in question.

The major subdivision of headings within a country's balance of payments accounts is between the *current account* and the *capital account*. Within the former there are two further categories of account. The *visible account* documents trade in physical goods, such as raw materials, while the *invisible account* identifies any trade involving the service sector, such as banking or insurance services. In contrast the capital account identifies any transactions involving investment flows. For example, investment by Toyota in Britain would enter on the credit side of the British capital account and as a debit in that of Japan. Similarly, should a foreign investor choose to deposit monies in a British bank, this would also represent a credit item for Britain's capital account. In addition to investors' perception of the relative strength of different economies, the direction of investment flows also depends on the relative rates of interest between different countries. Thus by raising its interest rates a government can try to raise the level of investment flowing into the country.

If overall credits exceed overall debits, the balance of payments is said to be in *surplus*, whereas if overall debits exceed overall credits it is said to be in *deficit*. Indeed a country can be in credit for certain items in its balance of payments account, for example its visible balance, yet experience a deficit elsewhere, for example in some part of its capital account. If a person persists in spending more than he or she earns on a day-to-day basis, incursions will need to be made into savings and eventually debts may be incurred. A balance of payments deficit can have a similar effect, such that currency reserves are reduced and international debts accumulated. On this count alone, a persistent balance of payments deficit is not deemed to be a desirable outcome of macroeconomic policy, and therefore as a policy it cannot be sustained indefinitely.

Maintaining a satisfactory rate of economic growth

The rate of economic growth of an economy is the percentage in-crease in its national output over a fixed period of time, usually one year. This can be distinguished from the *potential growth* of a country, which is that which would be derived if all its resources were to be used efficiently. A country's ability to grow depends on the quantity and mix of resources it has at its disposal, together with the way in which they are combined. Resources include the labour force (and its degree of training), capital stocks (and the level of technology endowed in them at any given point in time), land and raw materials (for exam-ple productive farm land and reserves of coal, gas and oil).

Immediately after the Second World War the need for economies to grow quickly was taken to be self-evident. Western governments inter-vened actively in their economies to promote low unemployment, and in doing so they tried to provide their business sector with the confi-dence to take entrepreneurial risks. With hindsight it is possible to identify the mid-1950s as a watershed marking the end of postwar reconstruction and the emergence of an international boom period. Between 1960 and 1973, world production grew at an unprecedented rate, averaging 5.5 per cent per anum. This was a period of cheap energy, rapid technological change and a general increase in expecta-tions, which provided the momentum for such growth to take place. The subsequent decline in world growth can be attributed to a number of factors, for example the destabilising inflationary pressures that emerged throughout the world economy and the overdependence of the world economy on oil, an energy source whose price increased rapidly dur-ing the 1970s. When oil prices rose, money had to be diverted from other activities in order to meet higher fuel costs, leaving a smaller residual for growth-enhancing expenditure.

Economic growth is usually measured with reference to one of two basic indicators: gross domestic product (GDP) and gross national product (GNP):

- *Gross domestic product*: a country's GDP is measured by estimat-ing the value of the flow of goods and services it produces over a given period of time, usually one year. This measure makes no distinction between the output of domestic firms and that of foreign-owned firms operating within the domestic economy.
- *Gross national product*: in contrast, GNP is a measure of the value of domestic output (goods and services) within a given period of time, *plus* the earnings of nationals who earn monies from their investments abroad, *minus* the earnings of foreign nationals in the domestic economy.

A number of points should be noted about the estimation of a country's GDP or GNP. First, to avoid *double counting*, the value of products that are inputs into another production process should be excluded from the calculations. Only the value of *final goods* and *investment goods* should be included. Second, If *market prices* are used in calculations, then we may get a distorted picture of GDP or GNP since their value depends on the level of indirect taxes and subsidies being levied on them. This can be a problem if we are using time series data. Thus economists often make a distinction between GDP (or GNP) at *market prices*, which includes indirect taxes and subsidies in the value of a good or service, and GDP (or GNP) at *factor cost*, which excludes indirect taxes and subsidies. Third, regardless of whether a factor cost or a market price measure is being used, care must be taken with respect to the effects of *inflation* on the market price of goods and services. For reasons already explored in Chapter 1, time series data are best compared according to the prices prevailing in a particular year. Fourth, international comparisons of GDP or GNP need to take into account differences in population between countries. Per capita measures (in other words GDP or GNP per head) provide a more accurate insight into how wealthy countries really are. Finally, by definition GDP and GNP figures are *gross* figures. They take no account of the depreciation of capital and hence the level of production that is needed simply to replace worn-out machinery. Some writers refer to *net national product (NNP)* figures, though these are not usually cited in everyday publications because of the difficulties that can emerge in formally defining depreciation.

POLICY INSTRUMENTS USED BY GOVERNMENTS

Although any government in power has a large armoury of policy instruments at its disposal, it is often convenient to consider them under one of four basic headings: fiscal policy, monetary policy, exchange rate policy and supply-side policy. It is not the intention to use this section to provide a detailed analysis of the implications of using any one of these, merely to identify the main characteristics of each approach. Their economic implications in terms of the success each has afforded past and present governments will be considered in more detail in Chapter 8.

Fiscal policy

Fiscal policy involves the use of monies raised through taxation in order to 'manage' the level of demand within an economy. The emergence of fiscal policy as a credible policy option can be attributed directly to the work of John Maynard Keynes, whose influence set the tone for government policy for 25 years after the end of the Second World War.

The use of fiscal policy is a recognition by government that it need not passively accept increases in unemployment brought about by short-falls in aggregate demand within an economy, but instead that imbal-ances can be corrected through the regulation of its own spending and a willingness to incur a budget deficit. Central to the approach is a belief in the existence of a *multiplier* process, by which a unit in-crease in government expenditure generates an even greater increase in aggregate expenditure as monies are passed on from one economic agent to another. If the multiplier is large, then fiscal policy can be a powerful instrument for controlling economic activity, providing that inflationary pressures are not created. When price stability becomes a problem, fiscal policies are often supplemented by a *prices and in-comes policy*, which places an artificial 'lid' on inflationary pressures.

Monetary policy

Monetary policy refers to government attempts to achieve its objec-tives by manipulating the rate of growth of the money supply, the level of interest rates and the ability of banks to lend money to their cus-tomers. A central feature of the monetarist (advocates of the relative importance of monetary policy) philosophy is adherence to some form of the *quantity theory of money*. Although this concept predates Keynesian economics, it was repopularised by the leading monetarist writer Milton Friedman during the 1950s and postulates a direct causal link between the rate of growth of the money supply and the rate of inflation (dis-cussed in Chapter 8).

For over 25 years after the Second World War, monetary policy was viewed by the government as a separate and minor supplement to its fiscal strategy, which was geared explicitly towards achieving full em-ployment. From the 1970s onwards, when unemployment and infla-tion seemed to be increasing simultaneously (known as *stagflation*), monetary policy moved to centre stage with the principal objective of controlling inflation, which was perceived to be one of the causes of the high level of unemployment that had begun to emerge. Monetarists believe that a government's fiscal and monetary policies are interre-lated, rather than discrete entities, such that any attempt to control the rate of inflation must be accompanied by a reduction in government spending, the cause of money supply growth and high interest rates.

Exchange rate policy

Strictly speaking, the rate at which a currency is exchanged for the currencies of other countries can be used by governments as a policy instrument or a defined policy objective, or indeed it can be viewed as a constraint on the use of other policy instruments and the achievement of other policy goals.

Broadly speaking, in the postwar era countries have adopted one of two forms of exchange rate management. The first involves countries agreeing to fix the rate at which their currencies are exchanged for each other (within predefined limits). Where necessary, governments must intervene actively in the currency markets in order to protect these parities against potentially large fluctuations. Examples of this type of system include that negotiated under the Bretton Woods Agreement and the European Exchange Rate Mechanism. The second approach simply allows currencies to fluctuate against each other according to market forces. In practice, governments have not been prepared to allow their respective currencies to float freely, preferring instead to intervene if the exchange rate of their currency was in danger of falling too low (because imports had become too expensive) or rising too high (because exports had become difficult to sell). This is known as a 'managed' or 'dirty' float.

Although the Bretton Woods Agreement was intended as a policy instrument to facilitate and promote world trade, it soon became a constraint on Britain's attempts to engage in demand management. In particular, attempts to increase aggregate demand during recessionary periods prompted a flood of imported goods, which placed a downward pressure on sterling, a force the government was obliged to defend against. Another example of the value of sterling being used explicitly as a policy instrument occurred during the early 1980s when the government chose not to defend the value of the pound, (which was part of a managed float) in order to make British goods more competitive during a recessionary period. Later on in the 1980s however, the government chose to make the value of sterling an explicit objective in its attempt to 'shadow the Deutschmark', and in doing so enhance sterling's credibility in anticipation of its short-lived entry into the European Exchange Rate Mechanism.

The basic mechanics underpinning the determination of exchange rates in currency markets will be considered shortly, while the policy implications of Britain's exchange rate policy will be analysed at the end of this chapter.

Supply-side policy

A feature of the 1980s and 1990s have been attempts by the government to promote economic growth using 'supply-side' strategies (see Chapter 8 for more details). In essence these measures are microeconomic in flavour and involve attempts to make markets function more effectively: the removal of impediments to entrepreneurial activity; curtailing restrictive labour practices; reducing excessively high welfare payments; the introduction of measures to promote individual liberty; and the introduction of reforms to reduce the size of the public sector, which was perceived to be unresponsive and bureaucratic.

MODELLING THE WORKINGS OF AN ECONOMY: A SIMPLE KEYNESIAN ANALYSIS

The remainder of this chapter is divided into two main sections. This first section considers the composition and implications of a simple Keynesian model; the second provides a brief overview of how currency markets operate. It is well worth spending some time considering each of these sections. Although they both use a highly simplified framework, when set against what actually happens in the real world, they identify some of the relationships that governments of all political persuasions need to be aware of when they engage in policy making. Ultimately they will be seen to provide a backdrop for the policy-oriented discussion contained Chapter 8, not only in terms of the period when Keynesian policy was dominant, but also in more recent times when monetarist principles superseded Keynesian ones.

A simple Keynesian model – demand management in theory

As we have already seen, demand management is an attempt by governments to influence the prevailing level of economic activity by initiating changes in the level of its own expenditure. In order for such a policy to be carried out successfully, it is necessary for a government to have an accurate measure of the value of the flow of goods and services arising from economic activity within a given period of time. There are three basic ways of making such an estimate, each of which is used in the 'Blue Book'.

The *income approach* identifies the incomes accruing to all the factors of production used in the production of goods and services. By definition, this includes profits but excludes payments made by government to identified societal groups, for example to pensioners, since this is a transfer of money from one part of society to another (via the tax system) for which no production has actually taken place. The second approach is known as the *expenditure approach*. This aggregates all the expenditures associated with the purchase of *final goods and services*. Care must be taken to avoid the double counting that would result from including expenditure on *intermediate goods and services* (which will ultimately become final goods and services themselves) and to take account of any taxes and subsidies that artificially distort the level of expenditure on goods and services within any given time period (by definition, taxes and subsidies may vary from year to year). The final approach is the *output approach*, which aggregates the *value added* at each stage of production by productive enterprises in the economy. Again, this value needs to reflect the price distortions that arise from taxes and subsidies levied on output.

In theory all three approaches should generate the same figure. However, and not surprisingly, measurement problems result in three different figures emerging and as a consequence national income figures represent a compromise between the three. Often these figures (when modified for the effects of inflation and expressed in per capita terms) are used as a comparative measure to define how the level of 'well-being' of an economy has changed over time, either domestically or in comparison with other countries. However it should be recognised at the outset that this is a summary statistic that says nothing about, for example, how incomes are distributed between members of the population or the rate at which economic activity is causing the environment to deteriorate. The following analysis will proceed with reference to the expenditures that takes place in an economy over any given accounting period. Four basic categories of expenditure can be identified: consumption expenditure, investment expenditure, government expenditure and net export expenditure.

Consumption expenditure

Consumption demand is the aggregate expenditure made by households on goods and services during a given period of time. On average it contributes to around two-thirds of all expenditure taking place in the British economy. Just which commodities should be included in calculations of consumption expenditure is not totally clear. Whereas expenditure on such things as food and electricity can be explicitly related to the accounting period in question, the benefits to be gained from buying a car or a house can extend over several time periods. However, for the purposes of national income accounting, the purchase of a car by a householder is counted as consumption expenditure whereas the purchase of the house is classified as investment expenditure (see the section on investment). It should also be noted that purchases of second-hand goods are excluded from consumption expenditure estimates since they will have been included in previous accounting periods and hence would lead to double counting. Such purchases are simply a transfer of ownership. However, the services of people who facilitate such transfers of ownership should be included in consumption expenditure figures.

Prior to the pioneering work of Keynes, it was believed that the division of income between consumption and saving was determined by the rate of interest. Specifically, that consumption expenditure was negatively related to the rate of interest whereas savings were positively related. Although Keynes accepted the idea that the rate of interest does play an important role in influencing consumption decisions, he argued that the *level of income* is a more significant determinant. This gave rise to what has become known as the Keynesian *consumption function*, an expression that assumes planned consumption comprise two elements. First, *autonomous consumption* is expenditure that does not vary with income. This is associated with the purchase of the most basic of necessities, and if the worst comes to the worst these may need to be financed out of savings or borrowing. Second, *income induced consumption* is determined by the aggregate level of disposable income in an economy (that is, income less taxation, and after the addition of any benefits). Ignoring taxation for the time being, the Keynesian consumption function is often assumed to take the basic form

$$C = \alpha + \beta Y \tag{7.1}$$

where α denotes autonomous consumption and β is known as the *marginal propensity to consume* (or *mpc*). The marginal propensity to consume represents the proportion of each unit of currency that is devoted to increased consumption. For example, in the case of the hypothetical equation

$$C = (£)10 \text{ billion} + 0.7Y \tag{7.2}$$

autonomous expenditure is £10 billion and the mpc is equal to 0.7. This means that for each £1 they receive, consumers will spend 70p and save 30p (in practice Keynes recognised the fact that the mpc will fall as income rises, giving rise to a non-linear consumption function). Keynes proposed that the ratio of consumption expenditure to income (C/Y), known as the *average propensity to consume* (or *apc*), will fall as incomes increase. Since at zero income individuals engage in autonomous consumption, the marginal propensity to consume will be *less* than the average propensity to consume.

Once the consumption function equation is specified, as in Equation 7.2, it is possible to determine the level of consumption expenditure associated with any level of income. For example, if income is assumed to be £45 billion, then the value of consumption expenditure will be £41.5 billion. This outcome is depicted in Figure 7.1, where income is measured along the x-axis and expenditure is measured along the vertical (y) axis.

At this point it is customary to introduce what economists often refer to as the 45° cross diagram. Consider Figure 7.2. It can be seen that a 45° line has been added to the previous diagram. This measures all the points at which income = output = expenditure, an identity that has been considered earlier in this work.[1] It can be seen that the consumption function $C = \alpha + \beta Y$ crosses the 45° line once, namely at point Z. This point is associated with the level of income (Y^*) at which households plan to spend *all* their income. There is no saving or dissaving talking place. At levels of income below Y^* dis-saving takes place since planned expenditure exceeds income. Conversely, for incomes greater than Y^* saving will take place since planned expenditure is less than income. The level of income Y^* is known as the *equilibrium income.*

If we know the equation of the consumption function, it is possible to calculate the equilibrium level of income. Let assume again that the consumption function is $C = 10$ billion $+ 0.7Y$ (from now on we shall drop the pound sign from the equation). From our previous analysis we know that:

income (Y) = output (Q) = expenditure (E)

(at this point expenditure only consists of consumption expenditure, namely C). At the equilibrium point:

$$
\begin{aligned}
Y &= C \\
Y &= 10 \text{ billion} + 0.7Y \\
Y - 0.7Y &= 10 \text{ billion} \\
0.3Y &= 10 \text{ billion} \\
Y^* &= £33.33 \text{ billion}
\end{aligned}
\tag{7.3}
$$

Thus it can be seen that the equilibrium level of income is, in this case, £33.33 billion.

Investment expenditure

Within any given period of time, economic agents will purchase investment goods such as new buildings (for example houses and factories),

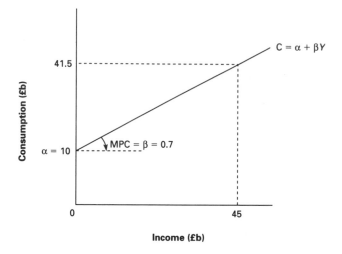

Figure 7.1   The Keynesian consumption function

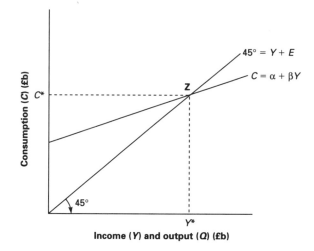

*Figure 7.2   Equilibrium income and the Keynesian 45º cross
diagram*

new machinery (for example a computer or a steamroller) and holdings of stocks (for example bricks, prefabricated structures and finished
goods). As noted above, the distinction between what is 'consumption'
and what is 'investment' may appear somewhat arbitrary in the case of
calculating the national accounts. Recall that expenditure on housing
is treated differently from expenditure on cars. However, this explanation does not tell the full story. If a householder buys a car or van to

travel to and from work and for leisure travel in general, the purchase is indeed classified as 'consumption', whereas the purchase of an identical vehicle by a self-employed builder is deemed to be an 'investment'. The distinction seems to rest on whether the vehicle is being used for 'gratuitous' purposes (by the householder) or whether it serves as an input into a particular production process (building).

When referring to investment it is important to distinguish between *gross* investment and *net* investment. Specifically, the former refers to *all* investment expenditure taking place over a given period, whereas the latter adjusts the figure downwards to take account of any investment expenditure on replacing depreciated or worn-out capital goods.

Two interrelated factors determine the level of investment that takes place in any given year: the *rate of interest* and *business expectations*. When considering the first of these it is important to make a distinction between the *real* interest rate and the *nominal* interest rate. The real interest rate takes account of the effect of inflation. Thus, if a person lodges a sum of £100 with a bank that promises to pay an annual rate of interest of 10 per cent, he or she would receive £110 at the end of the year. However, if during the year average prices increase by 4 per cent, then at the end of the year the person in question will need £104 to purchase goods and services that had cost £100 at the beginning of the year. As a result the person is only £6 better off in real terms and hence has received a real interest rate of 6 per cent rather than 10 per cent.

When deciding whether or not to undertake a particular type of investment, economic agents have to consider whether they will finance it through borrowed monies or use their own resources (for example retained profits). In either case an assessment needs to be made as to the future rate of inflation, since this will provide an insight into (1) the real interest rate that will have to be paid on borrowed monies, and (2) the forgone earnings from retained funds that would otherwise have been invested with a financial institution or lent to other economic agents. The lower the future real rate of interest, the greater the perceived stream of profits from a particular investment, and therefore the more likely it is that it will go ahead.

At any given real rate of interest, the business community will form expectations about the future prospects of the economy. If the economy is in recession and there appears to be no immediate prospect of recovery, then many entrepreneurs will be deterred from making investments if they are not confident about the potential profitability of a given venture. Conversely, if the economy appears as if it will strengthen in the future, then profit expectations will be much higher for a given programme of investment, and this will encourage entrepreneurs to take a risk.

In our analysis it is assumed that planned investment is autonomous expenditure and may simply be added to any autonomous consumption within the economy. For example, if planned investment (I) equals £22 billion and the (Keynesian) consumption function can be represented by the equation $C = 10 + 0.7Y$, then consumption expenditure plus investment expenditure ($C + I$) will simply be $32 + 0.7Y$. This addition to total expenditure in the economy (consumption plus investment) will lead to a parallel and upward shift in the expenditure line, such that for all levels of income $C + I$ will be £22 billion higher than the line depicting the original consumption function. This is shown in Figure 7.3. It can also be seen that $C + I$ is associated with a higher level of equilibrium income. Recall that the equilibrium income associated with the consumption function $C = 10 + 0.7Y$ is £33.33 billion. With the additional £22 billion expenditure arising from investment expenditure, it is possible to estimate the new equilibrium income as £106.66 billion.

Government expenditure

The government is an important purchaser of goods and services. Many of the things we take for granted result from government expenditure: hospitals, schools, roads, the armed services and so on. This expenditure involves the purchase of new buildings and new capital equipment, the wages paid to teachers, doctors, civil servants and other employees, the financing of everyday running costs, for example heating and lighting, as well as the monies spent to prevent the depreciation of existing buildings, structures and capital equipment. When economists consider 'government spending' within the context of estimating aggregate expenditure, they are referring explicitly to the purchase of *goods and services*. Thus the monies the government pays out to individuals in benefits, for example unemployment benefit, housing benefit or the state pension, are merely *transfers* from one group of society to another rather than a payment for a good or service. For this reason *transfer payments* are excluded from estimates of government expenditure in the national accounts. However transfer payments are usually included in general estimates of *public expenditure*, which we shall consider in more detail in Chapter 8. In terms of the framework being constructed, government expenditure is treated as an autonomous variable. Thus when G is added to the $C + I$ line there will be a parallel shift in the schedule and, as a result, a new level of equilibrium income. The mechanics of this shift are identical to those identified in Figure 7.3. From now on the sum of these expenditures $C + I + G$ will be referred to as aggregate expenditure (AE).

However this outcome only tells half the story. Government spend-

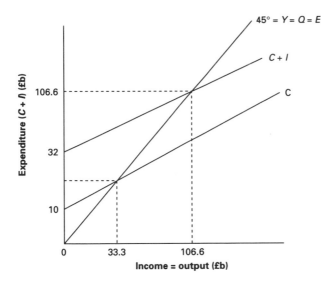

Figure 7.3   Equilibrium change from the addition of investment expenditure

ing cannot take place unless money is raised to finance it. This may be achieved in two basic ways. First, money can be *borrowed* from other economic agents through the sale of bonds (which pay a fixed rate of interest) or bills (whose return reflects the difference between the price the purchaser pays for the bill and the sum at which the government redeems it at some future, predefined date). The second and most important means of raising money is through *taxation*. This is a compulsory transfer of money from non-government economic agents to the government. *Direct* taxes are levied on wealth, for example the wages of individuals, the profits of firms and transfers of capital from one economic agent to another. The most obvious example is income tax. Conversely *indirect taxes* are monies levied on the goods or services that householders, firms and other economic agents buy. An example of this is value added tax (VAT). In terms of the consumption function element of the aggregate expenditure curve, the decision by government to raise direct taxes will effectively reduce consumers' marginal propensity to consume. For example, in our previous example it was assumed that the consumption function took the form

$$C = \alpha + \beta Y \qquad\qquad (7.4)$$

where α denotes autonomous consumption and β is the mpc. In previous examples, α was assumed to equal £10 billion while the income coefficient (β) implied an mpc of 0.7, or that 70p is spent for every pound received. If we now assume that the government chooses to finance some of its expenditure by levying an income tax, we must redefine the basic consumption function so that it relates directly to national income. Specifically it will take the form:

$$C = \alpha + \beta(1 - t)\, Y \tag{7.5}$$

where t denotes the rate of income tax. For example, if the chosen rate of income tax is 20p in the pound then it means that individuals only receive 80p for every £1 they earn. Assuming that householders still wish to spend the same proportion of their disposable income, namely that their mpc is 0.7, then they are spending 70 per cent of every 80p they receive. When consumption expenditure is related to national income, the implicit marginal propensity to consume becomes 0.56. Specifically, we may write:

$$
\begin{aligned}
C &= 10 \text{ billion} + 0.7\,(1 - t)\, Y \\
&= 10 \text{ billion} + 0.7\,(1 - 0.2)\, Y \\
&= 10 \text{ billion} + 0.7\,(0.8)\, Y \\
&= 10 \text{ billion} + 0.56Y
\end{aligned}
\tag{7.6}
$$

Thus the effect of a government choosing to raise revenue through direct taxation will be to reduce the slope of the consumption function: the higher the rate of taxation, the flatter the slope of the aggregate expenditure line will be. This can be seen in Figure 7.4, where the introduction of income tax reduces mpc, causing the aggregate expenditure curve to pivot downwards from *AE* to *AE'*. The parallel shift from *AE'* to *AE"* is the amount of government spending that takes place once these taxes have been levied.

Aggregate expenditure may now be estimated as:

$$AE = Y = \alpha + \beta(1 - t)Y + I + G \tag{7.7}$$

Thus if α = £10 billion, I = £22 billion, G = £50 billion and t is 20p in the pound, then:

$$
\begin{aligned}
AE = Y &= 10 \text{ billion} + 0.56Y + 22 \text{ billion} + 50 \text{ billion} \\
&= 82 \text{ billion} + 0.56Y
\end{aligned}
$$

$$
\begin{aligned}
Y - 0.56Y &= 82 \text{ billion} \\
0.44Y &= 82 \text{ billion} \\
Y &= 186.36 \text{ billion}
\end{aligned}
$$

It is also possible to determine whether, at this equilibrium point, govern-

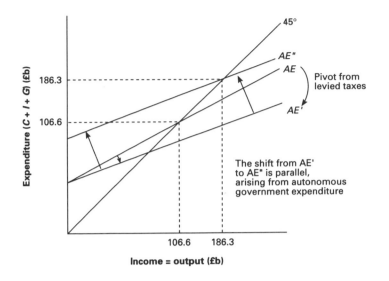

Figure 7.4   The effect of investment taxation on economic activity

ment receipts are greater than, less than or equal to government expenditure (ignoring other forms of government income). At an equilibrium income of £186.36 billion, tax receipts will be 0.2 multiplied by £186.36 billion, which equals £37.27 billion. However, since we have assumed that government spending is equal to £50 billion, it is managing a deficit of £12.73 billion, an amount that needs to be raised from other sources. If it wishes to reduce this figure then it may be decided to reduce its overall level of spending and/or increase the rate of income tax, both of which are electorally unappealing. Furthermore any increase in income tax and/or reduction in government spending will, by definition, reduce the level of equilibrium income.

Net export expenditure

The term *net exports* refers to the difference between expenditure by overseas consumers on domestically produced goods and services and expenditure by domestic consumers on foreign-produced goods and services. Thus if British consumers buy foreign products of a greater value than foreigners' consumption of British goods and services, the value of net exports will be negative. Broadly speaking, the demand for imported and exported goods and services depends on the economic conditions prevailing in domestic and foreign markets, the relative price of products produced domestically and abroad, together with the effects of ongoing changes in currency markets.

    The assumption we shall make is that the level of goods and services demanded abroad (exports) is independent of the amount of economic activity prevailing in the domestic economy. Hence foreigners' expenditure on domestically produced goods is another example of autonomous expenditure. In contrast, import levels will be assumed to be related positively to the level of economic activity taking place within the domestic economy. Thus as incomes rise, so too will imports. Hence we may write:

$$M = mY \tag{7.8}$$

where M denotes the value of imports, Y is the level of aggregate income within the domestic economy and the coefficient m is what economists call the *marginal propensity to import* (mpm). For example, if the mpm is 0.3 it means that 30p of every £1 worth of income is spent on foreign-produced goods and services. Countries that need to import products (be these raw materials, intermediate goods or finished products) are said to have a *high marginal propensity to import* whereas countries that are more self-sufficient are said to have a *low marginal propensity to import*. The meaning and policy-making implications of this term will be explored in greater detail shortly.

Total aggregate expenditure

We are now in a position to compress all four types of expenditure into an aggregate expenditure curve. This measures all *planned* expenditure within an economy over a given period of time for each level of national income. As we have already seen, this is made up of autonomous expenditure and income-induced expenditure. Algebraically, the acknowledgement of foreign trade means that Equation 7.7 becomes:

$$
\begin{aligned}
AE &= C + I + G + X - M \\
&= \alpha + \beta(1 - t)Y + I + G + X - mY
\end{aligned}
\tag{7.9}
$$

If, in addition to the values identified earlier, $m = 0.3$ and $X = £30$ billion, then the equilibrium income can be calculated as follows:

$$
\begin{aligned}
AE = Y &= 10 \text{ billion} + 0.56Y + 22 \text{ billion} + 50 \text{ billion} \\
&\quad + 30 \text{ billion} - 0.3Y \\
&= 112 \text{ billion} + 0.26Y
\end{aligned}
$$

$$
\begin{aligned}
Y - 0.26Y &= 112 \text{ billion} \\
0.74Y &= 112 \text{ billion} \\
Y &= £151.35 \text{ billion}
\end{aligned}
$$

If actual spending (and hence actual incomes) is below the equilibrium of £151.35 billion, then economic agents can only realise their plans if their demands are taken from firms' stocks. As a result, production will rise as firms attempt to recover this unplanned reduction in their stocks. This attempt by firms to restore their stocks to previous levels will cause them to hire more workers, increase output and hence increase GDP. On the other hand, if actual GDP is greater than £151.35 billion, planned expenditure is less than real income and stocks begin to rise. Because of this rise in stocks, firms will curtail their production in order to reduce this unplanned growth in their stocks. Thus either way there is a tendency for an equilibrium to emerge where firms do not experience any unplanned changes in their stocks and hence are not forced to change their (planned) level of output.

The multiplier

For a government committed to the containment of unemployment as its primary macroeconomic goal, the desirability of any given equilibrium level of income depends on the degree to which it can employ the available workforce. If the equilibrium generates unemployment above the politically tolerable level, there is a rationale for additional government spending to take the place of spending that has not occurred through natural market forces affecting the economy. Conversely, if this equilibrium is above that associated with full employment, the government should curtail its spending in order to prevent inflationary pressures from emerging within the economy. For a government to intervene successfully, it needs to be aware of the degree to which its own spending will generate additional spending within the economy. This question relates to a term used frequently by economists: the *multiplier*. If the 'multiplier' is large, then a given unit of autonomous expenditure is passed around the economy many times – from firm to firm and from economic agent to economic agent – thus stimulating economic activity. The larger the multiplier, the smaller the amount of money the government needs to inject into the economy to generate an increase in economic activity, and hence reduce unemployment. If, at the most extreme, the multiplier is unity, this simply means that a sum of autonomous expenditure is being received by economic agents in return for particular goods and services, but they choose subsequently not to pass this money on any further.

In a recent article Ball and Wood (1995) note that past researchers have disagreed as to the number of construction-based jobs that are generated by additional government spending. In the case of a £1 million increase (1992 prices) in public expenditure, past estimates have varied between 27 and 71 jobs. These differences reflect the assumptions adopted in different studies, for example the size of the multiplier and the degree to which additional expenditure has an upward impact on input prices (thereby reducing the real value of the additional expenditure). Nevertheless Bale and Wood's own analysis was able to show that the multiplier effect is work-specific, so that, for example, repair and maintenance will produce three times the number of jobs per £1 million spent (32 new jobs) than new civil engineering work (10.5 new jobs).

Calculating the multiplier

To illustrate the basic principles that underpin the multiplier process, let us initially consider the case of an economy with no government intervention or dealings with foreign countries. In this case, total planned expenditure will simply be in terms of consumption expenditure (by firms and households) and investment expenditure. Taking the figures used in our previous examples, we know that when the consumption function = £10 billion + 0.7Y, and autonomous investment = £22 billion, there is an equilibrium income of £106.66 billion. Now let us assume that planned investment by firms increases by £10 billion, prompted by an increase in the expectations of entrepreneurs. This increase will provoke a parallel shift in the aggregate expenditure schedule from AE_1 to AE_2. Readers should now be able to prove for themselves that this increase of £10 billion will in fact swell the equilibrium level of income from £106.66 billion to £140 billion, an increase of £33.34 billion. This is the *multiplier effect* in action.

A clue as to why this happens can be derived from Figure 7.5, which contains two ajoining sets of axes. In each diagram two aggregate expenditure curves have been drawn: AE_1, mirroring aggregate demand before the autonomous increase in private investment; and AE_2, depicting the level of aggregate expenditure after it. It can be seen that the aggregate expenditure schedules in the left-hand diagram have a relatively steeper slope than those in the right-hand diagram. This has resulted in a larger increase in equilibrium national income from the same £10 billion rise in investment. Put another way, the rate at which national income increases in response to any change in autonomous expenditure depends on the slope of the aggregate expenditure curve, and hence the marginal propensity to consume.

If the marginal propensity to consume is high, then the recipients of the additional spending (for example the extra workers taken on by firms that win contracts for new construction projects, commissioned by firms engaging in extra investment) will spend a large proportion of the income they receive, and this will be passed on to other economic agents within the economy (for example shops), who will also spend a

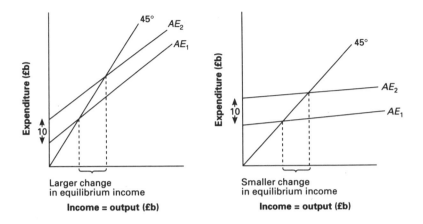

Figure 7.5   The multiplier effect

relatively large proportion of any additional monies they receive. Since each recipient of the additional expenditure is hypothesised to spend a large proportion of it, each pound generates additional incomes further and further down a potentially long line of economic agents.

In contrast, if the marginal propensity to consume is very low then in relative terms, recipients of the additional income are holding onto a large proportion of it. Since a large proportion of the additional expenditure is not being passed on to others, then its impact on the activities of other economic agents diminishes quickly, and hence it has a much more limited impact on the overall national income of the economy.

The multiplier is therefore a numerical measure of the responsiveness of an economy to expenditure changes, and hence is a coefficient with which we can multiply any given change in autonomous expenditure to derive the new equilibrium income.

A simple multiplier proof

The simplest formulation of the multiplier can be derived with reference to the marginal propensity to consume. Specifically, we may write:

$\Delta Y = \Delta C + \Delta$ autonomous expenditure
$\Delta Y = b\Delta Y + \Delta$ autonomous expenditure
$\Delta Y - \beta \Delta Y = \Delta$ autonomous expenditure
$\Delta Y(1 - \beta) = \Delta$ autonomous expenditure
$\Delta Y = 1/(1 - \beta) \times \Delta$ autonomous expenditure   (7.10)

where $1/(1 - \beta)$ is the simple multiplier equation. Thus, if the marginal propensity to consume is 0.7, then the multiplier equals 3.33 and every £1 of autonomous expenditure increases the equilibrium income by £3.33. In terms of our £10 billion increase in investment expenditure, we now know that it will increase the equilibrium income by 3.33 x £10 billion, which equals £33.33 billion (the new equilibrium income equals £100 billion + £33.33 billion). Had the marginal propensity to consume been 0.4, the multiplier would have been 1.66, since:

$$1/(1 - \beta) = 1/(1 - 0.4) = 1/0.6 = 1.66$$

In this case the equilibrium income would only increase by 1.66 x £10 billion, or £16.66 billion.

Now let us take the analysis a stage further and assume the existence of a government that is prepared to intervene actively in the economy by raising revenues to prevent the emergence of unemployment. If we also assume that the only source of government revenue is direct taxes, then the previous analysis has already shown us that taxation will exert a downward influence on the marginal propensity to consume, and hence upon the multiplier. Formally, we need to redefine our equation to take account of the fact that we are now interested in the marginal propensity to consume from national income rather than disposable income. Following on from previous analysis, our equation now becomes $1/1 - \beta(1 - t)$. Thus if $\beta = 0.7$ and $t = 0.2$, then the multiplier becomes $1/1 - 0.56 = 2.27$. In other words, whereas the £10 billion increase in investment expenditure increased the equilibrium income by £33.33 billion when the multiplier was 3.33, when the government levies taxes at a rate of 20p in the pound the increase is reduced to £22.7 billion. As we have already seen, the need for government to engage in the unpopular activity of raising taxes stems from its perceived need to spend in order to avoid uncorrected market failures (for example an insufficient number of hospitals) and a politically unacceptable level of unemployment (itself a market failure).

Deflationary gaps and inflationary gaps

When the equilibrium income (Y^E) is below that which would fully employ a nation's workforce (Y^F), a *deflationary gap* is said to exist. This can be seen in Figure 7.6 Assuming that the private sector cannot be encouraged to increase investment expenditure (for example private sector investors do not expect an improvement in the economy), then this deficiency can be offset by additional government spending. An increase in spending equal to the distance X will encourage additional consumption expenditure, and as a result correct the shortfall that has occurred. If the government knows precisely what the multiplier is,

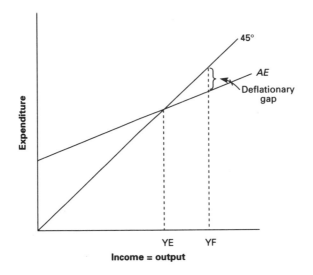

Figure 7.6 A deflationary gap

then it is possible to determine how much additional expenditure it needs to commit to the economy.

In contrast, if the economy is operating at an equilibrium income that is *above* that needed fully to employ its workforce, an *inflationary gap* is said to have emerged. This outcome is not desirable because it will create inflationary pressures, since the expenditure plans of economic agents are associated with a greater level of output than the economy can produce, even when it is working at full capacity. In the absence of imported goods (to be considered shortly), economic agents will bid up the price of the goods and services that are available as they compete against each other. This outcome is depicted in Figure 7.7. The inflationary gap can be measured in terms of the distance Z. In order to reduce the level of planned expenditure from that associated with Y^E to that associated with Y^f, the government may choose to curtail its own expenditure.

In the case of either a deflationary gap or an inflationary gap, the government may also recognise that the size of the multiplier depends on the rate at which the government levies income tax to help finance its own expenditure. The higher the rate of tax, the smaller the multiplier. Thus either situation may prompt a change in aggregate expenditure by a reduction in the tax rate *and* a change in the level of its own level of expenditure. Readers may wish to explore this possibility under the assumption of both a deflationary gap and an inflationary gap. Ultimately, the mix of these complementary options will also depend on the degree to which the government is committed to a balanced budget.

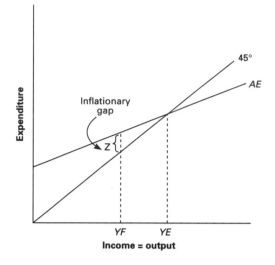

Figure 7.7   An inflationary gap

The multiplier for an economy that trades with foreign countries

The analysis to date has concentrated on a simple economy that does not trade with foreign countries. If it does have dealings with the rest of the world, then we have already seen that there is not only an autonomous addition to aggregate expenditure as foreigners buy domestically produced goods, but also leakages from the economy as monies are spent on imported goods. This latter expenditure is income-induced and, as a result, it must play a role in a revised multiplier equation. Specifically we must add the marginal propensity to import into the denominator of the equation, so that we get:

$$\text{multiplier} = 1/1 - \beta[1 - t] + m \tag{7.11}$$

where m denotes the marginal propensity to import. Thus if domestic residents spend 30p in every pound on imported goods, the rate at which tax is levied is 20p in the pound and the basic marginal propensity to consume is 0.6, then the multiplier will be:

$$\text{multiplier} = 1/1 - 0.6(0.8) + 0.3 = 1 - 0.48 + 0.3 = 1.21$$

Had the same economy been closed to international transactions the multiplier would have been 1.92.

THE DETERMINATION OF EXCHANGE RATES

The exchange rate is the price at which one currency is exchanged for another. Let us consider the relationship between the currencies of Britain and France, namely sterling and the franc. We shall assume that £1 is exchanged for 8 francs (£1 = F8). If a change in economic circumstances (considered shortly) precipitates a change in this exchange rate such that £1 = F5, then sterling has fallen in value relative to the franc, whereas if the reverse happens and £1 = F10, then the pound has gained in value relative to the franc. In reality the currency market is multidimensional and changes take place in the relative value of all the world's currencies. Thus sterling may increase in value relative to the franc yet simultaneously decrease in value relative to the US dollar. However, for the purposes of this analysis we shall restrict ourselves to a simple two-country case.

In order to understand the way in which a simple market for currency operates, we need to consider both demand and supply factors as they affect one of the two currencies in question. We shall use an example that initially considers the demand for French francs.

Demand factors

Let us assume that the price charged by French plasterboard manufacturers is 8F per square metre. At an exchange rate of £1 = F8, this implies a sterling price for French plasterboard of £1 per square metre (ignoring all other costs associated with importing and distributing the product in question). If the exchange rate were to fall to £1 = F5, then the price of French plasterboard would rise to £1.60 per square metre in British markets. Similarly, if the exchange rate changed from £1 = F8 to £1 = F10, then the price in Britain of French plasterboard would fall to 80p per square metre. Elementary demand theory would lead us to expect that in the first scenario the British demand for French plasterboard would fall (since its price in Britain has risen) whereas in the latter case it would rise (since its price in Britain has fallen). A fall in the demand for French plasterboard would also lead to a reduction in the demand for French francs (used to buy the imported plasterboard), whereas an increase in demand would increase the demand for francs for the opposite reason.

Supply factors

Let us now consider the factors that affect the supply of francs. Just as British firms and individuals are willing and able to buy plasterboard from France, French consumers also demand British products. If the value of the franc is high relative to that of sterling, then British goods and services will be relatively cheap for French consumers (*ceteris paribus*) and more will be demanded. This means that more pounds will be demanded by French importers and they will use francs to buy them. Similarly, if the value of the franc is low relative to the pound, then British products will become more expensive to French consumers. This will not only precipitate a fall in the demand for British goods but also a fall in the demand for sterling.

The currency market

We are now in a position to present the above information diagram matically. In Figures 7.8 and 7.9 the vertical axis measures the value of the franc in terms of sterling, while the horizontal axis measures the quantity of francs. The demand curve D_0 denotes the initial demand for francs by British consumers and firms who wish to buy French goods and services. Conversely, the supply curve S_0 depicts the initial supply of francs, derived from the degree to which French firms and households buy British goods and services. The following analysis will highlight two basic currency market systems: one where the rate at which one currency exchanges for another is determined totally by market forces (known as a freely floating system); and one where market forces are suppressed through government intervention such that a fixed rate of exchange is maintained (this may be the policy of one government or as part of a collective agreement, as in the case of the Bretton Woods Agreement or, more recently, the European Monetary System).

Freely floating exchange rates

When currency exchange rates are allowed to float freely, the equilibrium exchange rate is determined by the interaction between the demand curve and the supply curve for the currency in question, which in this case is the franc. In Figure 7.8 this occurs at E_0.

If French goods are perceived as highly desirable by British consumers, so that they are willing and able to buy more of them at any given price, then the demand curve will shift to the right, from D_0 to D_1. Assuming that the supply curve remains unaltered, this means that the rate of exchange will change from E_0 to E_1. Thus the change in taste of the British public has led to an increase in the value of the French franc. If, in contrast, there is an increase in the demand for British goods by French firms and households, this will cause the supply curve of francs to shift to the right, from S_0 to S_1. If we assume in this instance that the demand curve remains unaltered, this will mean a fall in the exchange rate from E_0 to E_2.

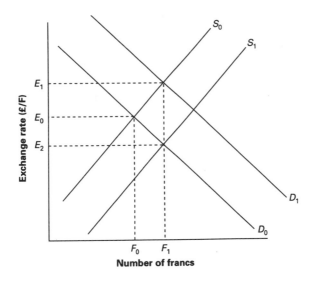

Figure 7.8   Freely floating exchange rates

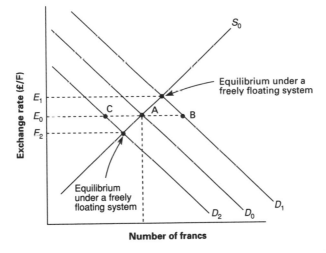

Figure 7.9   Fixed exchange rates

Fixed exchange rates

Let us now assume that the French government chooses to intervene in the currency market and to guarantee the convertibility of its currency at a particular rate of exchange. This is represented in Figure 7.9 as E_0.

Let us further assume that there is again a change in fashion that leads British consumers to buy more French goods and services. This will lead to a rightward shift in the demand curve. Under a freely floating system there would be a new equilibrium exchange rate at E_1. However, at the predetermined rate of exchange of E_0, there is an excess demand for francs equal to the distance AB. In order to preserve the rate of exchange at E_0, francs will need to be printed to compensate for the shortfall, and these will be sold for pounds at E_0. These pounds become part of the foreign reserves held by the French central bank.

If French goods and services cease to be desirable to British consumers, then the demand curve for francs will shift to the left, namely from D_0 to D_2. In this case unbridled market forces will prompt a fall in the exchange rate from E_0 to E_2. However, if the French government chooses to defend the franc and preserve the exchange rate of E_0, it must demand francs equal to the distance CA. This can only be done by selling some of its sterling reserves at the exchange rate E_0. If the demand associated with D_2 becomes a permanent feature of France's trading relations with Britain, then the French government may find itself unable to sustain the exchange rate E_0 over a long period of time since it will be perpetually running down its foreign reserves. In such a situation it may choose to *devalue* its currency. This may be done in two ways: the French government could simply choose a new, lower rate of exchange, at which it would guarantee convertibility for its currency, or it could allow the franc to float freely towards its true market value and then use this new equilibrium as a basis for further intervention.

As we shall see in Chapter 8, the currency market has been an important battleground for governments since the Second World War. Britain's desire to remain within the constraints of the Bretton Woods fixed exchange rate system proved to be an important constraint on successive governments' ability to use Keynesian economic policies effectively. More recently, Britain's reluctance to join the European Exchange Rate mechanism, thereby surrendering the flexibility of a freely floating currency, became a major source of concern about Britain's commitment to the European Union. Britain's subsequent inability to stay within the confines of the ERM, despite the extreme pressures to which sterling was subjected by currency speculators, did nothing to convince commentators of Britain's standing within the European and World economy.

8 The Construction Industry and Macroeconomic Policy, 1945–95

INTRODUCTION

This final chapter analyses the interface between the construction industry and the macroeconomic policies that have been pursued by successive postwar governments. Drawing on the theory outlined in the previous chapter, the discussion focuses initially on the emergence of Keynesian economics, which underpinned the macroeconomic thinking of the two main political parties until the 1970s. It will be seen that during much of this period the construction industry adopted a somewhat complacent attitude, prompted by the 'easy profits' of postwar prosperity and public expenditure growth. However the macroeconomic instability that arose from the late 1960s gradually required construction firms to become not only more cost conscious but also to pay greater attention to the characteristics of the product they were supplying to clients and the wider environmental implications of building activity.

The election of Margaret Thatcher's Conservative government in 1979 brought a new approach to the way in which the British economy was managed. Gone were the trappings of Keynesian orthodoxy and its emphasis on correcting variations in the level of unemployment. In its place was a new approach based on monetarist concern about inflation. Specific emphasis was given to the relationship between inflation, the money supply and public spending. In addition a new philosophy was unleashed, which stressed the possibility of kick-starting the economy through a reduction in government spending and a series of microeconomic measures intended to increase incentives within the economy.

Despite a boom period during the late 1980s, which produced an increase in demand for construction work, the construction industry has had to endure two major recessions since 1980. This has resulted in the industry becoming more streamlined, with inefficiencies being squeezed out as firms competed for a smaller number of available contracts. However the 1990s have also emerged as an era of potential, not only because of signs of economic recovery, but also because of the opportunities that exist in the newly liberalised European market.

THE RISE AND FALL OF KEYNESIAN ECONOMICS

In order to understand the economic and political philosophy under-pinning some of the economic policies enacted in the postwar period, it is important to consider briefly the problems that emerged in the twenty years preceding the Second World War and the emergence of John Maynard Keynes as one of the most influential economic thinkers.

The interwar years: the emergence of John Maynard Keynes

The interwar years were largely a period of economic hardship, sym-bolised by rising unemployment and a slump in world demand. In the case of Britain, economic difficulties emerged for a number of reasons: an ageing technological base, an overvalued pound, and an inherent 'smugness' that partly contributed to Britain's inability to respond to increased international competition. These problems were compounded by the Wall Street Crash in the United States in 1929, which led the Americans and ultimately the rest of the industrialised world into an era of trade protection.

By today's standards, there was only limited government interven-tion in response to these problems, since government thinking was pre-dominantly market-oriented, and as a result the economic downturn was interpreted as a temporary period of disequilibrium. For example it was thought that the increase in unemployment brought about by the decline in economic activity would be resolved naturally by a re-duction in wage rates. With a parallel decline in interest rates, invest-ment would increase, and with it the demand for labour. These factors would combine to create new incomes and greater economic activity. According to Keynes however, a general reduction in wages has the opposite effect – it reduces aggregate spending rather than prompts an increase in it. In his view, therefore, a decrease in aggregate demand should be met by an expansionary package of public spending, financed by a managed budget deficit. Via the *multiplier effect* (see Chapter 7), the increased spending would not only create incomes for workers di-rectly employed by the spending programme (for example on road construction), but also generate extra incomes as their demand for goods and services increases. However, during a period when it was deemed prudent for a government to balance its budget and simply provide the mechanism that would promote market stability, his interventionist views contradicted official thinking. Keynes was not a socialist – his theories should be seen as attempts to provide a remedy for the shortcomings of the capitalist economy rather than a desire to destroy it.

The Midlands and the southeast of England were able to attract growth industries such as motor vehicles, consumer durables and chemicals, and as a result they were able to withstand the rigours of the depression. As these industries continued to grow during the 1930s, so did the demand for associated products such as housing. However, unprecedented levels of structural unemployment in areas that depended on primary industries, for example shipbuilding and coalmining, prompted the government to reorientate its economic philosophy. For example monies were directed to employment-creating public works programmes. Nonetheless these initiatives remained tentative because, unlike previous policies, there was no established economic theory to justify them. This emerged in Keynes' highly influential book, *The General Theory of Employment, Interest and Money* (1936), which marked the beginning of what many commentators refer to as the 'Keynesian revolution'. In Britain, widespread official acceptance of Keynesian economics did not emerge until the wartime coalition government produced its White Paper on Employment Policy (1944), a document that arguably provided the foundation for government policy for the next two and a half decades.

Lessons learned from the First World War promoted the government to take responsibility for the allocation of resources and the regulation of markets from the onset of the Second World War. As the war neared its conclusion, the government had to decide how to manage the transition from a wartime economy to the needs of a modern peacetime country. Politicians were well aware of the economic problems that emerged after the First World War and were determined that history would not be repeated. The wartime coalition government had committed itself to maintaining a high and stable level of employment and this was embraced by the incoming Attlee government of 1945 as its primary economic objective.

The postwar years

Although illness resulted in the premature death of Keynes in 1946, his writings had convinced governments that the level of unemployment that would emerge after the war lay directly within the domain of government control. However concerns about the degree to which the recovering economy could absorb its labour force ran parallel to a need to correct Britain's widening trade imbalance. Government policies were targeted on fostering export markets at the expense of domestic consumers, a factor that prompted a major devaluation of sterling in 1949. Although formal attempts were made to restrain the rate of increase of prices and wages, the control of inflation was not deemed to be a serious problem and was accepted as inevitable during a period of rationing and shortages. Furthermore the bank rate was held at its prewar level of 2 per cent in order to promote postwar investment.

Economic growth was not identified explicitly as a goal, given the precarious state of the war-damaged economy – growth would be an inevitable consequence of a successful reconstruction programme.

Attlee's Labour government was responsible for implementing the proposals for a new welfare state (encompassing health, education and social security) – the framework of which had been set out in the Beveridge Report in 1944, under the auspices of the wartime coalition government – together with its desire to carry out a programme to nationalise certain strategic industries (for example the railways, gas and coal). Despite Churchill's popularity as wartime leader, the Conservative Party was linked strongly to the old order and the Great Depression. The electorate was attracted to the new interventionist approach, and it was believed that this would steer a crippled economy towards the prosperity of a new modern age.

Just as the Conservative Party's undoing was its association with the interwar depression, the postwar Labour government became linked to the austerity that persisted after the Second World War. Thus, despite a relatively smooth transition to a peacetime economy, the Conservative Party was reelected in 1951 and remained in power for thirteen years. Although the Conservative Party was ideologically committed to private ownership and the unbridling of market forces, it only introduced a limited programme of denationalisation between 1951 and 1964 and no significant changes were made to the newly established welfare state. Unlike today, there was a high degree of consensus between the two major political parties, directed specifically towards the objective of full employment. The 1950s saw the British economy settle into a pattern that became known as *stop–go* (a process that arose from the economy's long-standing supply-side sluggishness), as well as an increasing propensity to import the goods it needed and a commitment to the Bretton Woods system of fixed exchange rates.

Stop–Go

To understand what is meant by the term 'stop–go', let us consider a stylised set of events that typified the British economy. Assume that for one reason or another there was an increase in unemployment. As we have already seen, the standard Keynesian response to this would have been a programme of expansionary fiscal policy. Because the world economy was expanding rapidly at that time, the government did not need to run up a large budget deficit in order to encourage private sector investment. However, a balance of payments deficit on the current account soon emerged as imports of raw materials and finished goods increased to meet the extra demand that had been created. This was not only detrimental to Britain's balance of payments, but also placed a downward pressure on sterling, resulting in speculators doubting Britain's commitment to maintaining a fixed exchange rate under the Bretton Woods Agreement. With speculators anticipating a devaluation of sterling (and therefore selling their holdings of pounds), the government's desire to maintain the pound's credibility as a premier international currency (by not devaluing it) became a constraint on its ability to follow its Keynesian instincts. The government was forced temporarily to sacrifice its objective of full employment – it reversed its expansionary fiscal policy and tightened its monetary policy through increased interest rates and the introduction of a restrictive credit policy. This reduced the demand for imported goods, but at the same time it prompted an increase in unemployment. When unemployment levels eventually became politically unacceptable, the authorities responded by increasing government spending and introducing a less restrictive monetary policy. The whole cycle then started again.

Despite the uncertainties arising from the four-to-five year cycles that were associated with stop–go, the average levels of unemployment ranged between 1.2 per cent and 2.3 per cent during the 1950s, figures significantly lower than the 5 per cent that had been anticipated in the Beveridge Report. Throughout this period inflation too remained low and reasonably stable, averaging 3 per cent. However Britain's rate of economic growth was poor when compared with those of its international competitors. For example, between 1955 and 1960 Britain's average rate of growth was 2.8 per cent per annum compared with 6.3 per cent in West Germany, 4.6 per cent in France and 9.7 per cent in Japan.

The trend set in the 1950s continued more forcibly into the 1960s with more accentuated balance of payments difficulties and constant battles to preserve the international status of sterling. Early in the decade attempts were made to address the problem of Britain's poor growth record. The incoming Labour administration (1964) built upon the framework that had been established by the outgoing Conservative government. In 1962 the Conservatives had established the National Economic Development Council (NEDC) in an attempt to create a forum for industrialists, trade unions and key government ministers to formulate long-term plans and to make forecasts that were intended to make firms take a more positive view of Britain's economic prospects, adjust their output upwards and hence make a higher rate of economic growth a self-fulfilling prophecy. However the NEDC was not a specific government department, and as many key players were suspicious of 'planning' in government and industry, its recommendations fell on deaf ears. In contrast the new Labour government gave the initiative a formal governmental outlet through the newly created Department of Economic Affairs (created 1964, abolished 1969). Although the resulting plans had greater credibility and indeed were incorporated into government policy in a process known as *indicative planning*, a series of deflationary measures intended to stave off another sterling crisis in July 1966 put an end to what had become known as the 'National Plan'. Continued pressure on sterling eventually forced the government to devalue by 15 per cent in November 1967, a move that brought temporary relief from balance of payments difficulties after 1969.

The breakdown of the Keynesian consensus

Although governments recognised that there was a need to control inflation throughout the postwar period, it took until the late 1960s for inflation to manifest itself as a highly significant problem. Until then, creeping inflation had been seen to be a small price to pay for the benefits of full employment. However attempts to contain price increases through a series of prices and incomes policies during the 1960s brought limited success and were soon discarded by the newly elected Conservative government of 1970. Rather than introduce a series of deflationary policies, a voluntary prices and incomes policy was soon reintroduced in order to suppress the continued inflationary pressures.

However, with unemployment approaching one million, the government felt the need to initiate an expansionary economic policy. The massive increase in government spending that took place in 1972 prompted what became known as the 'Barber Boom' (after Anthony Barber, the chancellor of the exchequer at the time). Unlike in previous fiscal expansions, Britain was freed from its exchange rate constraints by sterling's removal in the same year from the now unstable Bretton Woods Agreement. Sterling was allowed to float. When trade unions and industry were unable to agree on a further voluntary policy in 1972, a compulsory prices and incomes policy was introduced. This provoked industrial unrest, and the strength of the National Union of Mineworkers ultimately led to the reelection of a Labour government in 1974.

The new Labour government inherited an economy in which inflation was starting to explode. This was the result of a number of factors: the expansionary spending of its predecessor; the inability of the Conservatives to control banking activity; and the impact of the rapid increase in oil prices, which caused input costs to rise rapidly. Nevertheless the Labour government did little to control wage inflation during its first year of office because it did not want to antagonise the trade unions. Although incomes policies were seen as being contrary to the spirit of free collective bargaining, the unions agreed to a voluntary incomes policy in mid 1975. Although subsequent renewals of the voluntary incomes policy seemed to be holding back price increases, the government was unable to secure union agreement to an extension of the policy in 1978.

Crowding out

The 1970s was the decade when the Keynesian consensus between the two major political parties began to break down. From all available evidence, Keynesian policies were failing to provide a remedy for the simultaneous increase in inflation and unemployment (known as stagflation) during the 1970s and were therefore falling into disrepute. Keynesian orthodoxy – which emphasised the need to fine-tune the economy to counteract variations in the economic cycle – was replaced by a new, longer-term framework based on monetarist concerns about the need to control inflation by reducing the rate of growth of the money supply (and hence adhering to the quantity theory of money) and the level of public spending.

Sustained increases in inflation during the 1970s brought about a rapid rise in public spending. Throughout the 1960s and early 1970s public expenditure was planned in *volume terms* (discussed later), that is, with reference to achieving pre-defined objectives rather than a need to remain explicitly within a spending budget. With inflation accelerating, government departments were committed to ever-increasing levels of expenditure as the costs of existing spending programmes rose. According to some commentators, this increase in public spending was having a destabilising effect on the private sector and was therefore detracting from Britain's ability to compete abroad. This was the basis of what became known as *crowding out*, expounded most explicitly by Bacon and Eltis (1976).

Crowding out can take two basic forms. *Physical crowding out* arises when the public sector pre-empts resources that would have been used by the private sector. Because many services provided by the public sector are not bought and sold in the market place, they must be financed though taxes, which, by definition, are diverted from income and profits. *Financial crowding out*, on the other hand, arises because any increase in public spending must be met by an increase in the supply of money and/or increased borrowing. According to the monetarist literature, an increase in the money supply will increase prices, thereby making manufactured goods and services less competitive abroad, which has a detrimental effect on the balance of payments. Furthermore, if this inflation is unanticipated a misallocation of resources may result as economic agents misinterpret market signals. If the government chooses to increase its level of borrowing, then it is likely that interest rates will be raised to encourage investors to hold extra government securities. If interest rates increase, then two problems may follow.

First, interest-sensitive expenditure will be curtailed, exerting a dampening effect on the demand for houses and other consumer durables as well as on business investment decisions. Second, a rise in interest rates may increase the attractiveness of British investments to foreigners, thereby pushing up the value of sterling relative to other currencies. An appreciation in the relative price of sterling makes it harder for firms to sell their products abroad. Given this analysis, it may be no surprise that Robinson (1986, p. 42) felt compelled to refer to the relationship between the PSBR, the money supply and the rate of interest as the 'Bermuda Triangle of economics'.

Changes in public expenditure planning and control

During the 1950s it was recognised that the Treasury had lost control over the level of public expenditure being incurred each year. This prompted the setting up of a Treasury committee, chaired by Sir William Plowden, which published in 1961 what subsequently became known as the Plowden Report (*The Control of Public Expenditure*, Cmnd 2432).

The system by which future public expenditure was determined prior to the Plowden Report had five key defects. First, public expenditure was determined annually, and as a result tended not to take into account its implications for future years. Second, the Treasury negotiated individually with each spending department. The Cabinet received no indication of the ultimate sum of these separate proposals until they were put together in the final stages of the planning process. Third, individual departments, and indeed the Treasury itself, tended to use the volume and structure of the previous year's expenditure as a guide to its commitments for the following year. This exerted an upward pressure on individual departments' spending programmes. Fourth, estimates were drawn up without recourse to a consistent framework against which 'value for money' could be defined, or indeed in terms of the level of public expenditure the economy as a whole could sustain. Finally, the pressures of the Keynesian-led ideology that dominated both major political parties resulted in the effectiveness of ministers being defined in terms of the budgets they could secure for their respective departments. As a result the cabinet was dominated by ministers whose underlying interest was to increase public expenditure.

Thus although government departments that overspent relative to the estimate presented to parliament faced the threat of intervention by the Public Accounts Committee, the decisions they were making lacked a coherent economic framework against which they could be analysed. The recommendations of the Plowden Committee were fourfold:

- that public expenditure should be viewed in context of the medium term rather than a single financial year;
- that public expenditure should be planned in *volume terms* (in other words, in terms of the physical goods and services that would be bought) and in relation to the performance of British economy;
- to set departmental spending within the context of an overall figure defining public expenditure as a whole;
- to improve the mechanisms by which public expenditure was evaluated and appraised.

The first three recommendations were completely consistent with the Labour government's ill-fated attempts to adhere to *indicative planning* during the mid 1960s. Central to the new approach was the *public expenditure survey (PES)*, a process supervised by a committee of top civil servants from the spending departments (chaired by a Treasury civil servant), known as the *Public Expenditure Survey Committee (PESC)*. Each annual PES spending 'round' adopted a five-year time horizon, with plans rolled over one year. As a result it was possible to identify the future implications of present spending programmes. Future spending projections were then considered in the light of an assessment by the Treasury's own economists of future economic performance (the medium-term economic assessment), and this exercise was used to identify the volume of resources that could be devoted to public expenditure. Consistent with the new emphasis on the medium-term implications of public expenditure plans, was acceptance of the need to use appraisal techniques such as cost–benefit analysis and cost-effectiveness analysis to evaluate major investments. By the mid 1960s, for example, the Ministry of Transport had set up an Economic Planning, Directorate, which began to develop economic appraisal techniques and to explore the use of computer-based technology to run what were relatively sophisticated mathematical models. As we saw in Chapter 4, economic appraisal techniques such as cost–benefit analysis were developed in the United States during the 1950s and began to arrive in Britain a decade or so later. Indeed, by pre-empting the Plowden recommendations, the appraisal of the M1 motorway by Coburn, Beesley and Reynolds (1960) can be seen as the start of this approach in the UK.

Unfortunately this process was soon encountering difficulties. The first emerged as a result of the inflation of the late 1960s and early 1970s. As we have already seen, the economic context of the Plowden Report was one in which inflation was historically low. With planning being undertaken in volume terms under the assumption of 'constant prices', inflation meant that expenditure programmes bore little resemblance to the resources that were actually being committed (leading to the term 'funny money'). However, ministers had no incentive to address the inflation problem and assess alternative means of delivering services. The second problem with the PES system was that, by definition, it was a *planning* process rather than a *monitoring* exercise. There was no inbuilt machinery to force ministers to keep to their plans in subsequent years. Greater macroeconomic instability inside and outside the economy, together with the inability/unwillingness of lower tiers of the public sector to stick to their limits, meant that ministers were less able to plan ahead with confidence.

The degree to which total government expenditure (central government plus local government) had grown over the postwar period can best be seen with reference to the fact that when expressed as a percentage of GNP, it amounted to 26 per cent in 1920, had risen to 39 per cent by 1950 and in 1975 stood at 54 per cent (Hockley, 1979, p. 100). It should be recalled from Chapter 7 that these percentages do not mean that government expenditure contributed 54 per cent to GNP – government expenditure includes transfer payments, which are excluded from GNP and GDP figures.

As we have seen, the 1970s was a period of growing macroeconomic difficulty. By 1975 the Labour administration was attempting to exert control over local government spending (through the newly formed Central Council for Local Government Finance), the National Health Service (by slowing down the supply of resources to the different regional health authorities) and the nationalised industries (by imposing external finance limits – EFLs – to constrain their ability to borrow funds). However, the need to take further steps ceased to be an issue when the government was forced to borrow from the IMF in order to support its spending programmes in March 1976. The restrictions the IMF imposed on the government in order to qualify for the loan brought about a number of changes to the PES system.

First, the high degree of macroeconomic uncertainty that now characterised policy making meant that the use of a five-year time horizon for planning was increasingly less relevant. As a consequence it was reduced to three years.

Second, significantly, the government introduced *cash limits* to certain areas of spending as an appendage to the volume planning process. When the rate of inflation exceeded expected levels, the cash limits would squeeze volume expenditure. Hence these limits provided a financial constraint on the services that could be bought (though this did not apply to demand-led expenditure such as unemployment benefit). Thus there was now an incentive for public spending departments to seek efficiency savings in order to make their cash allocation go further. However the precise mix of services that could be bought in a given financial year was less transparent from the outset than under the former volume-only planning system. Furthermore, the existence of cash limits provided a disincentive for spending departments to consider the long-term implications of their spending programmes, thereby leading to a potential misallocation of resources. These measures helped contain the growth in public expenditure during what remained of the Labour Party's term of office.

The 1979 election not only brought a change of administration, namely a Conservative government, but also a change in economic philosophy. As we have already noted, the view that the level of economic activity (and hence the level of unemployment) fell within the domain of the government was replaced by one that saw the role of government as providing the right economic environment within which economic agents could operate. Emphasis was placed on the control of inflation (a factor that promotes resource misallocation and affects international competitiveness), the creation of incentives in the labour market and within industry, and the containment of public expenditure (due to its 'crowding out' effects).

It should be emphasised that the reforms of the PES did not represent a complete change in policy direction. Instead it was an acceleration of a process that the previous Labour government had already started. Cash limits were extended to an even wider variety of services and the idea of volume planning was abandoned. As a result, PES is now explicitly directed towards *inputs* rather than *outputs*. Furthermore its role as an instrument to plan future spending has disappeared. From the point of view of public spending at the local government level, central government has not only specified the amounts local authorities need to spend in order to maintain 'adequate' services, but also the level of expenditure that can be raised through local taxes formerly rates, then the community charge and now the council tax). Furthermore, as we shall see shortly, attempts have also been made to reduce public spending through the privatisation programme (which passes on public expenditure to the newly privatised companies) and the process of contracting out. Recently the chancellor of the Exchequer announced a radical overhaul of the way public spending will be planned and controlled in the future. This seems to reaffirm the government's desire to keep a tight control on public spending (see below). From April 1998 resource accounting systems will be introduced in central government departments, and at the turn of the century commercial style accounts will become the basis for planning and controlling public expenditure. Central government departments will have to show more systematically how their expenditure has contributed to their policy objectives, with the emphasis on output indicators.

The construction industry during the years of Keynesian consensus

From the end of the Second World War until the beginning of the 1970s the construction industry operated in a relatively stable economic environment. As a result firms were able to identify markets in which they had a comparative advantage without having to worry about the reliability of the price signals they were receiving. In sectors where there was a potential for extracting size economies, firms were able to organise themselves in a manner more associated with the manufacturing sector (see Groak, 1994). Growing markets could be exploited by formalising procedures. Larger contractors enhanced their competitive strength by vertical integration, both forwards and backwards: quarrying companies became engaged in road building; companies involved with public sector house building set up plants to manufacture prefabricated housing units; and civil engineering firms saw the advantages of integrating backwards in order to secure supplies of road stone and aggregate.

Business confidence in the construction industry was typified by the housing market, where a combination of demographic factors, rising real incomes and mortgage concessions meant that demand outstripped supply. This process of expansion was not even hindered by supply-side bottlenecks such as land shortages. Larger firms were able to concentrate on first-time purchasers, with an emphasis on a highly standardised product that could be turned over quickly. The more risky and specialised market was left to smaller and more localised firms.

However by the early 1970s the economic uncertainties that had begun to characterise the economy caused this bubble to burst, with supply beginning to exceed demand for the first time since 1939. Past confidence had led to house prices being pushed rapidly upwards. However, with the economy now facing difficulties from stagflation, these prices had become uncompetitive with respect to household earnings and the high interest rates that had been brought in by the government in an attempt to regain control of the money supply during and after the 'Barber Boom' (which by definition increased mortgage prices). Builders not only found themselves facing rising input costs and falling house prices, but also the prospect of paying higher interest charges on loans on land (whose value was falling) and work in progress. The easy speculative profits that had accrued from investing in land banks began to evaporate. Indeed, firms that had borrowed excessively when demand was buoyant found themselves facing liquidation. In order to compete against the second-hand market, surviving house builders built smaller houses, tried to improve efficiency and worked for lower profit margins. Whereas buoyant markets had encouraged firms to integrate vertically during the 1960s, the 1970s could only support 'quasi-integration' via joint ventures, where links between suppliers and building firms were established in the short term to cover a specific contract.

The environmental implications of construction activity

The late 1960s and early 1970s was not only a period when economists and politicians began to reveal their concern about an apparent breakdown of the Keynesian consensus. It was also a time when fears began to be aired over the ability of the Earth's ecosystems to support the unbridled pursuit of economic growth. It is inevitable that the construction industry has found itself at the centre of a snowballing concern about the relationship between economic progress and the environment. The inputs used in the construction process can consume a large amount of energy: steel, 30 MJ/kg; portland cement, 4–5 MJ/kg; and ceramic bricks, 8.5 MJ/kg (Agopyan, 1991, p. 969). Similarly, the quarrying of sand, gravel and rock – aggregates used extensively for road building and other construction-related activities – can lead to a deterioration of the countryside and coastal areas, both from an ecological and a scenic point of view. Their subsequent transfer to geographically dispersed sites not only leads to further consumption of energy but also increases the amount of particulate matter in the atmosphere. The construction industry is also a major producer of waste products, and the disposal of building debris raises significant waste management issues.

However, in any environmental debate about construction activity we must be careful to draw a distinction between the types of structure firms are sometimes asked to construct and the designs/types of material that are subsequently used in the building process. The pressure to build is something for which we all must accept some degree of responsibility, whereas the latter reflects the response of the construction industry to technology that is more resource-efficient and ecologically benign. The aim of this sub-section is to consider, albeit briefly, some of the thinking that permeates economics literature devoted to environmental issues and to then identify ways in which the construction industry is changing in response to it.

The evolution of environmentalism

Although the 1980s is the period usually associated with the growth of environmental concern, its roots rest firmly in the late 1960s and early 1970s. As we have seen, the postwar era was characterised by the pursuit of full employment, and with it an acceptance of the desirability of sustained economic growth. For some economists this process could continue almost indefinitely, as the price mechanism will act as a stimulus to change and technological progress, and as a result it will counter the tendency to deplete natural resources, both renewable and non-renewable. For others, however, the price mechanism and unbridled economic progress is always bound to be detrimental to the environment. Furthermore, the fragility of the rapid growth enjoyed by Western economies was exposed by the two oil crises in the 1970s. Alternative approaches have ranged from broadly traditional policies that take explicit account of the environment to more radical prescriptions in which the pursuit of economic growth is explicitly rejected. In other words, the rationale we have already considered when discussing the concept of externalities has been taken at its broadest and most far reaching. In this respect, it should be recognised that government intervention in markets should not be piecemeal, but coordinated and non-compartmentalised. The term that permeates the environmental economics literature nowadays is *sustainable development*. The most widely used definition of the term is a relatively recent one (Brundtland Report, 1987, p. 43): 'development that meets the need of the present without compromising the ability of future generations to meet their own needs'.

A fivefold set of 'rules' to promote sustainability are outlined by Turner, Pearce and Bateman (1994, p. 59) and are paraphrased below:

- Any shortfalls in the market system and indeed failures by the government to provide the right signals (for example with respect to resource pricing and property rights) should be corrected.
- The ability of renewable resources, such as fish stocks, to regenerate should not be compromised by over-harvesting; pollution needs to be controlled to prevent the deterioration of ecosystems and the natural ability of the earth to absorb benign waste.
- Improvements in technology should reflect shifts from non-renewable to renewable natural resources.
- The development of renewable natural resources should be exploited at a rate equal to the development of substitutes.
- Economic activity must be reflect the 'carrying capacity' of the natural resources available to us – given current uncertainty about the full environmental implications of economic activities, a 'precautionary approach' should be followed with wide safety margins.

The response of the construction industry to environmental pressures

The degree to which these issues relate to the construction industry is addressed by Ofori (1992, pp. 380–1). He argues that the construction industry should respond to the environmental challenge through the promotion of the following actions:

- Economising on the use of such resources as timber through recycling and the development of new materials.
- Developing construction and other materials that are capable of withstanding extreme conditions (weather and man-made pollution).
- Making use of safer materials that are associated with lower levels of pollution and health risks.
- Adopting practices that reduce the amount of soil erosion.
- Developing technologies and practices that encourage the use of existing structures and developed land that has fallen into dereliction, thereby reducing the pressure on undeveloped green areas.
- Finding more energy-efficient ways of producing and maintaining construction materials.

In some respects, changes in the political agenda are already driving the construction industry down this road, for example the introduction of controls on the energy consumption of new buildings, the tightening of permitted levels of air and water pollution, and the need to subject new developments to an environmental impact assessment at the planning stage. However, according to Ofori the industry should not simply be 'defensive'. Instead it needs to be 'offensive' such that professional bodies, trade associations and individual firms:

> anticipate opportunities and prepare to meet the changed nature of the items it will be required to design, construct and manage, the new materials it might have to use and the processes it will have to adopt; and . . . to make its contribution to the overall effort being made to address the environment (ibid., p. 370).

THE THATCHERITE 'REVOLUTION' AND THE CONSTRUCTION INDUSTRY, 1979–95

As discussed in the previous section, the 1970s brought a change in economic and political outlook. It was a period when monetarist thinking began to permeate economic policy making, made explicit by the ideas put forward by the Conservative Party while in opposition and imposed upon James Callaghan's Labour administration by the IMF. The failure of Keynesian policies to provide a remedy for stagflation increased the need to control inflation and public spending in order to reestablish economic stability, and hence create the environment required for unemployment to fall. This approach became the centrepiece of the Conservative government's medium-term financial strategy (MTFS), implemented in 1980.

The medium-term financial strategy

Underpinning the MTFS was acceptance of a long-standing hypothesis known as the quantity theory of money. This specifies a correlation between the rate of growth of the money supply and the rate of price increases. The theory was originally developed by the American economist Irving Fisher (1867–1947) and was repopularised by Milton Friedman (1912–). Specifically, the quantity theory of money (or more simply, the quantity theory) states that a stock of money (M) multiplied by the number of times it turns over, or its velocity (V), equals the average level of prices (P) multiplied by the volume of transactions (T), or $MV = PT$. This implies that the price level is determined by the interaction of the other three variables. Assuming that the velocity of money and the number of transactions do not fluctuate significantly and will return naturally to some equilibrium value, then changes in the money supply will be the major determinant of price changes within an economy. Thus if the quantity theory is to underpin a government's macroeconomic policy, there needs to be an unambiguous definition of what the money supply actually is.

Generally, there are two basic categories of money – *narrow* and *broad* – and these can be subdivided further into more precise categories – that are usually referred to by the letter 'M' with a numerical subscript, for example M_0, M_1, M_2 and so on. By definition, narrow money definitions relate to real spending power and hence are concerned with notes and coins in circulation and easily accessed bank deposits. Broad money definitions additionally recognise *potential* spending power and include long-term bank deposits and financial assets that cannot be converted immediately into cash.

Initially it was one of the broad money definitions that was favoured by the government – 'sterling M_3', or £M_3, renamed M_3 in 1989. Projections were made for the money supply (as target bands) and for the public sector borrowing requirement (PSBR) over a four-year period (expressed as a percentage of GDP) from 1980–1 to 1983–4. The aim during this period was to reduce the rate of growth of £M_3 such that it would lie within a band of 7–11 per cent at the beginning of the period, but would rest somewhere within a band of 4–8 per cent by the end of it. This was to be facilitated by an increase in interest rates in order to encourage saving. Increased saving meant that less money would be used for transactions, thereby necessitating a smaller money supply. During the same period real government spending was to be reduced to enable the PSBR to fall from 3.75 per cent to 1.5 per cent of GDP. While the government's ability to keep the money supply within its predefined limits would be an explicit measure of its performance, it was recognised that public spending would be sensitive to variations in economic activity (for example a rise in unemployment would increase the number of benefit claimants) and hence the achievement of this aim was never going to be central to overall policy.

It soon became obvious that the government was failing to meet both its explicit money supply projections and its implicit PSBR targets, a pattern that was to repeated in subsequent years. This failure seemed to prompt a search for the 'right' money supply definition by which the government should be judged. By 1982 it was resorting to three definitions: $£M_3$, plus PSL_2 (an even wider broad money definition) and M_1 (narrow). By 1983 M_1 had been replaced by an even 'narrower' definition of money, M_0, a measure that proved to perform well with respect to government projections. The fact that the government seemed to be chopping and changing in order to find the 'right' money supply definition tended to detract from the straightforward message of its medium-term financial strategy. Nevertheless, although the government seemed unable to hit its own targets consistently, the money supply (regardless of the definition adopted) was contracting.

Between 1980 and 1984, the rate of inflation fell from 18 per cent to below 5 per cent, suggesting that the government's tight monetary stance was a success. However this was also a period of world recession. The ability of the British economy to weather this storm was hindered by the high interest rates that had been imposed by the government in an attempt to control inflation and by a rise in the value of sterling, the latter having been brought about by the same rise in interest rates plus the effects of North Sea oil, which had encouraged speculators to invest more heavily in Britain. The high interest rates prompted healthy firms to postpone their investment decisions and forced struggling firms to close down.

The decision of the government not to intervene actively in the financial markets during the early part of the decade meant that exporting firms found it increasingly difficult to compete in world markets. As a result unemployment rose rapidly, eventually peaking at over three million in 1986. This placed a limit on the ability of workers to extract large wage claims from their employers. Overall, however, the period from the early to mid 1980s saw consumer expenditure begin to rise as real incomes rose (tax cuts allowed average earnings to grow faster than inflation) and credit became easier to obtain. Over time, this impetus was to fuel the rapid rise in aggregate demand that emerged between 1985 and 1988. This 'loadsamoney' mentality manifested itself most explicitly in the upwardly spiralling house prices that typified the optimism of the time.

Another important factor to note is that the government's apparent success in reducing both inflation and unemployment meant that money supply targets were pursued less vigorously. In addition $£M_3$ became less important as a target variable due to its persistent overshooting of the top end of the band that had been set for it. From 1985 was 'monitored' rather than 'targeted', and in 1987 it was discarded. Emphasis was given to the more easily controlled narrow money (M_0). Eventually a new broad money supply definition, M_4, was adopted. Unlike $£M_3$, it explicitly recognised the enhanced status of building societies within the banking system, and hence was less likely to fluctuate when depositors switched their monies between banks and building societies.

Although the MTFS remained in place, the government's commitment to controlling inflation by the mid-1980s manifested itself in the attention it began to give to sterling's value on the foreign exchange market. This change in approach reflected the recognition that sterling's relationship with other currencies, particularly with the Deutschmark (DM) as the dominant European currency, was linked to inflation rates at home. By allowing sterling to 'shadow' the DM, whose continued strength reflected the stability of the premier European economy, rather than to lose value against it, inflationary pressures would (in theory) be suppressed.

The rationale for this approach was twofold. First, despite reluctance in some quarters, Britain was signalling its intention to subject sterling (and indeed the government's own room for manoeuvre) to the confines of the European Exchange Rate Mechanism (ERM). The government's unwillingness to join the ERM throughout the 1980s continued to fuel the opinion that Britain's commitment to the EC was not total and was more in keeping with a desire to make choices from a 'pick and mix' menu. Second, and more immediate to the domestic economy, such a policy would reduce the likelihood of industry granting inflationary pay awards since they would not ultimately be underwritten by a reduction in the international exchange value of sterling. However, with North Sea oil adding to the strength of the pound, initial increases in domestic interest rates (which would also help to bring down the money supply) were reversed to prevent speculative pressure from pushing the pound beyond the politically sensitive £1 = DM3 level.

The impact of lower interest rates and post-1987 election income tax cuts meant that the economy moved rapidly into a boom. The inevitable rise in inflation forced the government to raise interest rates again, and between May 1988 and October 1989 they doubled from 7.5 per cent to 15 per cent. These rises prompted an appreciation in the value of sterling from around DM3 at the end of 1987 to DM3.25 by the beginning of 1989. By October 1990 the chancellor of the Exchequer, Nigel Lawson, felt able to commit sterling to the ERM, albeit at the high rate of DM2.95 to the pound and within a 'wide' ± 6 per cent band. However, high interest rates were needed to keep sterling within its agreed band in order to appease speculators who were concerned about the underlying weakness of the British economy and the increases in German interest rates following reunification. Although this helped to suppress inflationary tendencies, unemployment rose as Britain was again unable to withstand another worldwide recession. It was now obvious that Britain had entered the ERM at an unsustainable rate of exchange. Sterling was increasingly targeted by speculators during 1992, and despite heavy intervention in the international money markets sterling went into freefall and was withdrawn from the ERM on 16 September.

Without this constraint the government was able to take action to encourage consumption and investment expenditure: interest rates were cut and sterling was allowed to find a lower market value. Although the government continues to set ranges for the growth of M_0 and M_4, it has recognised with hindsight since the late 1980s that achievement of these ranges, year in, year out, would be more through luck than judgement. Thus money supply ranges are not set as explicit targets by which government performance should be assessed.

Since the end of 1992 the government has aimed to manipulate inflationary expectations through periodic reference to inflation targets, set initially within a range of 1–4 per cent. While remaining a policy of low inflation, the MTFS has moved away from quantity theory and has tended to emphasise the role of interest rates, public spending control and an implicit public sector incomes policy. Whereas the boom period of the mid to late 1980s allowed the government to set itself targets and achieve negative PSBR figures (such that revenues exceeded expenditure, thereby allowing previous debts to be paid off), the recession that has characterised the economy for much of the 1990s created a springboard for a rapid rise in the PSBR. This has implications for the money markets as higher government spending impacts on interest rates. As a result, the government is now placing a high degree of emphasis on the need for fiscal contraction (for example through public spending reductions) to run alongside its explicit counterinflation strategy.

The medium-term financial strategy and the construction industry

Until the breakdown of the Keynesian consensus, the pursuit of full employment meant that the construction industry was highly susceptible to changes in government policy due to the labour-intensive nature of the production process. Thus when the government adopted an expansionary economic package (increased public spending and a reduction in tax and interest rates), rising demand fed into the system and quickly created new jobs in the construction industry. However, when the government was forced to curtail its spending there was a curtailment of job opportunities. Although the booms and depressions associated with the stop–go cycle were predictable, particularly in hind-sight, there nevertheless existed a high degree of uncertainty that dis-couraged all but the very largest companies from thinking beyond established practices that encouraged the subcontracting of work to specialist firms and discouraged marginal spending on investment and training.

Prior to the general election of 1979, the two main political parties were already signalling that they intended to reduce the priority given to public sector construction activity (housing and non-housing). In the private sector, housing demand was dampened by increases in the minimum lending rate in June 1979, while declining business confi-dence reflected Britain's continuing poor economic performance at home and abroad. Thus it was no surprise that the construction industry was to experience difficulties in most sectors of activity from the outset of the Conservative government's first term of office. With the Conserva-tive government set to manage the economy according to a new economic philosophy, the construction industry faced a revised mix of uncertainties.

As we have seen, the incoming Conservative government put explicit emphasis on the control of inflation and the need to reduce public spending. The impact of the latter was to make the construction industry less dependent on the public sector for its work. For example local authority expenditure on non-trunk and non-motorway roads contin-ued to be put under pressure by the continued enforcement of cash limits. Furthermore reforms in the public housing sector (see below), together with the passing of nationalised industries into the private sector, further undermined the relative importance of the public sector to the construction industry. Thus to fill its order books, rather than having the fall-back position that had been facilitated by the desire of past Keynesian governments to reduce unemployment through fiscal expansion, the construction industry now found itself at the mercy of private sector confidence. In the case of the business sector, only small unit development in the Midlands and the north, together with general repair and maintenance work, provided the construction industry with opportunities as the recession began to bite hard. Overall the value of new private industrial work tumbled from £1856 million in 1980 to £1409 million in 1982 (*Housing and Construction Statistics 1982–92*, 1990 prices).

From 1981, however, private house building started to make a sig-nificant contribution to total output. This was a reflection of greater optimism by house builders and the greater willingness of large firms to develop more than the housing estate at the same time. In 1978 the total number of private sector dwellings under construction or com-pleted in Britain was 161 597. By 1980 this figure had fallen to 102 204 but it rose to 144 969 two years later and continued its upward trend to reach over 182 175 by 1986. In monetary terms, new orders for private house construction stood at £2648 million in 1981 and peaked at £5432 million in 1988 (*Housing and Construction Statistics 1982–92*). By 1983 this optimism had begun to be felt in industry and there was an increasing amount of capital expenditure despite high interest rates. This seemed to reflect the fact that the government's tight monetary policy had been successful in making the British economy more competitive by reducing inflation from 18 per cent to just under 5 per cent.

Whereas the early part of the 1980s was characterised by a lack of demand for construction activity, the mid to late 1980s saw private sector confidence swell. The government had by now chosen to pursue its anti-inflationary strategy through the foreign currency markets, rather than by a tight monetary policy. By 1987 the economy was rushing into a boom and with it came a rapid increase in industrial construction. Public expenditure on infrastructure also grew rapidly between 1987 and 1990, and indeed, unlike most other sectors of the construction industry, it continued to grow while recession began to take hold of the economy. Most of the growth was accounted for by Channel Tunnel project, rapid increases in the privatised utilities' investment programmes and an expanded roads programme. Thus, whereas the total value of construction output had stood at £34 820 million in 1982 (*Digest of Data for the Construction Industry*, 1995: 1990 prices), it had risen to £41 130 by 1985, £51 998 by 1988 and peaked at £55 307 by 1990.

Although this was a significant growth period for the construction industry, it should be noted that between 1965 and 1974 the average value of all construction activity (again in 1990 prices) was just over £44 200 million, a figure that was only exceeded three times during the 1980s (1987–9). Between 1983 and 1989 the number of construction firms (regardless of size) fell and rose again. In 1983 the total number began to decline from just over one million to 935 000 in 1985, before returning to one million in 1989. As we saw in the previous section, however, the optimism of the late 1980s was soon quashed by the reemergence of recession as the government saw the need to contain the rise in inflation by imposing higher interest rates. This affected the construction industry in two ways.

First, private sector investment fell rapidly, forcing construction firms to submit lower tenders in order to compete for work in a contracting market. In the case of the housing market, house sales were slowed by the general increase in unemployment and the prospect of higher mortgage repayments. Indeed in growth areas such as the south-east, where house prices had risen rapidly in the face of short-term property shortages, the term 'negative equity' became the watchword, with home owners finding themselves paying off mortgages that exceeded the value to which their properties had fallen as a result of the recession. In other words, the demand curve for housing had shifted inwards, resulting in a significant reduction in the equilibrium price and providing a disincentive to house builders. For example, in 1988 the total number of private sector houses under construction or completed stood at 195 295, almost two and a half times the figure for 1980. By 1990, however, this figure had fallen to 110 437. In 1988 the value of new private housing output had risen to almost £7.8 million (1990 prices), whereas by 1993 this figure had fallen to £5.5 million.

Even more significant was the decline in private commercial construction work: from £11.3 million in 1990 to £6.5 million in 1993. Only expenditure on infrastructure output grew between 1989 and 1993: from £4 million to £7 million. Now, however, with work on the Channel Tunnel complete and the contraction of the roads subsector in the wake of general expenditure cuts, the outlook for this sphere of activity appears depressing. Overall the recession has seen the total value of all new work and all repair and maintenance work fall from £55.3 million in 1990 to £48.5 million in 1993 (*Digest of Data for the Construction Industry 1995*).

Second, construction firms that had borrowed money from banks and other lending institutions found themselves having to repay more than they could earn in a depressed market. Many of the very small firms that were able to survive did so because they could undertake subcontracting work at the cheapest rate because of their very low overheads (for example by operating from home using a vehicle that doubled as a family car), and simply remained in business because in a recession there was little if any economic rent to be accrued. Thus although the number of construction company insolvencies and individual bankruptcies had shown an upward trend throughout the 1980s, despite the boom period in the latter stages of the decade, a massive increase occurred from 1990 onwards. Whereas 1638 companies had become insolvent in 1989, in 1990 the figure rose to 2445, reaching 3189 by 1993. Individual bankruptcies in the same three years were 1652, 2348 and 4361 respectively (*Digest of Data For the Construction Industry 1995*).

Whereas the nature of the industry enabled it to adjust quickly in response to the need to streamline operations and the increased availability of construction work between 1983 and 1989, the rapidity with which firms of all sizes could exit or were forced to exit the industry became even more apparent during the 1990s. By 1993 the total number of firms within the industry stood at 753 200, a fall of over a quarter of a million from its 1989 peak (*Housing and Construction Statistics 1983–93*).

The Conservative government's supply-side strategy

In the run-up to the 1979 general election, the Conservative Party put considerable emphasis on the need for a programme of microeconomic reforms aimed at promoting greater market efficiency and improving Britain's ability to compete in foreign export markets. These *supply-side* policies were to influence all sectors of the economy and they remain part of government policy today. The policies fall into three basic categories: those affecting the labour market, the capital market and the provision of goods and services.

The labour market

In the case of the labour market, the government held the view that there was a need to increase incentives and reduce the power of the trade unions, the latter being seen as having held the country to ransom during the 1970s. This view has manifested itself in reductions in the real value of welfare benefits for the unemployed (thereby encouraging jobless people to seek work actively), reductions in the marginal rates of direct taxation (which gives workers more take-home pay) and laws intended to prevent 'secondary picketing' and enforced 'closed shops'. The set-piece confrontation between the government and miners in 1983 provided confirmation of the government's intentions.

The capital market

The government's desire to increase competition in the financial markets is most associated with the year 1986. The Building Societies Act (1986) enabled building societies to widen their sphere of activity beyond that of mortgage lending to provide a wide array of customer services, ranging from the provision of cheque accounts to estate agency, insurance broking and general financial consultancy. The increased importance of building societies within the financial sector reflects the government's introduction of the new broad money supply definition discussed earlier (M_4). Nevertheless, it should be recognised that only the very largest building societies are able to compete effectively against the high street banks.

The second and most important change to take place in 1986 became known as the 'big bang' and was associated with the widespread deregulation of the financial sector via the Financial Services Act. The Act set up the Securities and Investment Board (SIB) to oversee the system, with the power to delegate supervision to approved self-regulatory organisations such as the Financial Intermediaries, Managers and Brokers Regulatory Association (FIMBRA). However the electronic linking of financial markets ultimately resulted in tragedy. The rapid growth in electronic trading within an already buoyant market forced share prices above their equilibrium value when the overall market for financial securities was taken into account. When investors finally took stock of this situation it resulted in the crash of October 1987, initially in New York, then in London. This negative bandwagon effect also reflected the more immediate impact of technology on the financial services sector. Although share prices recovered subsequently, there remains a danger that a similar decline could be triggered if share prices again become unsustainable.

The provision of goods and services

By the time the Conservative government had been elected in 1979, almost everyone was familiar with the party's desire to 'roll back the frontiers of the state'. This simply meant that there was an intention to promote greater competitiveness and wider consumer choice by removing or reducing the level of government intervention in the provision of certain goods and services, for example those of the nationalised industries, the National Health Service and local government. This was reflected in a five-dimensional process of reform:

- Encouraging 'popular capitalism' by floating shares in nationalised industries (for example British Gas and British Telecom) and instituting the 'right to buy' scheme, which enabled a greater number of council house tenants to buy their houses.
- Deregulating certain industries, for example via the Financial Services Act (see above) and the Transport Act (1980), which aimed to revitalise competition in the provision of bus and coach services.
- Requiring public sector bodies to open up their activities to private sector competition through compulsory competitive tendering (CCT).
- Introducing a major reform of local taxation, most notably the community charge or 'poll tax' (later replaced by the council tax, discussed below).
- Reforming the National Health Service. Unlike previously a clear distinction is now made between those who demand health care and those who supply it.

Obviously not all these changes are of direct relevance to the construction industry. Thus in order to provide a flavour of the reforms introduced by the Conservative government, attention will focus on three interrelated changes. First, the need for governments and other public sector bodies to provide the opportunity for private sector organisations to tender for work previously undertaken 'in-house', known as compulsory competitive tendering; second, the implications of council house tenants having the explicit right to buy their property; and third, the reform of local taxation.

Compulsory competitive tendering

Prior to the election of the Conservative government in 1979, the relationship between central/local government departments or institutions and private sector companies tended to be one-sided. For practical reasons, the former have always needed to purchase goods from the private sector, for example vehicles, yet it was policy to employ their own labour forces to meet their service responsibilities rather than employ outside agency workers. Thus, with in-house suppliers protected artificially, they were seen as being inflexible, and lacking the incentive to make the efficiency gains often forced on private sector companies striving to remain competitive in a market situation. In the view of the incoming government, local government should provide private sector firms with the opportunity to put in tenders for local authority service work, a process that would lead to cost savings. Initially the government did not wish to impose its preferences directly upon local authorities,[1] hoping that the lesson would be learnt through example, such as that of Southend on Sea, where savings of almost £500 000 per annum were made when its refuse and cleaning services were contracted out voluntarily. However by the mid 1980s less than 10 per cent of the 456 English and Welsh councils had followed Southend on Sea's lead. Thus the government decided to draft legislation (the 1988 Local Government Act) to compel public bodies to put some of their services out to compulsory competitive tendering (CCT).

Put simply, CCT requires local authorities to allow private sector companies to tender for the opportunity to undertake services previously supplied by the organisation's own direct service organisations (DSOs), sometimes referred to as direct labour organisations (DLOs). If a DSO puts forward a superior bid to that of its private sector counterparts (or indeed if private sector firms choose not to bid) a clear distinction must be made between the DSO as a service provider and its client, namely the public sector organisation.

The potential benefits of CCT

- It encourages efficiency by making markets contestable rather than closed to competition (implicitly or explicitly).
- It requires local authorities to identify and set standards for the services they provide. These can then be enforced through penalty clauses and performance bonds.

- Because of the second point above, it emphasises performance explicitly in terms of *output*. In the past, input indicators were often used as a measure of performance – the size of the in-house supplier was often determined by political rather than economic factors.
- Suppliers have the opportunity to serve more than one local authority and hence achieve scale economies that could not be achieved by in-house organisations serving one authority.
- Cost savings can be redistributed towards other services.

The potential problems of CCT

- Private sector firms may make a lower bid than a DSO simply because they are unaware of what is required of them. If one firm wins the contract but defaults subsequently, the council may be left without the service in question.
- Private sector contractors may try to underbid the DSO and then renegotiate with the local authority after the DSO has been disbanded. This potential problem can be addressed within the specification of the initial contract.
- The benefits from CCT may be undermined if private sector firms collude and agree to marketsharing arrangements. As we have seen, this is a major problem in the construction industry.
- CCT is not a costless activity: contracts need to be specified, negotiated, awarded, monitored and retendered. Any benefits that may arise from CCT may be swallowed up by these transaction costs.
- Being in the public domain, DSOs have been required to meet more exacting employment standards than private sector firms. Cost savings may simply be accrued through a deterioration in employees' remuneration, training levels and working conditions rather than through greater efficiency *per se*.

Despite these potential problems, the benefits from CCT seemed explicit: construction work, as well as the provision of other services, would now be undertaken by the most cost-effective firm that could meet the criteria stipulated in the contract. Although this message seems straightforward, it must be argued that the playing field has not been level, and as a result DSOs have been at a competitive disadvantage. It has already been noted that the size of DSOs was frequently determined by political rather than economic considerations and that they were subject to the rigours of public sector accountability. Furthermore, DSOs used to be restricted to day-to-day public sector construction activity, which tended mainly to be minor repair work. As a result

DSOs have needed to employ a high proportion of labour to capital. Private sector firms on the other hand have always been able to compete for relatively larger contracts within the private sector, and as a result they have been able to organise their production in a more capital-intensive manner. Nominally, therefore, DSOs have appeared to be less efficient than their private sector counterparts. Where DSOs have organised themselves so as to be able to compete in the private sector, their lack of experience in a more commercial environment has detracted from their ability to compete on equal terms. Figures show that DSOs now contribute less to the volume of total construction output than they did during the 1970s, or indeed during any period since 1955. For example in 1975 DSOs contributed 13 per cent to total output. By 1985 this figure had fallen to 10 per cent, and since 1990 it has averaged only around 6 per cent (*Digest of Data for the Construction Industry 1995*).

The 'right to buy'

When viewed alongside its highly publicised programme of denationalisation and share floatation, the Conservative government's desire to extend home ownership as far down the income scale as possible, in particular by encouraging council tenants to buy the properties they were renting, resulted in the 1980s emerging as the era of 'popular capitalism'.

The need for local authorities to provide dwellings in response to a need for good-quality low-cost housing was recognised in the nineteenth century but not acted upon explicitly until the passing of the Town and Country Planning Act (1919). However, the major impetus towards the building of council housing followed the Second World War, and 90 per cent of the million houses built between 1945 and 1950 fell into this category. The 1950s saw a gradual end to the acute housing shortage and the emphasis was switched to slum clearance and increased private building, with public sector housing provision responding to macroeconomic fluctuations rather than ideological shifts. However, in the 1960s it was recognised that a substantial proportion of the current housing stock was becoming increasingly unfit for habitation. This prompted an increase in public spending such that the proportion of local authority completions to total completions had risen from one in three to one in two by 1968.

As discussed earlier, the 1970s was characterised by a rapid rise in the rate of inflation. With subsidised council rents being held below the rate of inflation, housing debt began to rise rapidly, and with it the level of Exchequer subsidy. During this period the decision to sell council houses rested with the individual authorities and generally sales remained few (for example in 1971 only 17 215 council houses were sold in the whole of England and Wales). However the Conservatives' introduction of the 1980 Housing Act meant that the option of whether or not to sell council houses was taken away from the local authorities. Tenants were guaranteed the right to buy, providing they had been tenants for three years or more (later reduced to two years), with an opportunity to claim the maximum discount of 50–60 per cent.

Faced with the obligation to sell their stock of council homes, a number of Labour-controlled councils showed great reluctance to implement the Act. For example, in Stoke on Trent the return of a Labour council by a majority of 57 to three was interpreted by the council as legitimising its stand against council house sales. Although it initially adopted a policy of processing applications slowly, the council's defiance withered under the threat of the process being administered centrally. Despite such pockets of resistance, by the end of the decade over one million dwellings had been sold under the right to buy scheme.

New legislation contained in the 1988 Housing Act also made it possible for tenants to opt out of local authority control altogether and transfer their properties to a housing association or other approved landlord, the properties subsequently being relet under 'fair rent' criteria. The same Act enabled housing action trusts (HATs) to take over run-down estates, renovate them and pass them on to a housing association or approved landlord. Because the better-quality houses have been sold off to tenants with above-average incomes, there has been a residualisation of the council housing stock. In other words, councils with declining resources have been left to maintain a poor quality and increasingly fragmented housing stock, and in some cases this has resulted in an enormous backlog of repairs and improvements.

Accompanying the 'right to buy' scheme was a reduction of the Exchequer subsidy on public housing, and council rents rose two and a half times faster than retail prices. This was predictable at a time when the government's supply-side strategy included a desire to promote labour market incentives. In the eyes of the government, council tenants were being too heavily subsidised and therefore were imposing an unreasonable burden on taxpayers. With two-thirds of council tenants in receipt of welfare payments, a large proportion of the increased council house rents was being paid for by means-tested housing benefit.

Local taxation

The reform of local government finance proved to be one of the Conservative government's most controversial policies, becoming a focus for extensive public debate and even acts of civil disobedience. Until April 1989 in Scotland and April 1990 in England and Wales, local authority expenditure was partly financed by a system of *domestic rates*, which were raised locally. These rates were a tax on private, industrial and commercial property. In the case of householders, the amount paid each year was a proportion of the 'rateable value' of the property they occupied, the rateable value being determined by the rent that would have been earned had the property been let out commercially on the open market. As with all taxes, the rating system was unpopular. Initially the response of central government was to hold down the domestic rate burden being inflicted on householders. Thus an increasing proportion of local government expenditure, which had risen rapidly from the end of the Second World War to the mid 1970s, became financed centrally through general taxation. Whereas in the mid 1950s, 55 per cent of local authority expenditure was financed through rates (domestic, industrial and commercial), this figure had fallen to 40 per cent twenty years later (Harrington, 1992, pp. 140–1).

This raises an important issue: electors were effectively able to vote for rises in local government expenditure with the knowledge that there would only be limited increases to their domestic rate bills. Indeed, by the mid 1970s less than 20 per cent of all current expenditure of local authorities was being financed directly by those who were voting for that expenditure. As discussed earlier, the 1970s saw attempts to reduce escalating public expenditure. After 1976, local authorities had to reduce their spending because central government financial support declined in real terms. This was the background to the changes the incoming Conservatives were to confront.

It has already been shown that the Conservative Party's aims included a reduction in public spending and the promotion of greater market incentives and self-reliance. In the case of local government this philosophy manifested itself in an attempt to make local populations aware of the costs of the public services they were voting for and to increase councillors' accountability to their electorate. In particular, a reduction in the real level of central government grants to local authorities gave councillors a simple choice between reducing their expenditure or raising local taxes. When councils opted for the latter, particularly some Labour-controlled councils, who rapidly elevated local rates, they were thwarting the central government's desire to reduce individual tax burdens. As a result the government attempted to exert greater control over local authority spending, initially by setting legal ceilings on rate demands (and indeed abolishing certain councils, for example the Greater London Council), and ultimately by abolishing household rates altogether and imposing a uniform business rate on industrial and commercial premises, irrespective of their geographical location.

The *community charge* (more widely known as the poll tax), which replaced domestic rates, was a personal tax levied on all adults irrespective of the size and quality of the house they lived in. Its logic was simple: rather than the main householder being solely responsible for paying domestic rates, all people over the age of 18 would pay a locally determined, flat-rate sum to help cover the cost of the services they were consuming. Although people on very low incomes were entitled to a discount, the overall impact of the community charge was *regressive*. In other words, it did not reflect *ability to pay*.[2] The gainers were households with a small number of high-income adults while the losers were households with a large number of low-income adults.

The government had expected that any criticism of the high community charge bills would be vented against the local authorities. Instead it was directed at the government itself. Faced with a potential vote loser and the massive cost of collecting monies from dissenting sections of the population who were refusing to pay, changes were made. Initially the grant aid given to local government was increased, paid for out of an increase in value added tax from 15 per cent to 17.5 per cent, thereby reversing the government's policy of the early 1980s. In early 1992 it was announced that the community charge would be abolished and replaced by a new local tax, the *council tax*.

The council tax was introduced in April 1993 and continues to the present. It is a compromise between the former system of domestic rates and the community charge. It returns to the concept of taxing property values but makes a reduction for single-person households. In contrast to the domestic rate, the council tax is based on the *capital value* of a property rather than its rental value. A residence falls into one of several bands, regardless of whether it is owner-occupied or rented (privately or from a housing association/local authority). For example, in the case of England the lowest band, A, covers all properties valued at £40 000 or below; band B covers properties valued above £40 000 but below £52 000; band C includes properties valued above £52 000 and below £68 000. The highest band, H, includes all properties valued at £320 000 and above. Separate scales exist for Scotland and Wales. Although the banding system eliminates the need to value each property individually, there are still areas of dispute in borderline cases. When a property is occupied by just one adult there is a 25 per cent reduction in the amount that is due, and if the property is unoccupied a 50 per cent reduction applies. Nevertheless the council tax retains some regressive attributes, this time because capital values are likely to increase less than proportionately to household income. Furthermore, individuals in band H in a given locality pay the same council tax, regardless of whether their property is worth £320 000 or £3 200 000. Unlike the community charge, however, the linking of payment to property value is more equitable, assuming that income and property are to a certain extent related.

THE EUROPEAN UNION AND THE CONSTRUCTION INDUSTRY

Britain's membership of the EU has played an increasingly important role in determining the activities and performance of the construction industry: it has affected the way in which work is undertaken; the standards that have to be met; the processes governing how firms bid for public sector contracts; and indeed the level of trade between member states in construction-related goods and services. This has become most pronounced since the advent of the *single European market* (sometimes also referred to as '1992', the inception date of the single market). The remainder of this chapter is divided into three subsections. The first briefly identifies the processes that led to the creation of the EU (or the European Economic Community – EEC – as it was called originally) from a British perspective. The second turns to the implications of the single European market, while the final subsection looks at the construction industry in a European context.

The evolution of the EU

The economic foundations of Europe were devastated by the Second World War. Europe's ability to produce exportable goods was limited by the domestic needs of the various economies, and with import needs soaring, foreign exchange reserves were running out rapidly. At this point the United States announced the Marshall Plan, by which it would provide aid to help the European economies find their feet. The United States did not want European countries to present individual shopping lists of needs. Rather it wanted its loans to be linked to progress towards European unification rather than a reaffirmation of the nationalism that had prompted hostilities in the first place.

The need for European cooperation was heightened by the emergence of the Cold War and the signing of the North Atlantic Treaty in 1949. One of the main problems was the postwar relationship between France and West Germany. The solution emerged through the work of Jean Monnet, who helped establish the European Coal and Steel Community (1952), an organisation intended to make war between France and West Germany 'materially impossible'. Specifically, France and West Germany, together with the Netherlands, Belgium, Luxembourg and Italy, agreed to treat all their coal and steel industries as one: by eliminating import duties and quota restrictions they would enjoy the potential efficiency gains of a single unified market. Britain was invited to join, but refused (though it signed an agreement of association in 1954) as Attlee was unprepared to allow vital products to be handed over to an 'undemocratic' body. Because Britain was then producing 50 per cent of European coal and 33 per cent of European steel, its absence was significant.

The success of the ECSC prompted member states to consider the implications of further economic integration involving a common market and an atomic energy pool. Britain originally participated in these talks but it soon became clear that Britain and the other six were at odds – Britain favoured a free trade area focusing on industrial goods while the other countries wanted to pursue a higher level of economic integration with an emphasis on agriculture. This conflict led to Britain withdrawing from the discussions.[3] An agreement, the Treaty of Rome, was eventually signed in 1957 and the EEC came into being in 1958.

Although Britain had committed itself to the European Free Trade Association (EFTA),[4] whose remit fitted Britain's own requirements, it soon found itself isolated economically. Consequently it sought membership of the EEC in the 1960s, but French anger about the way in which Britain had seemingly tried to derail the original negotiations delayed its accession until 1973. This represented the first enlargement of the EEC Six, which became the EEC Nine when Denmark and Ireland joined too. Subsequent enlargements have included Greece (1981), Spain and Portugal (1986) and Austria, Finland and Sweden (1995). It is likely that countries from the former Eastern Bloc will become members in the future. However, their accession will reflect the ability of their economies to evolve successfully into more market-oriented systems.

A detailed analysis of the economic performance of the EEC (subsequently referred to as the EC from 1987 and the EU from 1994) is beyond the scope of this text. Interested readers should consult such texts as El Agraa (1994), Artis and Lee (1994) and Hitiris (1994). The focus of the discussion to follow is the implications of what has become the key initiative of the EU, the single European market (SEM), and its implications for the construction industry.

The single European Market

The European Commission's White Paper 'Completing the Internal Market' (1985) initiated a seven-year programme to create a single European market. The Single European Act, which was signed in July 1987, not only introduced a series of additions (articles) to the original Treaty of Rome but also identified 31 December 1992 as the deadline for the completion of the SEM. Although the signing of the original Treaty of Rome had political as well as economic overtones, the catalyst for the creation of the SEM was economic. Specifically, it was recognised that European firms were unable to realise all their potential efficiency gains by virtue of the fact that Europe was made up of a series of fragmented national markets, often protected by implicit or explicit barriers to trade, rather than a single unified market, as was the case with the United

States. The aim therefore was to establish a dynamic and homogeneous integrated market based on common rules and equal conditions for competition, equipped with (if necessary) judicial backing. The programme's objectives can be summarised into five main points.

First, the removal of *physical barriers* that restricted the movement of goods (for example unnecessary border controls that acted as non-tariff barriers) and discriminated against individuals on the ground of nationality with respect to employment, remuneration, qualifications and working conditions. However, construction is but one example where it has proved difficult to obtain mutual acceptance of EU members' individual professional qualifications – the range of education, professional training and roles afforded to architects within the EU has led to considerable problems in implementing the architects' directive.

Second, the removal of barriers preventing competition between the suppliers of *services* within the community. Within this heading we may include the liberalisation of banking and insurance markets, securities trading, transport, telecommunications and information services, including the rigorous protection of intellectual property rights (such as patents, trademarks and copyright).

Third, the removal of *technical barriers* that promoted suboptimal production levels more suited to individual national markets than Europe as a whole. In the case of the construction industry, this has involved the introduction of agreed standards governing building activity, for example the resistance of building materials to fire, the durability of buildings and the strength/reliability of special structures (for example bridges).

Fourth, the removal of exchange controls that prevented or restricted cross-border *capital transfers* and thus maintained differentials in the price of capital.

Finally, the maintenance of a strong *competition policy* to prevent market forces from being distorted. This attempt to 'level the playing field' not only included standard issues relating to monopoly power and merger activity (see Chapter 6) but also procedures for public procurement. In the past, public sector contracts, such as that to undertake building projects, tended to favour local contractors and exclude foreign ones.

The potential benefits to be gained from a fully integrated SEM (as opposed to continuing with a fragmented 12-nation EC) were outlined in a multivolume document known as the Cecchini Report (1988). These included improvements in corporate efficiency, and hence a reduction in x-inefficiency and organisational slack; lower and hence more competitive prices at home and abroad to provide the opportunity to reap scale economies; and the incentive to increase research and development expenditures. In cash terms, the Cecchini Report suggested a figure as high as ECU 200 billion, though this figure was considered by many to be overoptimistic. Industries and customers of industries whose activities have been highly regulated and/or subject to low levels of competition will benefit most from the completion of the SEM. This not only includes financial services and motor vehicles but also construction activity.

Construction activity in the EU and the response of British construction firms

Although construction activity, wherever it is practised, has many unique features that distinguish it from other forms of industrial activity, it nevertheless has epitomised the need for a SEM. Just as it is localised at the national level, the industry being dominated by a large number of small companies and a few large companies, so too is it localised at the pan-European level, with the larger domestic firms seemingly best suited to meeting the specific characteristics of their own construction markets. In many respects, the British construction industry is well suited to meeting the new challenges of a more integrated European market since, alongside France, it has a large number of domestic firms that are capable of competing in international markets. In countries such as Germany and the Netherlands the emphasis remains with the smaller, more localised firm. Multinational firms that can offer a full range of services – from the feasibility study through to the construction phase and subsequent maintenance – will have the edge, particularly when it comes to private sector clients who demand the speed in design and construction that encourages adoption of the most up-to-date technologies. Smaller and less capable firms will find themselves working as subcontractors and being marginalised into accepting smaller and more basic contracts, such as those of the public sector.

Although the British construction industry has always been well suited to compete effectively in European markets from a structural point of view, it needs to face two interrelated issues. Neither can be levelled as an explicit criticism of the construction industry, but more of the 'British problem' that clouded Britain's initial response to the likelihood of a European common market in the 1950s. First, there remains general suspicion about the implications of initiatives emerging from Brussels. Second, there has always been a preference for markets outside Europe, particularly in countries where the need to speak a foreign language is less of a barrier, for example the Commonwealth countries, the United States, the Middle East and Africa. The pattern of geographical diversification by major British firms can be seen in Table 8.1.

During the 1970s British construction firms were able to exploit

Table 8.1   *Geographical diversification by four British majors in 1991: percentage shares in group turnover by origin of turnover*

Company	Britain	N. America	Europe	Rest of the world
Tarmac	85	9	5	0
Trafalgar House*	66	21	9	3
P&O	50	20	12	14
Wimpey	82	12	ns	6

* Trafalgar House's figures comprise the following: the Americas (treated above as N. America), Europe, the Middle East and Africa (Europe), and India, the Far East and Australasia (rest of the world).

Source: annotated from Ive, 1994, Table 4, p. 355.

opportunities arising from the expansion of building programmes in the Middle Eastern countries, prompted by their newly found oil wealth. Nonetheless Ive (1994) presents evidence to suggest that this attitude was changing in anticipation of '1992':

- By 1990, 34 of the 100 largest British construction firms were reporting that they were undertaking work in the EU, an increase of 12 over the previous year;
- There has been a general increase in cross-border takeover activity by British firms within the EU. In 1990 this amounted to ECU 5.9 billion – 35 per cent of total international spending on acquisitions, and a 57 per cent increase over the previous year. The most popular destination, however, remains the United States.

Notes

1 Understanding Economics and Economic Statistics

1. The specific regions used throughout *Regional Trends* are: the North, Yorkshire and Humberside, the East Midlands, East Anglia, the South East (itself subdivided into Greater London and the rest of the South East), the South West, the West Midlands, the North West, together with the more aggregated groupings of England, Northern Ireland, Scotland, Wales and Britain as a whole.

2 Demand and Supply

1. The Engel expenditure curve takes its name from the Prussian statistician Ernst Engel (1821–96), who argued that the proportion of income devoted to food, clothing and housing will diminish as incomes rise.
2. Many economics textbooks refer to a special category of goods that can be characterised by a positive relationship between quantity demanded and price. Commodities that do not obey the law of demand are known as Giffen goods, following the work of Sir Robert Giffen (1837–1910), who observed that when the price of bread increased, so did its consumption by poorer members of society. This behaviour reflects an idea that if the price of staple products increases, consumers are forced to cut back their consumption of other goods, and as a result they increase their consumption of the staple good. Conversely, when the price of the staple product falls, consumers can switch their demand to more 'luxurious' products. The implication is that the demand curve for Giffen goods is upward sloping.
3. Equation 2.6 converts to 2.7 through the following process:

$$\eta_P = (\Delta Q/Q)/(\Delta P/P)$$
$$= (\Delta Q/Q)(P/\Delta P)$$
$$= (\Delta Q/\Delta P)(P/Q)$$

3 Markets and Market Failure

1. Many introductory textbooks discuss cobweb models with reference to agricultural production. In this case the produce consumers buy in the marketplace reflects what farmers planned to grow in previous periods.
2. Under the 1915 Mortgage and Rent Restrictions Act.
3. In the past, council tenants theoretically had the opportunity to buy their council houses. However, this depended on the political persuasion of the local authority from which they rented the property. The 1980 Housing Act gave tenants the statutory 'right to buy' their houses, regardless of whether the local council agreed or disagreed with the sale.

4 The Economic Evaluation of Construction Projects

1. See M. Beesley, T. Coburn and D. Reynolds, 'The London–Birmingham Motorway – Traffic and Economics', *Road Research Laboratory Technical Paper*, no. 46 (London: Department of Scientific and Industrial Research, 1960).
2. For example the White Paper, *Nationalised Industries: A Review of Economic and Social Objectives*, Cmnd 3437 (London: HMSO, 1967).
3. For example, strong unionisation in low-risk jobs relative to high-risk jobs may lead to a smaller 'risk premium' being paid to the former group of workers.
4. SACTRA is the acronym for the Standing Advisory Committee on Trunk Road Assessment.
5. Some of the profits enjoyed by the owners of new motorway service stations will result from motorists being encouraged to undertake extra journeys due to the increased opportunities offered by the new road. However these journeys are normally included in other parts of the CBA, and therefore to include the profits derived from them would result in double counting.

6 The Organisation of Firms

1. 'Prisoners' dilemma' takes its name from the uncertainties that face two people who are being questioned by the police in separate interview rooms about a crime they have just committed. If they both remain quiet, they both receive a nominal jail sentence. However If one prisoner informs on the other, the former is allowed to go free while the implicated prisoner receives a long term of imprisonment. Because neither prisoner can guarantee the other's silence, the opportunity to walk out of the police station becomes so great that each is tempted to inform on the other. The result is that both are implicated and both receive a long prison sentence.

7 Introduction to Macroeconomics

1. Recall that the principle of the 45° line was used in Chapter 2 in the analysis of the Engel expenditure curve.

8 The Construction Industry and Macroeconomic Policy, 1945–95

1. With the exception of buildings, highways and maintenance, which were covered by the Local Government Planning and Land Act (1980).
2. Generally speaking, a regressive tax is one in which the proportion of income paid in taxes decreases as income increases. Conversely a progressive tax is one in which the proportion of income paid in taxes rises as income increases.
3. Britain tried to take the initiative in creating a free trade area in industrial goods, which was intended to include the six future EEC countries. However the six saw this initiative as an attempt to wreck the EEC. Britain was

perceived as wanting to enjoy the benefits of cheap Commonwealth food and free access to European industrial markets without making reciprocal concessions to European food producers.
4. EFTA's original members were Austria, Denmark, Norway, Portugal, Sweden, Switzerland and Britain.

References

Agopyan, V. (1991) 'Reduction of energy consumption in building materials', in A. Bezelga and P. Brandon (eds), *Management, Quality and Economics in Building* (London: E. & F. N. Spon).

Akintoye, A. and M. Skitmore (1994) 'Models of UK private sector quarterly construction demand', *Construction Management and Economics*, vol. 12, pp. 3–13.

Aqua Group (1990) *Tenders and Contracts For Building* (Oxford: BSP Professional Books).

Artis, M. and N. Lee (eds) (1994) *The Economics of the European Union* (Oxford: Oxford University Press).

Bacon, R. and W. Eltis (1976) *Britain's Economic Problems: Too Few Producers* (London: Macmillan).

Ball, M. and A. Wood (1995) 'How many jobs does the construction industry generate?', *Construction Management and Economics*, vol. 13, pp. 307–18.

Baron, T. (1983) 'The challenge for the UK housing industry in the 1980s and the planning system', *Construction Industry and Management*, vol. 1, pp. 17–29.

Bezelga, A. and P. Brandon (eds) (1991) *Management, Quality and Economics in Building* (London: E. & F. N. Spon).

Bowyer, K. J. (1993) *History of Building* (Powys: Attic Books).

Brownlie, S. M. and F. C. Harris (1987) 'A review of finance for large scale construction', *Construction Management and Economics*, vol. 5, pp. 115–21.

Brundtland Report (1987) *Our Common Future* (authored by the World Commission on Environment and Development) (Oxford: Oxford University Press).

Burgess, J. (1991) 'Economics of CCT: Part II', *Leisure Management*, April, pp. 58–9.

Carey, S. (1995) *Private renting in England, Report by the OPCS on behalf of the Department of the Environment* (London: HMSO).

Cecchini, P. (1988) *The European Challenge: 1992. The Benefits of a Single Market* (Aldershot: Wildwood House).

Central Statistical Office (1992) *Standard Industrial Classification of economic activities 1992* (London: HMSO).

Central Statistical Office (1993) *Social Trends 1993* (London: HMSO).

Chapman, D., T. Tyrell and T. Mount (1972) 'Electricity Demand Growth and the Energy Crisis', *Science*, 17 November, p. 705.

Clapham, D., P. Kemp and S. Smith (1990) *Housing and Social Policy* (London: Macmillan).

Clawson, M. (1959) *Methods of Measuring the Demand for and Value of Outdoor Recreation* (Washington: Resources for the Future Inc.).

Clawson, M. and J. Knetsch (1966) *The Economics of Outdoor Recreation* (Baltimore: Johns Hopkins University Press).

Coburn, T., M. Beesley and D. Reynolds (1960) *The London–Birmingham Motorway*, Technical Paper 46, Road Research Laboratory.

Cooke, A. (1993) 'Deriving Leisure Time Values for Visitors to Urban Sports Centres', *Leisure Studies*, vol. 12, pp. 2221–31.

Cope, H. (1990) *Housing Associations, Policy and Practice* (London: Macmillan).

Deaton, A. (1975) *Models and Projections of Demand in Postwar Britain* (London: Chapman and Hall).

Department of the Environment (various years) *Housing and Construction Statistics* (London: HMSO).

Department of the Environment (1971) *Planned Open Offices: Cost Benefit Analysis* (London: HMSO).

Department of the Environment (1977) *Policy For Inner Cities* (London: HMSO).

Department of the Environment (1978) *The Economic Assessment of Housing Renewal Schemes, Improvement Research Note 4–78* (London: HMSO).

Department of the Environment (1994) *Housing and Construction Statistics 1983–1993* (London: HMSO).

Department of the Environment (1995) *Digest of Data for the Construction Industry,* 2nd edn (HMSO: London).

Department of Transport (1987) *Values for Journey Time Saving* (London: HMSO).

Department of Transport (1992) (The Standing Advisory Committee on Trunk Road Assessment (SACRA)), *Assessing the Environmental Impact of Road Schemes* (London: HMSO).

Dolan, D. F. (1979) *The British Construction Industry* (London: Macmillan).

Dupuit, J. (1844) 'On the Measurement of the Utility of Public Works', *Annales des Ponts et Chausées,* 2nd series, vol. 8, translated from the French by R. Barback (1952) *International Economics Papers,* no. 2, pp. 83–110.

El-Agraa, A. M. (1994) *Economics of the European Community* (London: Philip Allen).

Employment Gazette (various months and years) (London: Department of Employment).

Ermisch, J. (ed.) (1990) *Housing and the National Economy* (Aldershot: Avebury).

Gratton, C. and P. Taylor (1991) 'Economics of CCT: Part I', *Leisure Management,* April, pp. 54–6.

Griffiths, A. and S. Wall (1993) *Applied Economics, An introductory course,* 5th edn (London: Longman).

Groak, S. (1994) 'Is construction an industry?', *Construction Management and Economics,* vol. 12, pp. 287–93.

Hanley, N. and C. Spash (1993) *Cost–Benefit Analysis and the Environment* (Aldershot: Edward Elgar).

Harrington, R. (1992) 'Money and Finance: Public Expenditure and Taxation', in M. Artis (ed.), *Prest and Coppock's The UK Economy* (Oxford: Oxford University Press).

Harvey, J. (1981) *The Economics of Real Property* (London: Macmillan).

Heald, D. (1983) *Public Expenditure* (Oxford: Martin Robertson).

Hillebrandt, P. (1985) *Economic Theory and the Construction Industry* (London: Macmillan).

Hitiris, T. (1994) *European Community Economics* (London: Harvester Wheatsheaf).

Hockley, G. (1979) *Public Finance, An Introduction* (London: Routledge and Kegan Paul).

Ive, G. (1994) 'A theory of ownership types as applied to the construction majors', *Construction Management and Economics,* vol. 12, pp. 349–64.

Jones, Lee, M. (1976) *The Value of Life* (London: Martin Robertson).

Keynes, J. M. (1935) *The General Theory of Employment, Interest and Money* (New York: Harcourt Brace).

Lansey, P. (1987) 'Corporate strategy and survival in the UK construction industry', *Construction Management and Economics*, vol. 5, pp. 141–55.

Leftwich, R. and R. Ekert (1985) *The Price System and Resource Allocation* (New York: The Dryden Press).

Mann, T. (1992) *Building Economics For Architects* (New York: Van Nostrand Reinhold).

Marin, A. and G. Psacharopoulos (1982) 'The Reward for Risk in the Labour Market: Evidence from the United Kingdom and a Reconciliation with Other Studies, *Journal of Political Economy*, vol. 90, no. 4, pp. 827–53.

Milne, R. and M. McGee (1992) 'Compulsory Competitive Tendering in the NHS: A New Look at Some Old Estimates', *Fiscal Studies*, vol. 13, no. 3, pp. 96–111.

Monopolies and Mergers Commission (1981) *Concrete Roofing Tiles, A Report on the Supply in the United Kingdom of Concrete Roofing Tiles* (London: HMSO).

Office of Populations Censuses and Surveys (various years) *General Household Survey* (London: HMSO).

Ofori, G. (1992) 'The environment: the fourth construction objective?', *Construction Management and Economics*, vol. 10, pp. 369–95.

Ofori, G. (1994) 'Establishing Construction Economics as an Academic Discipline', *Construction Management and Economics*, vol. 12, no. 4, pp. 295–306.

Parker, D. (1990) 'The 1988 Local Government Act and Compulsory Competitive Tendering', *Urban Studies*, vol. 27, no. 5, pp. 653–68.

Pearce, D. and C. Nash (1981) *The Social Appraisal of Projects* (London: Macmillan).

Peters, G. (1971) *Private and Public Finance* (London: Fontana/Collins).

Prais, S. and H. Houthakker (1955) *The Analysis of Family Budgets* (Cambridge: Cambridge University Press).

Pratten, C. (1971) *Economies of Scale in Manufacturing Industry* (Cambridge: Cambridge University Press).

Pratten, C. (1989) *Costs of Non-Europe*, vol. 2 (Brussels: European Commission).

Rafferty, J. (1991) *Principles of Building Economics* (Oxford: BSP Professional Books).

Robinson, D. (1986) *Monetarism and the Labour Market* (Oxford: Clarendon Press).

Royal Commission on Environmental Pollution (1994) *Transport and the Environment Eighteenth Report* (London: HMSO).

Sandford, C. (1969) *Economics of Public Finance* (Oxford: Pergamon).

Scarman, Lord (1981) *The Brixton Disorders 10–12 April 1981* (London: HMSO).

Seeley, I. (1983) *Building Economics*, 3rd edn (London: Macmillan).

Seeley, I. (1995) *Building Technology* (London: Macmillan).

Spencer Chapman, N. F. and C. Grandjean (1991) *The Construction Industry and the European Community* (Oxford: BSP Professional Books).

Stone, P. A. (1983) *Building Economy* (Oxford: Pergamon Press).

Turner, R. K., D. Pearce and I. Bateman (1994) *Environmental Economics: An elementary introduction* (London: Harvester Wheatsheaf).

Williamson, O. E. (1981) 'The Modern Corporation: Origins, Evolution, Attributes', *Journal of Economic Literature*, vol. 19, pp. 1537–68.

Willis, K. and G. Garrod (1991) *The Hedonic Price Method and the Valuation of Countryside Characteristics*, Countryside Change Centre working paper 14, University of Newcastle-upon-Tyne.

Glossary of Economics Terms

The aim of this section is to provide readers with a definition of many of the terms used in this text, which may prove useful when revising for examinations or undertaking written course work. The Glossary is organised alphabetically and hence readers will only have encountered all the terms cited below when the entire text has been read.

Aggregate demand   The overall demand for goods and services produced within an economy over a given period of time.

Aggregate expenditure   The total expenditure on goods and services produced within an economy in a given time period, namely the sum of consumption expenditure, investment expenditure, government expenditure and net export expenditure.

Average total cost   The total cost of producing a given output divided by the number of units produced. Thus if it costs £500 to produce 500 bricks, then the average total cost is £1.

Average revenue   Total revenue (see below) divided by the total number of goods sold. By definition, average revenue equals the price of the product in question.

Balance of payments   The difference between the amount a country exports and the amount it imports during a given period. If exports exceed imports, a country is said to have a balance of payments surplus, whereas if the reverse is true its balance of payments is in deficit.

Behavioural theories of the firm   A set of theories that reject the idea that firms can maximise given variables, such as profit. Behavioural theories emphasise the need for firms to compromise and to make side-payments in order to maintain a stable coalition between shareholders, managers and workers.

Blue Book   A name sometimes used for the (annual) official publication containing Britain's national income and expenditure accounts.

Boom   An expansionary phase of the trade cycle (see below).

Budget deficit   (Usually) when the government's income fails to meet its expenditure.

Budget surplus   (Usually) when the government's income exceeds its expenditure.

Capital   The general term given to such factors of production as factories, machinery, computers, vehicles and so on. Also a general term for financial assets.

Capital-intensive production   A process that uses a high proportion of capital inputs relative to labour inputs.

Cartel   An agreement whereby a group of firms act as if they are a single unit rather than competing independent sellers. Unless cartels are found to be in the 'public interest' they are deemed to be illegal. Cartel agreements (predominantly illegal) that embrace such variables as market share and price have been a regular feature of the construction industry.

Ceteris paribus   A Latin term that translates as 'other things being equal', that is, they remain the same. It is used frequently by economists when attempting to isolate the effects of all but one of the independent variables within a given function.

Cobweb model A dynamic model (that is, contains a 'time' dimension) that in its simplest form assumes the supply of a commodity in time t is a function of its price in the previous period (t - 1).

Collusion (as used in this book) An agreement between firms to cooperate with each other in order to avoid the costs of rivalry, for example through a cartel (see above).

Complements Complementary goods are commodities that are consumed together, for example cars and petrol. Thus we would expect that the demand for a good is inversely related to the price of the complement consumed with it.

Consumer surplus The difference between the amount a consumer pays for a good or service and the (higher) amount he or she is actually willing to pay for it.

Consumption expenditure Aggregate expenditure on the goods and services that are required to satisfy current needs.

Consumption function The mathematical relationship between consumption expenditure and the variables assumed to affect it. In its simplest form, consumption expenditure is assumed to be a function of income.

Contingent valuation A process used by researchers to discover how much consumers are willing to receive in compensation, or willing to pay, for a change in the quality of a good or service whose price is not determined explicitly by market processes, for example scenery or environmental quality.

Cost–benefit analysis (CBA) A framework used to aid the decision-making process by which all the costs and benefits of a project are expressed explicitly in monetary terms. CBA differs from CEA (below) in that it allows the decision maker to question project objectives and hence the desirability of the investment in question.

Cost-effectiveness analysis (CEA) A less 'demanding' framework than CBA (above) since it merely seeks to find the least costly way of achieving an already accepted objective. Unlike CBA, not all costs and benefits need to be put into monetary terms, and hence CEA is less open to the criticism that the economist is trying to 'quantify the unquantifiable'.

Cross-elasticity of demand A measure of the degree to which the quantity demanded of one commodity responds to changes in the price of another.

Cross-section analysis Analysis of data associated with a particular point in time (see time series analysis).

Crowding out Takes place when state intervention in the economy leads to a reduction in private sector activity. See physical crowding out *and* financial crowding out.

Deflationary gap A situation that occurs when aggregate expenditure is below that needed fully to employ a nation's workforce (see inflationary gap).

Demand The relationship between the amount of a commodity that consumers are willing and able to buy per unit of time and the price of that commodity.

Demand curve A graphical representation of demand. Price is measured along the vertical axis of the graph and the quantity demanded is measured along the horizontal axis.

Demand function An expression that identifies the precise relationship between quantity demanded and all the variables that can affect it (such as price, income and so on). Introductory economics texts place more stress on identifying the key variables that should be included in a demand function than they do on specifying their exact mathematical relationship.

Demand management   The attempt by a government to exert control over the level of aggregate demand by using fiscal and monetary policy (mainly fiscal).

Dependent variable   A variable whose value is determined by the value(s) of other variables. Thus in the case of a demand function (see above), 'quantity demanded' is seen to be dependent upon such variables as own price, income, taste and so on.

Depression   The contractionary phase of the trade cycle (see below).

Derived demand   A term that refers to the fact that the demand for some commodities does not reflect their own intrinsic value but instead a willingness and ability to consume another good or service. For example, petrol is demanded as a fuel for cars rather than because it is desirable to own petrol *per se*.

Division of labour   Occurs when a complex productive process is divided into smaller tasks that can be undertaken by different workers. Repetition enables each worker to become proficient in their designated task, enabling overall output to increase beyond that which would emerge if each worker had to master every individual task. This is also an argument for the continued existence of specialist building companies.

Duopoly   An industry containing two firms. A subset of oligopoly (see below).

Econometrics   The testing of economic relationships using statistical analysis.

Economic growth   A rise in the total output of a country over time. If output falls, economic growth is said to be negative.

Economic rent   A payment made to a factor of production in excess of the amount needed to keep it in its present use.

Economies of scale   Occur when increases in the scale of production, with factor inputs increased in the same proportion, reduce the average unit cost of production (the opposite applies to diseconomies of scale). Economies of scale are a more specific version of economies of size (below).

Economies of size   Occur when an increase in the scale of production, regardless of any change in the relative combination of factor inputs, leads to a reduction in the average unit cost of production (the opposite applies to diseconomies of size).

Elasticity of demand   *See* cross elasticity of demand, income elasticity of demand and price elasticity of demand.

Elasticity of supply   *See* price elasticity of supply.

Engel expenditure curve   A graph that measures the relationship between income and the amount spent on a particular group of commodities (for example food or leisure goods). Assuming that normal goods (see below) are likely to outweigh inferior goods (see below) within any commodity group, it is usual to expect an Engel expenditure curve to slope upwards.

Entrepreneur   A person who organises factors of production and is distinguished from labour by his or her willingness to take risks.

Equilibrium   A situation where opposing forces are in balance, so there is no tendency for change.

Equilibrium price   The price at which quantity demanded exactly equals quantity supplied.

Equilibrium quantity   The amount that is bought and sold at the equilibrium price.

Exchange rate   The amount of one currency that is needed to buy a unit of another currency (*see* fixed exchange rate and floating exchange rate).

Externalities   Externalities arise when the actions of one economic agent impact directly on the welfare of third parties who were not party to with the original decision. Externalities can be desirable or undesirable and can apply to individual householders or firms.

Factors of production Resources used to produce goods and services. There are three main factors of production: land, labour and capital (factories, machinery and so on). Some analyses include a fourth variable – entrepreneurship – which differs from general labour since it reflects a willingness and ability to take risks in order to exploit potential market opportunities. For simplicity, microeconomic analysis often refers to just two factors of production: labour and capital.

Financial crowding out Occurs when an increase in government borrowing leads to an increase in interest rates. It adversely affects firms whose activities are particularly sensitive to changes in interest rates, for example construction firms and firms that depend on export markets (higher interest rates lead to an appreciation of a country's international currency value, thereby making exports more expensive in the importing country).

Fixed exchange rate Governments agree to maintain a fixed rate of exchange (or maintain it within a narrow range of values) between their respective exchange rates irrespective of any market pressures that prevail.

Fixed factor A factor of production whose value cannot be changed in the short term. Usually this is assumed to be capital. In the long term such a distinction becomes irrelevant because all factors of production can be assumed to vary (see below).

Floating exchange rate Governments allow the equilibrium value of their domestic currencies to change in accordance with market pressures. A **dirty float** occurs when governments intervene in money markets in a systematic way in order to prevent wild fluctuations in currency values while remaining outside an explicit fixed exchange rate system.

Free rider problem Arises when some consumers of public goods (see below) do not reveal the full extent of their preference in the hope that others will bear the cost.

Game theory A body of theory used to illustrate the problems associated with asymmetrical information – the strategy/counterstrategy adopted by one economic agent directly affects the welfare of another. The framework is used frequently in the analysis of oligopolistic industries and can show, for example, that although cooperation between firms can be mutually beneficial, mistrust and the potential benefits from being first to break an agreement will lead to both firms becoming worse off (often referred to as **the prisoners' dilemma**).

Gross domestic product (GDP) The value of total output within an economy over a given time period. Includes output by foreign-owned firms as well as domestic ones.

Gross national product (GNP) Gross domestic product *plus* any incomes accruing to domestic residents from investments made abroad *minus* incomes earned by foreigners in domestic markets.

Hedonic price A shadow price (see below) for an attribute that is determined as a residual once the product characteristics that *can* be ascribed a market price have been accounted for. Hedonic pricing is often used in housing demand analysis.

Horizontal integration Horizontal integration is a merger between two firms at the same stage of production.

Identification problem A problem that can occur when a researcher tries to derive a single demand and/or supply curve (under the *ceteris paribus* assumption) using time series data, when in reality the demand/supply curves are shifting with time.

Income elasticity of demand   The measure of responsiveness of quantity demanded to changes in consumers' income. Normal goods (see below) produce positive income elasticities while inferior goods (see below) generate negative income elasticities.

Independent variable   A variable whose value determines the value taken by another (dependent) variable.

Inferior good   A good or service that is bought less as incomes rise (the reverse of a normal good). No commodity can be defined strictly as inferior: it may be inferior for high-income groups but normal for lower-income groups. Also, product inferiority is a function of quality, so low-quality versions of a product may be inferior while superior versions of it remain normal.

Inflation   An increase in the general price level that results in a reduction in the purchasing power of a given sum of money.

Inflationary gap   Occurs when aggregate expenditure is in excess of that needed fully to employ a nation's workforce.

Infrastructure   Facilities whose existence is necessary if an economy is to survive and grow. Examples include roads, railways, airports, bridges, telecommunications, sewerage, housing, schools and so on.

Intermediate goods   Goods and services that are inputs into further productive processes.

Isocost line   A line that identifies all the factor combinations a firm can use for the same outlay.

Isoquant   A line that identifies the minimum factor combinations (usually capital and labour) that can be used to produce a given output. Isoquants are drawn as smooth lines, implying that an infinite range of potential factor combinations can be used for each level of output, in reality only a limited number of efficient capital–labour combinations exist. Where only one process exists, the isoquant assumes an 'L' shape.

Labour-intensive production   A process that uses large quantities of labour relative to capital inputs.

Macroeconomics   The analysis of broad economic aggregates (as opposed to individual decisions by households and firms) such as price level, unemployment, economic growth, balance of payments and so on.

Managerial theories of the firm   A set of theories that emphasise the willingness and ability of a firm's managers (as opposed to its owners) to maximise or influence variables that are advantageous to them rather than to the economic agents who actually own the firm.

Marginal benefit   The increase in total benefits enjoyed by an individual after consuming one extra unit of a particular commodity.

Marginal cost   The increase in a firm's total costs brought about by increasing production by one extra unit, or the cost incurred by an individual from consuming an extra unit of a product.

Marginal revenue   The increase in a firm's total revenue brought about by increasing production by one extra unit.

Market   A market is created when buyers are able to communicate with sellers. It may be location-specific, such as a shop, or simply exist through telephone or postal communication.

Merit bad   A product that a 'paternalist' society views as undesirable. Consumption of a merit bad is discouraged through taxation, education (for example about the health risks associated with cigarette smoking) or an outright ban (for example drugs).

Merit good A product that a 'paternalist' society views as desirable. Its consumption is encouraged through subsidies or promotional programmes (for example the promotion of exercise), or it is made a legal requirement (for example education).

Microeconomics The study of individual decision-making units, for example consumers, households or firms.

Minimum efficient scale The lowest output at which long-run average costs are minimised.

Model A predefined set of mathematical relationships (usually simplified) that attempts to capture the key features of real-world economic processes.

Monetarism A school of thought that emphasises the importance of monetary phenomena in determining economic activity.

Money supply The total amount of money in circulation in an economy. Usually a distinction is made between 'narrow' and 'broad' measures of the money supply such that 'narrow' measures tend to refer explicitly to money in its more day-to-day sense and 'broad' measures include, in addition, less liquid financial securities which cannot be converted instantaneously into cash.

Monopolistic competition A market structure in which a large number of firms exist but produce a slightly different product and/or are geographically isolated from each other. As a result, firms can exert some control over the price they charge and face a downward sloping demand curve.

Monopoly In theory, an industry controlled by a single producer. In practice the term also refers to duopolistic and oligopolistic market structures.

Multiplier effect Occurs when an injection of expenditure into an economy leads to an increase in GNP in excess of the original injection.

Normal good A good or service whose consumption rises with income.

Normal profit Profit just sufficient to induce an entrepreneur to remain in his or her present line of activity. In diagrams it is subsumed in the entrepreneur's cost curves.

Normative economic statement A value judgement that cannot be tested empirically.

Oligopoly An industry that contains a small number of firms (*see also* duopoly).

Organisational slack Arises when payments need to be made in order to maintain the stability of coalitions within firms.

Perfect competition A situation where a very large number of price-taking firms exist within an industry.

Physical crowding out Arises when an expansion in state activity causes resources to be diverted from the private 'market' sector into the public 'non-market' sector.

Positive economics A branch of economics that is concerned with developing empirically testable hypotheses (which can be accepted or refuted using appropriate evidence).

Price discrimination Occurs when a firm sells its product at different prices in different markets for reasons other than relative cost differences. Examples include bulk buying and charging different prices to different consumer groups.

Price elasticity of demand A measure of responsiveness of quantity demanded to changes in the own price of a good or service.

Price elasticity of supply   A measure of responsiveness of quantity supplied to changes in the own price of a good or service.

Price taker   A person or firm with no influence over the price of a commodity.

Principal agent problem   Arises when a firm's owners are unable to monitor the day-to-day running of a firm. Manager(s) run the firm in accordance with their own personal utility function rather than that of the firm's owner(s).

Private benefit   A benefit that accrues to an individual.

Private cost   A cost incurred by an individual.

Private good   A commodity that, if consumed by one person, cannot be subsequently consumed by another.

Producer surplus   The difference between the price a producer is willing and able to charge to supply a unit of good or service and the price he or she actually receives.

Production function   A mathematical expression that identifies the maximum output that can be achieved from alternative input combinations.

Public good   A commodity that can be consumed simultaneously by more than one person, for example streetlighting. In its purest sense, individuals can consume identical amounts of the good, but in reality the relative amounts will differ (*see* quasi public good).

Public sector borrowing requirement   The amount by which public expenditure exceeds revenue.

Quasi public good   A commodity that has the main attributes of a public good but individuals do not necessarily receive the same quantity of it.

Rationality   An assumption that decision makers are fully informed about the consequences of their actions.

Real income   Income measured in terms of the goods and services it can be used to purchase over time.

Returns to scale   Refers to how output changes when all inputs are changed by the same proportion. Returns to scale can be increasing, decreasing or constant. If, for example, a doubling of a firm's inputs causes output to rise by a factor of three, returns to scale are said to be increasing.

Shadow price   A price that economists ascribe to commodities that are not traded in markets.

Short run   A time period in which factors of production, usually land and capital, cannot be varied.

Social benefit   A benefits that accrues to society as a whole (including the original decision taker(s)).

Social cost   Costs that are imposed on society as a whole as well as on the original decision taker(s).

Substitutes   Goods that are perceived as being alternatives for each other, for example bungalows and semidetached houses.

Supernormal profit   Profit in excess of normal profit (see above).

Supply curve   A pictorial relationship between what producers are willing and able to supply in a given period of time and the price of the commodity in question, *ceteris paribus*.

Supply function   An expression that specifies the relationship between quantity supplied and the variables that can affect it (for example price, technology and so on).

Time series analysis   The analysis of data associated with particular variables over a period of time. By definition, a time series analysis may force the researcher to confront the impact of inflation on his or her data set over time.

Total revenue The sum of money a firm receives from selling its output. Total revenue is calculated by multiplying the product's price by the number of units sold.

Trade cycle A term that refers to the oscillating performance of an economy from boom to depression.

Unemployment There is no single definition of unemployment. Distinctions are sometimes made between those people who wish to work and cannot get a job (involuntary unemployment) and those who prefer leisure to working (voluntary unemployment).

Utility The satisfaction or pleasure derived by an individual from consuming a good or service.

Utility function A mathematical expression that identifies the relationship between the different commodities from which a consumer derives utility.

Variable factor A factor of production whose level can vary in the short run. This is usually assumed to be labour.

X-inefficiency Organisational and technical inefficiencies that prevent a firm from maximising its profits.

Index